Washington State Government and Politics

Washington State Government and Politics

Edited by

Cornell W. Clayton
Lance T. LeLoup
Nicholas P. Lovrich

Washington State University Press
Pullman, Washington

Washington State University Press
PO Box 645910
Pullman, Washington 99164-5910
Phone: 800-354-7360
Fax: 509-335-8568
E-mail: wsupress@wsu.edu
Web site: wsupress.wsu.edu

Library of Congress Cataloging-in-Publication Data

Washington state government and politics / edited by Cornell W. Clayton,
    Lance T. LeLoup, and Nicholas P. Lovrich.
        p. cm.
    Includes bibliographical references.
    ISBN 0-87422-273-7 (pbk. : alk. paper)
    1. Washington (State)—Politics and government—1951- I. Clayton,
Cornell W., 1960- II. LeLoup, Lance T. III. Lovrich, Nicholas P.
JK9216.W37 2004
320.4797—dc22

                                                            2003028292

Table of Contents

Section III

Foreword

THIS IS OUR STORY, and it is never quite complete. Washington State's rich, quirky, and utterly fascinating experiment with self-government is always taking unexpected twists and turns as the ingenious and creative people of the Evergreen State continue evolving.

That is only fitting, given our history. We are rooted in the ancient wisdom and the love for resources and nature's bounty that gave—and give—our citizens such a sense of place, a spiritual and material grounding that provides the strength to sustain a pioneer spirit of renewal, experimentation, and daring—even as we plunge headfirst into the twenty-first century.

As made clear in this volume, Washingtonians are a people of contradictions, who seem to revel in questions and challenges, always presuming that new answers and solutions will emerge. Our forebears were exemplars of both tradition and reform as they carved out a new life in a sometimes brutal land. They combined, as we do today, the sunny optimism that once reflected itself in utopian settlements, and a sense of meritocracy, with the pioneer's no-nonsense concentration on the things that are truly important.

As the 42nd state, Washington borrowed liberally from our elders to the east, with a cut-and-paste constitution from the best of other states. Likewise, we adopted laws and the basics of politics and governing from around the country. Yet somehow, it seemed to be integrated in a way that was fresh, original and ever-changing.

As pioneers made their way westward, they left behind some of the hidebound ways of the East, where patrimony and status led to machine politics and circumscribed, predictable, and hierarchical ways of conducting government, politics, and daily life.

In the West, a meritocracy developed as people left behind the old rules and verities. Lewis and Clark's Corps of Discovery famously included a woman and a black man when they all voted, on Washington soil, about where to overwinter. Washington's earliest draft constitution, never adopted due to delays in Congress approving statehood, included the vote for women.

The state later became the first with a voter-approved abortion-rights law and state Equal Rights Amendment; became one of the first to elect a woman governor and other statewide female officeholders; and has the nation's highest percentage of women legislators. Although the state struggled with the same racial problems as the rest of the United States, including treatment of Native Americans and people of color, Washington also developed a reputation as a melting pot that welcomes minorities into the fabric of life. Blacks won election to high offices, including King County executive and mayoral posts, and Gary Locke, the son of immigrants, was elected as the first Chinese-American governor.

As Governor Locke pointed out in his first gubernatorial campaign, Washington turned out to be an ideal place to live out "the great American dream."

The sons and daughters of Washington—and their commercial and political endeavors—have been as diverse as the landscape itself. The same state that was once famously described as "the Soviet of Washington" for its radical labor leanings also was the state that dumped a sitting Democratic Speaker of the House and became the country's most enthusiastic recruits for the "Republican Revolution" of 1994.

Early voters and leaders evidenced a considerable skepticism about concentrations of power, either in the government or in the private sector. That wariness sticks with us today. And so our endlessly fascinating story continues to unwind. What will the next plot turn be?

This volume, *Washington State Government and Politics,* provides some snapshots of a work in progress that will be of interest to both the student of government as well as the more casual reader. It provides a fascinating look at the "big picture" of an evolving state, including fascinating case studies, such as the emerging use of the initiative process and new ways to manage environmental conflicts.

There are many common themes throughout the book. As a front-row observer at the state Capitol for more than thirty years, the most interesting to me is the conflicted feeling people have about government, a regular love-hate affair. In his chapter about the legislature, for instance, Todd Donovan talks about people being "dissatisfied with state government in general and their legislature in particular. Yet...public opinion polls show that voters give their [own] legislators relatively high marks. So we have an apparent paradox—a well-functioning, well-regarded state legislature that is the frequent target of the public's wrath."

In her chapter titled "Direct Democracy in Washington," Carolyn Long traces the fascinating rise of the initiative and referendum process as one of the ways Washingtonians take lawmaking into their own hands—and effectively handcuff their elected representatives in the process.

Indeed, in recent years, interest groups from across the political spectrum have stepped up their use of the initiative process as a way to circumvent the legislature and take their case directly to the voters. Although conservative anti-tax rebel Tim Eyman was credited—or blamed—for putting the initiative process on centerstage, starting with $30 car tabs in 1999, education advocates, unions, and environmentalists also found it to be a useful tool. The legislature has found budget-writing increasingly difficult as initiatives bind it with spending and tax limits, revenue reductions, and new spending mandates. In the year 2000 alone, the voters mandated billions of dollars to be spent, in perpetuity, for annual salary increases for public school teachers and for class-size reduction—while at the same time severely limiting property-tax growth.

Although lawmakers have toyed with curbing the exercise of the initiative process, few took state Senator Ken Jacobsen seriously when he proposed abolishing "direct democracy" in 2003. Tim Eyman announced that he was setting up a for-profit initiative factory, and legislators acknowledged that initiatives are here to stay—a shadow government, as I have taken to calling them.

Although the casual reader is certainly free to flip to the chapters that look most intriguing, a reading of the entire volume will give a more comprehensive feel for Washington State government and politics.

The first section of the book gives a behind-the-scenes look at public opinion, parties, and political participation. John Pierce, Nicholas Lovrich, and Stuart Elway, in their dissection of public opinion, note that "Government 'of the people, by the people and for the people' compels those who govern to keep a watchful eye on what the people prefer to be done in their name."

They discuss the development of "political culture" and the social capital that binds people together to collectively attempt to influence. Interestingly, they say diverse Washingtonians share many reflections on the world. "Political cynicism is clearly the most important of those broadly shared perspectives on politics among contemporary Washingtonians," they write. At the same time, the authors note an enduring optimism and note that respondents give high marks to government for the quality of colleges and universities, protection of natural resources and the environment, prisons, schools, and social and health services. Only transportation gets a failing or poor grade overall.

In their view of Washington's political parties, Andrew Appleton and Ashley Grosse describe the workings of the parties in a state that is "distrustful of the partisan division of political life" and tries to circumscribe their power.

As a result of the "blanket" primary adopted during the Great Depression—as an initiative to the legislature sponsored by labor and the Grange—parties were not even permitted to finally determine their own nominees for the November general elections. The popular system, under challenge in the courts as of this writing, has given voters the right to pick and choose their favorites for each office, without regard for party label of the candidate.

Still, the authors point out that parties enjoy a significant role in politics and government, particularly in organizing and financing campaigns.

In their chapter on interest group politics, Robert Herold and Jeff Gombosky give a behind-the-scenes look at the pressure groups that have long attempted to influence governmental and legislative decisions, particularly in the areas of public domain politics and urbanization.

They describe the state's Progressive and Populist roots, asserting that reforms have resulted in a relatively weak state administration that has always had difficulty governing. This weakness has created a governing vacuum into which interest groups have moved. They use the Columbia River, logging, and Boeing as examples of where pressure politics have been evident.

Carolyn Long's chapter on initiatives traces their development, historical roots, and how they have been used throughout modern history. She discusses the rise of the initiative industry, including use of "mercenaries and bounty-hunters" who gather signatures for pay. She outlines the role of the courts in evaluating, and often invalidating, initiatives.

In their chapter on the state constitution, Cornell Clayton and Stephen Meyer explain our basic social contract, spelled out in broadest fashion—in roughly 40,000 words, compared with the 6,000 in the U.S. Constitution. Like fashion, it has changed with the times to reflect evolving values and approaches, with more than ninety amendments since statehood. The document provides for a shattered administration and divided power, reflecting the public desire for checks and balances and diffuse centers of power. They note that the framers were "strong advocates of popular sovereignty" and sought to circumscribe corporate power and special interests.

David May, in his work on the state judiciary, talks about the "nexus between the political and legal worlds," making a compelling case that the supposedly apolitical world of the courts is anything but. Most judges have to regularly stand for election and must try to "balance the legal need for judicial independence with a political need for accountability and responsiveness." The chapter describes the workings of the various levels of the court, shedding light on probably the least understood branch of government.

Steven Stehr and Steven Ellwanger, in their essay on the executive branch, touch on the "ambivalence toward government, coupled with a heavy reliance on the services it provides." They discuss the rise of the modern administrative state, including uneasy and shifting relations with the federal government, power-sharing among independently elected officials, and restive relations with the taxpayers. We get a glimpse into the bureaucracy and the basic programs of government—the nuts and bolts of services that mean "government" to the average citizen.

David Nice and Erin Otte follow up with a discussion of the office of governor. The chief executive, the embodiment of government, often is hemmed in by political realities—a divided executive branch, sometimes tempestuous differences with the legislature, and a power base that is not always up to the task at hand.

"Americans are relatively ambivalent about representative government," Todd Donovan writes in introducing his look at the legislature. In Washington, this tension is underscored by the rise of initiatives, he notes. He describes the decennial ritual of redrawing district boundaries, the rise of the professional staff, the increasing power of parties in organizing the legislature, turnover and competitiveness of elections, and basics like lobbying and the committee structure.

In their chapter on budgeting, Lance LeLoup and Christina Herzog zero in on the legislature's single most important, and difficult, task of determining budget priorities and how to pay for them. The challenges of the new century, including initiatives, party competition and close divisions, and the ravages of periodic recessions are covered.

In a chapter that illustrates public policy development and twenty-first-century problem-solving, Edward Weber and Tetyana Lysak offer a hopeful coda for the book. They trace the emergence of a new paradigm, a more collaborative problem-solving method that is being used with some success in environmental and natural resource areas.

They say that "topdown, government-goes-it-alone, coercive approaches" to problem-solving do not have to be the dominant story line, but can give way to "devolution, collaboration, citizen participation, and area-based comprehensive, integrated approaches to public problems." That's a mouthful, but it reflects what the authors call "a robust array of new approaches to problem-solving."

And so our story continues. How will we, and government, evolve? As we vote by mail and by Internet, will we vote more often and representative government morph into plebiscites? Will citizen empowerment change? Will structures of government and delivery of services change? Can trust in government be restored?

Stay tuned.

David Ammons
Olympia, Washington

Foley Institute Sponsorship

As we move further into the twenty-first century, our educational institutions must facilitate a better understanding of the social, political, historical, and economic dimensions of the challenges ahead. *Washington State Government and Politics* is a step in this direction. It paints a detailed, relatively comprehensive picture of the current structure, processes, character, and substance of Washington State's political dynamic, along with key public policies. As such, the book is a natural extension of the educational and research missions of one of the primary sponsors of this volume, The Thomas S. Foley Institute for Public Policy and Public Service, as well as the land-grant mission of Washington State University, where the institute resides.

The Foley Institute is proud to sponsor this volume. We think that readers will find it informative, thought-provoking, and an invaluable asset contributing to civic literacy as pertaining to the study of state government.

The Foley Institute

The Thomas S. Foley Institute for Public Policy and Public Service was established in 1995 at Washington State University (WSU) in Pullman, Washington. The Institute, named in honor of Thomas S. Foley, former speaker of the U.S. House of Representatives and former U.S. Ambassador to Japan, was created to foster programs in three general areas: 1) student and educational programs, 2) public education and public service, and 3) public policy research.

Student and Educational Programs

The Foley Institute is a leader in efforts aimed at improving undergraduate and graduate educational opportunities. The institute awards scholarships and fellowships to students who have demonstrated academic excellence and desire to pursue public-service-oriented careers. An internship coordinator is available to arrange student placements in legislative offices, public agencies, and non-profit organizations. Invited speakers from across the world regularly address WSU classes on topics of contemporary concern.

Public Education and Public Service

The nation is currently in the midst of a crisis in public confidence in the ability of our democratic institutions to work effectively. The Foley Institute makes an important contribution in fostering civic literacy, community involvement in public decisions, and a commitment to public service. Annual programs such as the Congressional and Presidential Scholar Lecture and the Civil Society and American Governance Lecture bring national, state, and local experts to campus to spark lively discussions and community awareness on a variety of topics.

Public Policy Research

The Foley Institute sponsors Public Policy Symposia featuring policy specialists, elected officials, and other experts on problems facing all levels of government. The institute also supports public policy research conferences on a wide variety of domestic and international issues. Examples include events focusing on endangered salmon in the Pacific Northwest, the relationship between the decisions of the Rehnquist Supreme Court and congressional policymaking, the implications of globalization for international trade, the need for reform of the institutions and policies governing American public lands, the ramifications of deregulating the United States' electric power supplies, and racial profiling, to name but a few. The Institute also maintains a competitive Summer Graduate Fellows program that assists WSU doctoral students with their research programs.

The Foley Congressional Collection

The institute is also the home of the Thomas S. Foley Congressional papers, library, artwork, photographs, and other memorabilia. The gift of the Foley collection means that WSU is the depository of over sixty years of state and federal congressional history. The complete inventory of Foley materials is available on the World Wide Web at <http://www.wsulibs.wsu.edu/holland/masc/foley/page.htm>

—Edward P. Weber, Director
The Thomas S. Foley Institute for Public
Policy and Public Service
Washington State University

Chapter One

Public Opinion and Political Culture in Washington State

John Pierce, Nicholas P. Lovrich, and Stuart Elway

The Meaning of Public Opinion

THE SUBJECT OF PUBLIC OPINION is a frequent topic of political discussions, both in private conversations and in the mass media. Moreover, public opinion has been the subject of some of the classic works of contemporary political science (V.O. Key, Jr. 1965). Public sentiments on specific issues constitute a key political lever and resource in policy advocacy. Political candidates and established politicians alike frequently put their own "spin" on public opinion to achieve their own ends. Unfortunately, the term is used in so many differing ways that it lacks common understanding. It is important, therefore, that the concept be carefully defined at the outset.

The meaning of the term *public* can depend on the use to which it is applied (Pierce, Beatty, and Hagner 1982). Most often, we think of the public as the group of individuals who are found within some kind of formal political boundary. So, it might be the *American public,* or in the case of this book, the *Washington State public.* But there are other, more refined possible definitions. The *attentive public* is one such term, describing individuals who have an ongoing interest in politics, who know the major elements of their public institutions and political processes, and who pay close attention to political developments. *Issue public* is another refined concept often used by social scientists who study public opinion. This term refers to the portion of the citizenry that is especially interested in and cares about any outcomes arising over discussions and policy making in regard to a specific issue. For example, avid hunters may pay very close attention to hunting regulations and policy discussions concerning those regulations, but others may be uninterested in and inattentive with respect to that dimension of politics and public affairs.

The particular meaning attached to the term "public opinion" is important, because any boundary drawn around the individuals residing within a public jurisdiction may make a difference in the characterization of the content of the "public opinion" of that political entity. Scholars or politicians may pay particular attention to the opinions of the attentive public because they believe—with good reason—that citizens who pay attention to politics and follow public affairs are the most likely to vote and to seek to influence the thinking of their friends and neighbors. Interest group representatives, in contrast, are typically more interested in issue publics because their sentiments are critical to the effective mobilization of influence in the policy process. In order to raise money from persons with intense interests, to organize lobbying and electoral support for their cause, and to creative effective media communications to promote their views it is important that interest group representatives (e.g., environmentalists, right-to-life advocates, etc.) have an accurate assessment of their issue public's primary concerns. Whatever the definition adopted, the key point is that the boundary used to identify people affects judgments made about the character of public opinion in a political community.

Differences associated with varying understandings of relevant "publics" are most likely to occur when the issue or opinion in question is directly relevant to a particular interest in a community whose opinion is being described. When considering the opinions of individuals in regard to the clear-cutting of old growth timber, for example, it surely will make a difference whether the public being described includes only those who are directly affected economically by the policy or includes all of the citizens living in a particular jurisdiction.

There are other kinds of boundary issues that regularly come to play in the definition of public. For example, how old must an individual be to be included as part of public opinion? Should she be 16 (driving age), 18 (voting age), or 21 (legal drinking age)? What kind of citizenship requirements should be imposed for one to be included within the public? Must the person be a citizen, or should residency within the prescribed area suffice? What about convicted felons, or students whose homes are elsewhere but who reside in a residence hall at a university or college during the school year? How those boundaries of inclusion are set is important because they may determine the resulting opinion that is ascribed to a particular political community.

The second component to the concept of public opinion is *opinion*. Does one favor or oppose a particular position on an issue of public interest? That element of opinion is usually referred to as the *affective* element of public opinion. The *cognitive* element of opinion represents the dimension of human sentiment having to do with what one's *reasoning* is concerning an issue or person. For instance, is a ballot measure raising gasoline taxes to address traffic congestion and road repair seen as another attempt of an inefficient government to penalize its citizens for its own inability to operate within its proper means? Similarly, is the candidate standing for election seen as experienced, or as lacking in pertinent knowledge? Is an incumbent public official seen as ethical or opportunistic? Is a policy proposal seen as timely or out-of-date? These are all examples of the cognitive dimension of opinion. Finally, it is important to note that the true test of public opinion may be patterned *behavior* rather than attitudes. For example, many people claim to be "environmentalists," but may not act systematically to conserve energy, recycle, drive in car pools or take public transportation.

In describing the opinion of a public, by whatever definition, one is describing an aggregation or collection of individual opinions. For most issues affecting political life there is seldom a consensus among the citizenry. For many issues it is difficult to maintain that a public opinion actually exists. More commonly, a distribution of sentiments and predispositions—affective, cognitive, and behavioral—exists, which itself may have a number of characteristics. One of those characteristics is the degree to which a consensus exists. Generally, scholars require that there be 75+ percent agreement on a position to proclaim a consensus. If such widespread agreement does not exist, then a further question is fostered—i.e., what shape does disagreement take? Is public opinion spread along a continuum of some kind with equal percentages at various points, or are there groups of people widely separated from one another? The character of this opinion distribution may explain the presence or absence of conflict arising in the politics associated with this area of public opinion. Likewise, it is important to know the *intensity* with which people hold their opinions. Great division on some issue may mean little in terms of politics or conflict if nobody really cares. Similarly, there may be complete consensus on some topic, but if no one cares there may be no real need for public officials to respond to the preferences in question.

The Importance of Public Opinion

Given this discussion of the dimensions of the public and the elements of opinion, why should one care about public opinion—whether it be national in scope or that of the citizens of Washington State? There are several answers to that question.

Democracy. The most compelling reason for learning about public opinion stems from the dictates of democracy. The republican form of government under which we live accords substantial weight to public opinion. Popular sovereignty confers upon "the people" the awesome power of self-rule. Government "of the people, by the people, and for the people" compels those who govern to keep a watchful eye on what the people prefer to be done in their name.

The degree to which public policy matches public opinion is only one of several traits that make a governmental system democratic, however. Other criteria include the degree to which there is protection of individual rights to participate in the making of political choices, and to speak freely about those choices. Another is the degree to which all citizens have equal access to those rights and freedoms, including the choice of political leaders. Still another is the extent to which there is open competition among alternative seekers of political office, such as political parties and candidates.

The mechanisms through which some level of agreement between public opinion and public policy is produced have been referred to as *political linkage processes* (Luttbeg 1974). An obvious linkage mechanism is that of periodic elections. Political parties and individual candidates, in theory at least, actively compete for the votes of citizens, either on the basis of general ideological perspectives (e.g., liberal or conservative) viewed as overall guides to policy, or on the basis of differences on specific issues (e.g., favor the Endangered Species Act or wish to repeal it). Still in theory, voters in the public electorate then vote for candidates and/or incumbent officials according to the positions they state on ideological platforms (e.g., "no new taxes") or on issues deemed to be important to the public acting as voters. The winner, in principle, is the candidate for public office whose ideological stance and/or policy positions most closely match the voters' preferences. Election winners typically claim to represent "a mandate" to implement policy reflecting those preferences.

Another linkage mechanism exists between interest group members and their leaders, whose role it is to actively represent the interests of citizens who have policy preferences on policy questions but who are not able (for lack of time or knowledge of policy processes) to act on their preferences. Advocates of "pluralist democracy" argue that a wide variety of interest groups carry their unique positions to policy makers, bargain among themselves, provide the mass media with information about policy options, and—out of all this interaction—come to play a key role in the formulation of a public policy that approximates the distribution of preferences in the general public.

It is also possible to identify a linkage mechanism in cases where an "elite democracy" is in evidence. This term applies to a political jurisdiction that is governed by a process of open competition among individuals of uncommon influence or ability who claim to serve in the best interests of the general public. While the general public may not directly influence these elites, they take on the obligation of determining the public's preferences and reflecting those preferences in their public policy decisions.

While various mechanisms connect public opinion to public policy, one receiving considerable recent attention is that of *electronic democracy* (or e-democracy). This linkage mechanism entails citizens having open access to electronic terminals connected to a central server that records a multitude of actions taken on the periphery. Policy positions may be presented to the public, either in text form or in video format, and then citizens listen to the arguments, perhaps participate in those discussions themselves, and signal their choices through their own personal terminals.

Questions about this electronic approach to democracy challenge the degree to which it provides the opportunity for bargaining, compromise, and coming to agreement through mutual accommodation. Critics also contend that not all citizens have equal access to the resources required to participate effectively in e-democracy. In some contexts this inequitable access to computers and connectivity has been called the "digital divide" (Compaine 2001), suggesting that an unjust chasm in political influence and power exists between those who have access to these resources and the knowledge to use them, and those who do not. Scholarship on the digital divide often notes that the largest gulfs in access and ability occur between those parts of the public which are already in disadvantaged social locations—whether by income, education, or race and ethnicity—and those which already exercise disproportionate influence. In this case, then, electronic democracy might simply exacerbate problems of political linkage.

Theories of Public Opinion Formation

Why do people hold the opinions they do? Why does that question bear any relevance to an understanding of the opinions of the citizens of Washington State?

Political culture effects. Political culture is the mix of political behaviors, attitudes, cognitive beliefs, and values that characterize a political unit, such as a country or a state (Elazar 1994; Inglehart 1990). Political culture concerns "how things are generally done" in politics in a particular jurisdiction, and what norms or conventions exist to set the boundaries on acceptable attitudes and behaviors if one is to be part of the active citizenry. An adviser to President Franklin Delano Roosevelt once described the United States as being comprised of 47 states and the "Soviet of Washington." That remark indicated the presence of a very distinctive political culture in the Evergreen State, one that was considerably more radical (anti-establishment) than that of other states. A prevailing political culture is thought to affect how people who live in an area tend to be raised, tend to express their political sentiments and hopes, and what they tend to believe about politics. At the same time, as societies become more mobile and the numerous elements of mass media come to displace the influence of local newspapers, the external influences on the distinctive political attitudes of a state could erode its distinctiveness from other states. These forces would act as countervailing influences on a state's citizens. Perhaps as a consequence of these influences in the state and the large scale in-migration of citizens from throughout the country, one currently might be hard pressed to call it "the Soviet of Washington." Even so, remnants of that time in the state's history remain in some of the distinctive institutions and political practices in the state. Washington's dramatic Populist and Progressive reform eras left permanent anti-establishment legacies in Washington State politics, and those legacies are clearly seen in following chapters in this book on political parties, interest groups, the state legislature, and initiatives.

Period effects. In a country's history, the dominant features of certain periods have a powerful, formative effect on the way people behave in the political arena (Jennings and Niemi 1975). Among the most important kinds of period effects are those related to the economy and to war and peace. The Great Depression structured American values and beliefs for generations, leading to greater support for the growth of government and its involvement in maintaining economic stability. The Vietnam War, or the Watergate Scandal, or the destruction of the World Trade Towers are such visible and intense and deeply felt experiences that they can alter the way large portions of the public feel about politics. Again, the degree to which those period effects result in distinctive Washington State public opinion would depend on the degree to which they are uniquely relevant to the state or to the particular individuals who live in the state. The dramatic economic downturn of the beginning of the twenty-first century may come to have particular effects on Washington's citizens. The nation's economic problems were especially serious in high technology sectors, and Washington's unusual dependence on high technology industries—namely, aerospace and computer hardware and software—meant that the downturn hit that state's economy particularly hard. Washington had the highest unemployment in the country at one point during that period, and that experience may result in lasting changes in political attitudes and values among Washingtonians.

Political socialization effects. Much of what we believe stems from what we are taught, what we are "socialized" to believe (Greenstein 1965). The primary agents of socialization (those from whom we learn about politics) are our parents, our peer groups, our schools, and the mass media to which we are exposed. Historically, continuity in beliefs within nations (and within regions inside of nations) has been the norm because parents were the primary sources of political learning. Various changes in family structure and social mobility in recent decades have greatly diminished the effects of parental socialization, and have significantly increased the role of media.

Social location effects. What individuals come to believe may grow out of their position in the social structure of the country (Campbell et al. 1960). Individuals who are lower in the economic structure, or who perform different kinds of work, or who are systematically disadvantaged because of race/ethnicity, or who have historically occupied distinctive social and gender roles, may have different attitudes about important political issues. Those differences may grow out of the way in which the location in the social structure may be linked to alternatives in regard to a public policy, such as tax policy that differentially affects people in different social locations.

Personality/psychological effects. Many scholars who seek to explain why people hold particular opinions argue that beliefs, attitudes, and values are deeply rooted in the way those opinions serve particular needs of a person's personality (Sniderman 1975). Holding a particular opinion of disregard for other groups, for example, may reflect low self-esteem. Other scholars have argued that some global political classifications allow individuals to navigate the complex world of politics without undue effort. Holding highly favorable opinions toward Republicans, for example, allows one to evaluate particular Republicans favorably without going through the effort of assessing each one in terms of their positive and negative attributes.

Rationality. The rational choice approach to public opinion formation assumes that individuals are motivated to maximize their self-interest (Downs 1957). Borrowing from economics, this approach adopts the assumption that individuals know what their goals are, and, when confronted with public policy options, evaluate those options in terms of how they benefit or detract from those goals. Individuals calculate the costs and benefits involved, and support the alternative with the greater net benefits. When individuals lack complete information about the costs and benefits of policy options, they tend to turn to sources of guidance that have provided them with reliable cues for rational behavior in the past for guidance.

Summary. Any particular opinion held by an individual or by a collective public undoubtedly results from more than any one of the preceding theories regarding people's source of opinions. Nonetheless, when trying to determine why residents of Washington hold certain opinions, it may be helpful to look back at these various explanations to possibly assist in achieving a deeper understanding of public opinion in the Evergreen State.

Stability and Change in Public Opinion

Commentators and citizens alike enjoy discussing change in public opinion. "Has the public become more conservative?" "Has support for the governor fallen?" "Have citizens become more supportive of mass transit?" Unfortunately, answers to such questions are not easy to formulate. Indeed, fully understanding the degree to which public opinion is changing requires looking at both individual and aggregate (the public as a whole) levels simultaneously.

At the aggregate level, one is tempted to simply gauge the percentage supporting a particular opinion at two points in time to conclude whether change or stability is in evidence. But that evidence can be misleading. For example, one may find that the percentage supporting an income tax in Washington has not changed in recent years, and conclude that there is great stability in those opinions. That very well may not be the case, however. It may be that there has been a great deal of change, with many persons who used to favor an income tax no longer doing so, and an equal number of others who used to oppose an income tax now favoring it. The consequence is that, even though the overall distribution remains the same, there has been substantial change in opinions within the public. One might argue that it makes no difference because there still will be the same number opposing or supporting the tax policy. It may make a substantial difference, however, if those who are changing in a particular direction share particular characteristics that may lead to greater or lesser levels of participation in politics.

Looking at the question from another perspective, one may find that the overall distribution in support of the income tax has in fact changed over time, but no particular individual has changed her or his opinion. How could this happen? One way this could occur is by generational or cohort replacement. As older generations die off and leave the public, they are replaced by younger generations entering the public. Those groups entering and leaving may hold different views on public policy. Thus, even though no particular individual has changed an opinion over time, the overall public has changed in its distribution. Likewise, there are times when public boundaries change. For example, if a new group—such as young people after a change in voting age laws—is admitted into the electorate, and these people hold views that are different than held by the former collective, overall public opinion may change. Finally, a state may experience great tides of in-migration, and the newly arrived may bring with them very different opinions than those already established there. The in-migration of many persons from California to the Puget Sound area is one such significant factor in Washington State.

Political Culture

Political culture is the characteristic mix of attitudes, values, behaviors, and institutions that reflect a particular history and approach to politics. What distinguishes the political culture of Washington State, and how does that compare to the political cultures of other places in the United States? Most of the major political science research into questions of political culture in the United States has focused upon comparison at the state and city level. In Washington State, the state's largest cities to the east and west of the Cascade Mountains—Spokane and Seattle, respectively—are most often characterized as areas featuring quite different political cultures.

To date, the most influential classification of cities and states into types of political culture was developed by Daniel Elazar. In his work called *The American Mosaic* (1994), Elazar has suggested that there are three major types of political cultures in the United States: the *individualistic,* the *moralistic,* and the *traditionalistic.* He argues that any particular place holds a mix of those three culture types, but that nearly always one of these three cultures is predominant. Why an area exhibits a particular type of political culture reflects "the streams and currents of migration that have carried people of different origins and backgrounds across the continent in more or less orderly patterns" (229).

The individualistic political culture features a view of politics in democracies as constituting a "free marketplace," wherein the role of government is to be held to the very minimum required in order to "encourage private initiative and widespread access to the marketplace" (230). In this political culture, politics is dedicated to enhancing the success of individual needs. The moralistic political culture, in contrast, emphasizes the "positive potential" of politics, and sees the goal of political activity as "centered on some notion of the public good and properly devoted to the advancement of the public interest" (232). Citizens are expected to participate in political affairs, and there is an obligation to intervene in the activities of individuals if it is necessary to promote the public or common good. Finally, the traditionalistic political culture "…is rooted in an ambivalent attitude toward the marketplace coupled with a paternalistic and elitist conception of the commonwealth" (234). This political culture is dominated by elites whose primary goal is to maintain the existing social and political arrangements.

Where do the two major cities of Washington stand on the question of political culture when compared to other cities around the country? Table 1 presents Elazar's rating of Spokane and Seattle on each of the three major political culture dimensions, as well as the ratings he assigned to a group of other cities from around the country. Neither Seattle nor Spokane has any elements of the traditionalistic political culture, suggesting that there is an absence of any dominant force committed to sustaining the status quo through political activity. They differ from Atlanta in that regard, where traditional political values are the major theme of the culture. According to Elazar, Seattle has a minor strain of individualistic political culture, while the Spokane area has none at all. This might seem strange in the light of the popularly held view of Spokane as a more conservative city than Seattle, both in light of contemporary issues and in terms of historical events. But recall, Elazar is writing about the relative emphasis on the individual as opposed to the common good, and also that Seattle and Spokane really are quite similar in one important respect. The shared distinctiveness of Seattle and Spokane may be best expressed in their respective ratings on the dimension of *moralistic political culture.* The moralistic political culture is seen as the *sole* strain in Spokane, and as the major strain in Seattle. Recall that the term moralistic in this context does not refer to how "moral" the politics of the city are; rather, it refers to the relative emphasis placed on the common good as opposed to private interest. On this dimension, both Seattle and Spokane are more like the other Western cities of San Francisco, San Diego,

Table 1

Elazar Political Culture Types for Seattle and Spokane
and Selected other American Cities

City	Political Culture Types		
	Traditionalistic	Individualistic	Moralistic
SEATTLE	None	Minor	Major
SPOKANE	None	None	Sole
Atlanta	Major	Minor	None
Boston	None	None	Sole
Chicago	None	Major	Minor
Denver	None	None	Sole
Houston	Sole	None	None
Kansas City	None	Sole	None
Los Angeles	None	Minor	Major
Miami	None	Sole	None
Minneapolis	None	None	Sole
Sacramento	None	Minor	Major
Salt Lake City	None	None	Sole
San Diego	Minor	None	Major
San Francisco	None	Minor	Major
St. Louis	None	Sole	None

Source: Daniel J. Elazar, *The American Mosaic: The Impact of Space, Time, and Culture on American Politics* (Boulder, Colorado: Westview Press, 1994), pp. 242–43.

Sacramento, and Salt Lake City than they are like other cities across the country. For example, Seattle and Spokane differ greatly from Atlanta, Houston, Kansas City, and Miami.

Overall, then, the state's two major cities are similar in their dominant political cultures, and they are similar as well to other cities of the American West— and to Minneapolis, a city that lies in the same immigrant stream which moved across the northern reaches of the country. The political cultures of Washington's two major cities differ from many U.S. cities, especially those in the lower Midwest and the South.

Social Capital

One of the most important concepts in understanding the politics of a place is its level of social capital, itself based in the attitudes and values of citizens that constitute part of its political culture (Coleman 1990; Putnam 2000). Social capital has to do with the degree to which individuals trust each other, and assume good intentions on the part of others. If people trust each other they are more willing to join in social networks, and those social networks can be used to influence the character and the quality of their social and political environment. Individuals who trust other people are inclined to invest in interpersonal networks that benefit others because they have faith that those others can be trusted to reciprocate when the time comes that they are needed. This mutual trust binds people together in ways that allow them to exert greater collective influence than they would have individually. Many scholars argue that social capital is required to ensure democratic political practices featuring broad-based public involvement.

Some highly regarded observers of contemporary American society have argued that social capital is on the decline in America. Evidence of this decline is seen in a decrease in public involvement in political (e.g., voting) and social (civic organizations) activities, even those that are not explicitly political in form (Putnam 2000). Even such long-lived and highly revered organizations as the PTA have declined substantially in level of membership and range of activity. While some scholars dispute the claim that social capital is in decline (e.g., Ladd 1999), this apparent social trend is an important subject of study because major U.S. cities featuring higher levels of social capital tend to have higher quality city government services (Pierce et al. 2002) and feature higher quality health care services (Hendryx et al. 2002).

Table 2 displays scores for a number of U.S. cities on a measure of political and social trust expressed by their citizens. The higher the score, the higher is the level of trust, and thus the higher the level of social capital. Seattle's social capital score is among the highest of the cities listed, surpassed only by Minneapolis. Spokane's score, in contrast, is much lower than that of Seattle—although higher than a number of other major U.S. cities, such as Miami, Atlanta, and St. Louis. Hence, while Spokane and Seattle share a moralistic political culture, Seattle enjoys a higher level of social capital—and the concomitant higher levels of civic engagement and political participation.

Regional Differences on General Issues

Even within the metropolitan areas surrounding Seattle and Spokane, there may be significant differences among the communities and the kinds of political values held by their residents. One might expect, for example, the residents of Thurston County, the home of the state capital, to hold different attitudes than those of citizens in King County, the home of the state's largest city. Similarly, people in Spokane County can be expected to differ from King or Thurston county residents, and perhaps from the citizens of Kootenai County, Idaho, just a few miles across the border. Table 3 sets forth the percent of people agreeing

Table 2

Political and Social Trust Levels in Seattle and Spokane
Compared to Selected other American Cities

City	Trust Score
SEATTLE	205.75
SPOKANE	195.39
Atlanta	192.36
Boston	197.92
Chicago	199.01
Denver	200.86
Houston	176.06
Kansas City	184.66
Los Angeles	178.94
Miami	189.13
Minneapolis	210.08
Sacramento	190.90
Salt Lake City	205.16
San Diego	198.30
San Francisco	199.64
St. Louis	190.26

Source: Data for the calculation of political and social trust scores provided by the Leigh Stowell and Company market research firm of Seattle, Washington.

or strongly agreeing with a series of statements about contemporary public affairs in six counties in Washington, and one county in Idaho.

While there are some noteworthy differences among the residents of the different counties, all-in-all the gaps are not very substantial on most of the issues presented in Table 3. King County residents are least likely (32 percent) to say that "women's rights are receiving too much attention," while citizens who live in Snohomish Co., the home of Everett, are the most likely to agree with that statement (41 percent). Kootenai County, Idaho, residents are about in the middle of the distribution of the Washington State county results. Overall, it is clear that barely a third of the respondents in any county believe that the discussion of "women's rights" is getting too much attention.

On the question of whether "a few major corporations have all of the power," the percentage figures are much higher. In every county, well over half of the respondents believe that the country is run by major corporations. In Washington, the figure reaches as high as 66 percent in Thurston County, and the level is 68 percent in the Idaho Panhandle county of Kootenai. King Co. (54 percent)

Table 3

County Differences in Public Opinion on Political and Social Issues*

				County				
Issue	King	Pierce	Snohomish	Kitsap	Thurston	Spokane	Kootenai (ID)
Women's rights receiving too much attention	32%	40%	41%	34%	36%	35%	36%
Few major corps have all power	54%	59%	55%	59%	66%	59%	68%
Public officials interested only in people with money	66%	61%	64%	70%	58%	65%	69%
Everything changing too fast	43%	52%	52%	43%	57%	45%	54%

*The entry in each cell is the percentage agreeing or strongly agreeing with the statement along the side. Source: Leigh Stowell and Company market surveys of Seattle and Spokane.

and Snohomish Co. (55 percent) are close to each other, but even at that lower range more than half of the public agrees with the statement, reflecting pervasive political cynicism.

A related issue concerning who commands power in politics is raised by the statement: "Public officials are only interested in people with money." Nearly two-thirds of the respondents in the several counties agree with that cynical statement. In Kitsap Co. (Bremerton is the principal city), 70 percent of the citizens believe that people with money enjoy great advantage in contacting public officials, and in King Co. the comparable figure is 66 percent. On the other side of the Cascade Mountains, both the Spokane and the Kootenai samples are at the upper range of this cynical view of politics and of public officials. Indeed, the overall pattern confirms a broad belief that substantial distrust exists among American citizens about public officials.

Contemporary Americans indisputably live in a world of rapid economic, social, and technological change. Washington State is seen by many as being "on the leading edge" of that change, especially with the high technology elements of its economy in the Seattle area, and the social and cultural elements of its entrepreneurial prowess over the past two decades (e.g., Starbucks Coffee Houses spreading around the country, the ubiquitous presence of Microsoft in homes and offices across the country, and the popularity of the Seattle music scene). The residents of the several counties listed in Table 3 were asked the question of whether they agreed with the statement "everything is changing too fast." Ironically, perhaps, King and Kitsap county residents are least likely to agree that things are changing too fast, even though this is where most of the recent socioeconomic change has occurred. Citizens in Thurston Co. (57 percent) and in Kootenai Co. (54 percent) are the most resistant to the current pace of change.

Although not all regions of the state are included in these analyses, some worthwhile conclusions can indeed be tendered from this survey evidence. First, there are some regional differences in terms of the opinions their publics hold about important issues of politics. Second, substantial similarity exists across the Evergreen State in some respects; political cynicism is clearly the most important of those broadly shared perspectives on politics among contemporary Washingtonians.

Demographic Differences on General Issues

The body of research literature indicates that there is something important about a particular attribute such as gender or age or income that powerfully influences the way people view their political world. It may be that people in the same category, say under 40 years of age, have been subjected to the same forces of history (period effect), such as a war or a depression, and this shared experience has caused them to think a certain way about some aspects of politics. Or it may be that people in a particular socio-economic or demographic category share a stake or political interest in a particular issue. For example, women may feel differently about abortion or other women's rights issues than do men, or they may feel differently than men about whether there should be a universal draft for young men. Similarly, wealthy citizens tend to be more interested in capital gains tax reductions than are working class people. Tables 4–6 display the results of a survey of citizens in the Seattle area on a series of contemporary political issues, contrasting respondents by race/ethnicity, income, and gender.

Table 4

Racial/Ethnicity Differences in Opinions on Selected Political Issues*

| | Race/Ethnicity | | | | |
Issue	White	Black	Native American	Asian American	Multi-cultural
Women's rights are teceiving too much attention	38%	21%	31%	27%	44%
All young men should serve in the military	33%	27%	40%	31%	33%
Public officials only listen to people with money	60%	63%	71%	53%	52%
Politics is interesting	55%	53%	37%	50%	66%
A few major corporations hold all of the power	56%	61%	74%	51%	59%
Too many people are getting a free ride	66%	54%	69%	70%	71%

*The data are for the Seattle area public only. The entry in each column is the percentage agreeing with the statement. The white category of race/ethnicity includes Hispanic/Latino citizens.

On the issue of whether "women's rights issues are receiving too much attention," the least agreement is found among African Americans (21 percent), followed by Asian Americans (27 percent) and Native Americans (31 percent). The white survey respondents (38 percent) were nearly twice as likely as black respondents to agree with the statement. It is possible that these minority respondents are more sensitive to equity issues for historically disadvantaged groups in the population, and they are inclined to empathize with other disadvantaged groups. On most of the other issues, the racial/ethnic groups' opinions wrap around those of white Washingtonians, with the latter usually being someplace in the middle. Moreover, the differences among the non-white groups are sometimes quite substantial. Thus, for example, while only 53 percent of the Asian Americans polled believe that public officials only listen to people with money, fully 71 percent of the Native American respondents express that belief.

Table 5 displays the issue opinions of Washington residents of different income levels, contrasting those above and below $40,000 annual incomes. In most cases the opinions held are rather similar, save for several noteworthy issues. Perhaps not unexpectedly, people in families with annual incomes below

Table 5

Income Differences in Opinions on Selected Political Issues*

	Income	
	Above $40,000	Below $40,000
Women's rights are receiving too much attention	35%	35%
All young men should serve in the military	35%	30%
Public officials are interested only in people with money	53%	63%
Politics is interesting to me	62%	52%
Corporations have all of the power	48%	62%
Too many people are getting a free ride	38%	35%

*The results are Seattle area data only. The entry in each column is the percentage agreeing with the statement. Source: Leigh Stowell and Company market research firm, Seattle.

$40,000 are more likely to believe that "public officials are interested only in people with money." Likewise, they are more likely to believe that "corporations have all of the power." On the other hand, they differ very little on questions of women's rights, or universal male military service, or whether people are unfairly getting a free ride on the efforts of others.

Table 6 compares the opinions of men and women in Washington State on this same set of general political questions. Rather surprisingly, there are no significant male/female differences on the question of women's rights, nor on most of the other issues posed. The policy area where the biggest opinion differences between men and women arises appears in regard to military service. When asked whether "all young men should serve in the military" women are much less likely than men to support that statement (24% compared to 40%). Perhaps that difference is the result of women generally being seen as less supportive of military service and military action than men.

The Public Agenda

One of the most important functions of the public in a democracy is to define the problems and issues that those in decision-making positions should confront.

Table 6

Gender Differences in Opinions on Selected Political and Social Issues*

	Gender	
	Male	Female
Women's rights are receiving too much attention	36%	35%
All young men should serve in the military	40%	24%
Most public officials are only interested in people with money	61%	59%
Politics is interesting to me	58%	51%
A few major corporations have all of the power	54%	58%
Too many people are getting a free ride	70%	61%

*The results are Seattle area data only. The entry in each column is the percentage agreeing with the statement. Source: Leigh Stowell and Company market research firm, Seattle.

While citizens may not have the time or the relevant knowledge required to participate directly in the resolution of those policy questions, they can identify what they believe to be the appropriate topics that ought to be placed on the agenda for policymaker attention and public discussion.

A recent survey of citizens in Washington, Oregon, and Idaho asked respondents to indicate what they felt to be the most important problems facing their respective communities. Are Washington residents different in the problems they identify as pressing than their neighbors to the East and to the South? The findings displayed in Table 7 provide a partial answer to that question. That table sets forth the percent of respondents from each of the states that identified four specific areas as "major problems" concerning their respective communities. Each area represents a mix of related concerns that are combined into a single category. For example, the area of "crime" includes concerns with victimization, gangs, drugs, violence, and police misconduct. It should be noted that the totals in the table do not add to 100 percent because some people did not identify one or more of the major problem areas listed as affecting their community.

In only one area are Washington citizens particularly distinctive from their neighbors in the degree to which they see some issues as major problems. While Washington citizens are a little more likely than those from Oregon to see crime

Table 7

Public Perceptions of Most Important Problems Facing the Community:
Washington Compared to Oregon and Idaho*

| | State | | |
	Washington	Oregon	Idaho
Problem Area			
Crime[a]	21%	18%	19%
Growth[b]	34%	30%	33%
Economic[c]	5%	4%	4%
Quality of Public Life[d]	7%	14%	20%

*The entry in each cell is the percentage of the respective state publics identifying the problem area as the most important problem facing the respondent's community.

[a]Includes crime, safety, gangs, drugs, violence and police.

[b]Includes growth, growing too fast, over-development, infrastructure, traffic, population growth, new people-outsiders, immigrants.

[c]Includes housing, economy, cost of living, property values, jobs.

[d]Includes quality of life, small town atmosphere, schools, health care, social services, lack of youth activities, environment, pollution.

Source: Elway Research, Inc. for the *Seattle Times*/Northwest Cable News Poll, 2000.

as a problem, and to view population growth as a problem, they are substantially less likely than people from either Oregon or Idaho to mention a decline in the quality of public life as a major problem. From this perspective, then, the Washington public might be seen to be more satisfied with the overall quality of life in their state than are residents of Oregon and Idaho. On the other hand, the case may be that, though concerned about the quality of life, Washington residents find other issues to resonate more deeply with them, causing quality of life concerns to be somewhat understated. A partial answer to the question is found in results displayed in Table 8. This table reports the percentage of respondents in the three states believing that progress is being made in enhancing the overall quality of life in their state.

Table 8

Percent Saying Progress is Being Made in Various Areas:
Washington, Oregon, and Idaho Publics*

Areas of Progress	State		
	Washington	Oregon	Idaho
Overall Quality of Life	67%	72%	76%
Air and Water Quality	65%	63%	66%
Transportation	41%	57%	49%
A Place of Opportunity	67%	65%	72%
Race Relations	72%	66%	66%
Social and Health Needs	71%	70%	72%
Local Economy	72%	72%	70%
Affordable Housing	37%	43%	46%
Entertainment/Recreation	73%	73%	68%
A Place to Raise a Family	82%	82%	84%
Sense of Community	66%	75%	80%
Crime	57%	61%	58%
Education	65%	55%	58%

*The entry in each cell is the percent saying that progress is being made in the community in that particular area.

Source: Source: Elway Research, Inc. for the *Seattle Times*/Northwest Cable News Poll, 2000.

Contrary to what one might have concluded from Table 7, the results in Table 8 indicate clearly that Washington residents are less satisfied than those from the other two states concerning progress being made toward enhancing the overall quality of life in the state. But, it is noteworthy that even though Washingtonians are somewhat less likely to agree that overall progress is being made, still two-thirds of them are on the positive side of the question. On most of the issues listed, the citizens of the three states are close to each other in their view of progress, and likely to believe that progress is being made. However, there are several issue areas that are exceptions to the general rule.

For example, Washingtonians are much less likely than Oregonians to believe that progress is being made in the area of transportation—no doubt reflecting the now legendary magnitude of traffic congestion in the Puget Sound area. Washington residents are less likely to believe that progress is being made on the provision of affordable housing; barely a third of the Washington survey respondents feel progress has taken place. Washington residents also are less likely than those from either Oregon or Idaho to see progress being made in the area of sustaining "a sense of community" where they live. There are some policy areas, however, where Washingtonians are somewhat more likely to see progress being made—namely, those of education and race relations.

Participation in local community activities is one way in which citizens can give active voice to their opinions. High levels of community participation reflect high social capital, the kind of networking that allows citizens to exercise influence on the character of their local community. Table 9 displays the percent of respondents reporting active participation in community activities in Washington, Oregon, and Idaho.

The level of overall involvement by the Washington public is only slightly greater than that of Oregon, but substantially less than that of Idaho. The Idaho public is more likely to participate in community political activities and

Table 9

Percent Reporting Participation in Community Activities
Washington, Oregon, and Idaho Publics*

| | State | | |
Community Activity	Washington	Oregon	Idaho
Community Political Activity	39%	40%	46%
Contribution to Charity	88%	82%	88%
Community Social Event	61%	60%	73%
Contacted Public Official	29%	30%	39%
Volunteered Time	62%	58%	65%
Average Involvement Index	2.78	2.69	3.11

*The entry in each cell is the percent saying they engaged in that particular community activity. The involvement index is the number of activities in which the individual reports being involved. The index ranges from 0 to 5.

Source: Source: Elway Research, Inc. for the *Seattle Times*/Northwest Cable News Poll, 2000.

community social events, and to contact a public official. These differences may reflect the small-town nature of Idaho's population, where the community tends to be closer to the individual than is the case in the more highly urbanized states of Washington and Oregon.

What kinds of differences are obtained among Washington residents regarding their involvement in community activities? Table 10 shows the answer to that question in terms of individual attributes that often have been used to explain participation levels. The first is the level of education the individual has attained. As frequently is found in research on American political behavior, the participation level of Washingtonians is clearly differentiated by level of educational attainment. For example, Washingtonians who have attended graduate school average 3.3 acts of involvement, compared to only 2.3 by those who progressed no farther than high school. Similarly, individuals of color are less likely to be involved in community activities than are the non-minority citizens of the state. On the other hand, there are no differences between men and women in the Washington public with regard to their level of community involvement.

People who live in different parts of Washington often compare themselves, usually favorably, to those who live in other regions of the state. Do they differ in terms of their level of community involvement? The answer is yes. Residents of eastern Washington and those who live in central Puget Sound (Pierce and

Table 10

Average Levels of Community Involvement in the Washington State Public within Various Personal Demographic Categories*

Education	*High School* 2.28	*Some College* 2.82	*College* 3.04	*Graduate School* 3.30
Gender	*Male* 2.79	*Female* 2.77		
Region	*King Co.* 2.66	*Puget Sound* 2.92	*Western Wa.* 2.57	*Eastern Wa.* 2.96
Race	*White* 2.86	*Non-White* 2.22		
Home Internet Use	*Yes* 3.03	*No* 2.44		

*The entry in each cell is the average number of community activities in which the individual respondent participated, with a maximum of five and a minimum of zero.

Source: Source: Elway Research, Inc. for the *Seattle Times*/Northwest Cable News Poll, 2000.

Snohomish counties) are more likely to be involved in community activities than are those who live in King County and other parts of western Washington.

Finally, Table 10 shows the relationship of home Internet use to community involvement. Internet users are much more likely to participate in other community activities than those who do not enjoy such use. This is an important finding because there is considerable disagreement in the academic and popular literature on the relationship between Internet use and involvement in traditional community activities and networks (Katz and Rice 2002). Some social observers have argued that attachment to the technology involved in Internet use diverts individuals from their traditional personal connections and social networks. The singular focus on the desktop computer is hypothesized by some commentators to alienate individuals from their community. On the other hand, other scholars and social commentators argue that use of the Internet from home is a new way to reinforce traditional networks, albeit through an unconventional medium. The kinds of people who possess the resources to own and employ computer technology in the home are also people with individual attributes which typically lead them into community involvement. In particular, as we saw earlier, higher levels of education are associated with higher levels of community involvement, and both traits are associated with higher levels of Internet use.

Table 11 shows that Internet use is associated with differences in involvement on *each* of the community activities listed, albeit some more than others. In this table, the entry is an average score, where 1 is involvement in the activity and 2 is no involvement. Hence, the higher the score, the lower the level of involvement. These findings show that Internet users are more likely to go to political meetings in their community, to contribute to charities, to attend

Table 11

Average Level of Washington Public's Community Involvement
in Specific Activities, within Internet Use*

Community Involvement Activity	Internet Use	
	Yes	No
Community Political Meeting	1.55	1.76
Contribution to Charity	1.10	1.21
Community Social Event	1.35	1.48
Contacted Public Official	1.65	1.90
Volunteered	1.31	1.51

*The entry in each cell represents the level of involvement in the particular community involvement activity for Internet users and for Internet non-users. A lower number indicates higher level of involvement.

community social events, to contact public officials about their concerns, and to volunteer for community service. If anything, the use of the Internet may facilitate involvement in the local community for persons who are already inclined to do so, rather than displace those other traditional forms of civic engagement.

Government Performance

One of the most widely noted patterns in public opinion in recent decades is a significant decline in American citizens' confidence in the effectiveness of government performance (Putnam 2000). This troubling trend serves to undermine the capacity of government to address shared concerns, such as traffic congestion, environmental quality, public safety, and homeland security. It depresses the willingness of citizens to participate, along with their state and local governments, in collective activities intended to make their communities better places to live. This decline in willingness to engage in what are called *co-production activities* is revealed in such trends as a significant drop in contributions to United Way, declining donations of blood to the Red Cross and food to local food banks, lower participation in public safety programs such as Block Watch, and less joining of commuter-trip reduction programs to reduce traffic congestion.

Not all state government activities are viewed in the same light by Washingtonians. Some state government efforts are seen as being more effective in accomplishing public interest goals than others. Table 12 sets forth findings on how Washingtonians graded six distinct activities of state government that collectively make up the majority of the Evergreen State's budget. The survey find-

Table 12

Public Grades Given to the Performance of Different
Washington Government Activities

Activity	Grade assigned, by percent surveyed						
	A	B	C	D	F	DK*	GPA
Colleges and Universities	9	40	31	9	3	8	2.46
Natural Resources and Environment	10	35	34	13	5	4	2.34
Prisons	7	20	30	12	7	25	2.11
Public Schools	5	30	41	12	9	3	2.10
Social and Health Services	5	24	35	23	10	4	1.93
Transportation and Highways	4	16	25	33	21	1	1.47

* Don't Know
Source: Elway Research, Inc. Topline Data, June 3-6, 2002.

ings indicate that Washington's public colleges and universities are seen as doing a good job of meeting their responsibilities, with only 12% of the public awarding them poor grades of D or F. Natural Resources and Environmental Protection agencies do almost as well, receiving an average grade of 2.34 (grade of C). In contrast, Prisons (Department of Corrections) receive barely a C average at 2.11, as do public schools at 2.10. Even worse, Social and Health Services get a 1.93 average grade (D+), and the area of Transportation and Highways rates only a 1.47; over half of the public gives this area a D or F grade.

Conclusion

The citizens of Washington are inclined to have high expectations for their state government and their political leaders. The state's moralistic political culture invites these high expectations. This political culture was brought to Washington by its early settlers, and this perspective on politics was reflected in—and received reinforcement from—the Populist and Progressive reform movements which swept across the American West at the turn of the century. This same moralistic political culture continues in strong force today. As the following chapters will reveal, the moralistic political culture is reflected in the way in which political parties operate in the state, how interest groups have been both accommodated and regulated, how the initiative process has come to occupy a major role in the policy process, and how the major political institutions of state and local government have taken shape and tend to operate and interact.

Although the expectations of government entertained by Washingtonians tend to be rather high, their collective assessment of the current level of performance of the state's governmental institutions is quite low. Whether in regard to the resolution of Puget Sound traffic problems, the performance of public schools, the restoration of historic salmon runs, or providing affordable housing and health care coverage to the state's most disadvantaged citizens, the state's governmental institutions receive rather poor marks from their citizens. More vexing problems, such as reform of the state's inadequate and inequitable revenue and taxation system or broadening economic development beyond the congested Puget Sound region, seem beyond the reach of state and local government officials. Politics in the Evergreen State seem to be increasingly less deliberative and visionary, and more and more the subject of the fits and starts of temporary trends and fads. The less desirable unanticipated consequences of the state's deep Populist and Progressive roots have become increasingly evident in the frequent use of the initiative process to redirect public policies duly established by the deliberative work of esteemed commissions, the state legislature, and the governor.

The Evergreen State has come to a major crossroads in its history. One of its major employers, the Boeing Corporation, has moved its corporate headquarters away to Chicago. The state's major extractive industries—logging, mining and fishing—will never again attain their former levels of production. The "cheap power" available to industry and households alike in the past will no longer be present. The "dot com" boom of the 1990s became a bust in the early 2000s. Two former governors—a Democrat and a Republican—came out of retirement to attempt to rescue the state's higher education system from a decade-long decline in state support with an initiative to raise money for badly needed capital improvements. A blue-ribbon task force on tax reform headed by Bill Gates Sr. has proposed anew an income tax to balance out what it believes to be the state's seriously regressive and inefficient public revenue system. Will these and similar efforts by the state's opinion leaders succeed, or will the state's political institutions continue to disappoint the state's citizens? The chapters to follow will provide reasons for both optimism and concern in this regard. The Evergreen State has constructed an enviable governmental apparatus and legal superstructure, featuring some of the most progressive aspects of state government in the country. Its state and local agencies are generally staffed with first-rate career officials, well-educated and richly experienced to an uncommon degree. Despite these valuable assets, Washington's leaders and citizens nontheless face a considerable number of difficult challenges—items of unfinished business of democratic governance—in the years ahead. Only time will tell if Washington's governmental and community leaders can rise to the challenges facing them, and whether the state's citizens will do their part to support timely reforms and innovations.

References

Campbell, Angus, Philip E. Converse, Warren E. Miller, and Donald E. Stokes. 1960. *The American Voter.* New York: John Wiley and Sons.

Coleman, James S. 1990. *Foundations of Social Theory.* Cambridge, Mass.: Belknap Press.

Compaine, Benjamin M. 2001. *The Digital Divide: Facing a Crisis or Creating a Myth?* Cambridge, Mass.: MIT Press.

Downs, Anthony. 1957. *An Economic Theory of Democracy.* New York: Harper and Row.

Elazar, Daniel J. 1994. *The American Mosaic: The Impact of Space, Time, and Culture on American Politics.* Boulder, Co: Westview Press.

Greenstein, Fred I. 1965. *Children and Politics.* New Haven, Conn.: Yale University Press.

Hendryx, Michael S., Melissa M. Ahern, Nicholas P. Lovrich, and Arthur M. McCurdy. 2002. "Access to Health Care and Community Social Capital." *Health Services Research* 35: 307–18.

Inglehart, Ronald. 1990. *Culture Shift in Advanced Industrial Society.* Princeton, N.J.: Princeton University Press.

Jennings, M. Kent, and Richard G. Niemi. 1975. "Continuity and Change in Political Orientations: A Longitudinal Study of Two Generations." *The American Political Science Review* 18: 1316–35.

Katz, James E., and Ronald E. Rice. 2002. *Social Consequences of Internet Use: Access, Involvement, and Interaction.* Cambridge, Mass.: MIT Press.

Key, Jr., V.O. 1965. *Public Opinion and American Democracy.* New York: Knopf.

Ladd, Everett Carll. 1999. *The Ladd Report.* New York: The Free Press.

Luttbeg, Norman R. 1974. "Political Linkage in a Large Society." In *Public Opinion and Public Policy* (rev. edition), ed. Norman R. Luttbeg. Homewood, Ill.: Dorsey.

Pierce, John C., Kathleen M. Beatty, and Paul R. Hagner. 1982. *The Dynamics of American Public Opinion: Patterns and Processes.* Glenview, Ill.: Scott, Foresman and Company.

Pierce, John C., Nicholas P. Lovrich, Jr., and C. David Moon. 2002. "Social Capital and Government Performance: An Analysis of 20 American Cities." *Public Performance and Management Review* 25: 381–97.

Putnam, Robert. 2000. *Bowling Alone: The Collapse and Revival of American Community.* New York: Simon and Schuster.

Sniderman, Paul M. 1975. *Personality and Democratic Politics.* Berkeley: University of California Press.

Chapter Two

Washington State Parties

Andrew Appleton and Ashley Grosse

Introduction

P OLITICAL PARTIES IN WASHINGTON STATE have been characterized as historically and comparatively weak at the organizational level (Appleton and Deporter 1996). Prior to the modern era, party organizational development was restrained by two peculiarities that came to symbolize the uniqueness of the state at some level—namely, the "blanket primary" and the absence of party registration. Coupled with a weak set of laws regulating party finance and campaign spending, the party system in Washington State before the modern era remained perhaps less developed at an organizational level than party systems in many other states.

However, in the intervening period, two broad sets of changes have taken place in the environment surrounding the party organizations themselves that have catalyzed party development in the state. First, Washington has become a truly competitive state where the control of the state legislature, prominent statewide offices, and the composition of the federal congressional delegation have become intense fields of struggle for the major parties (Beck 1997, 37). Second, there have been challenges and changes to the legal regime within which the parties operate, most notably in the areas of campaign finance and the primary system.

Scholars have noticed the reinforcing effect that modified rules governing campaign finance have had on state parties. The growing salience of the "soft" versus "hard" money distinction under federal (and many state) rules actually served to recenter state party organizations in the election campaign process, and to cement their key position in the service-vendor model of the new political party. Exempt from many of the restrictions placed on national party organizations and political action committees, state party organizations became an important hub of money collection and distribution.

This chapter examines the impact of changing rules and environments on political parties in Washington State. We argue that recent events in the state allow us to use the case of its political parties to test two broad theories of party behavior that have been proffered in recent years: the theory of parties as adaptive organizations and the theory of the cartel party. Before turning to these two theories, however, we will provide a general overview of the development of the party system in Washington State.

The Development of State Parties

Two clear trends can be distinguished in the development of political parties in the Evergreen State. On the one hand, the state has been characterized by a political culture that contains many elements of populism, political independence, and indeed, overt anti-partyism. On the other hand, parties have been consistent in their attempts to both combat the more anti-party provisions of state law and to maintain their place in the political process. These two counter-trends can be discerned in the shape of the legal environment itself, which will be discussed in greater detail later; suffice it to observe at the outset of this discussion that political parties in the Evergreen State have used both the legislative and judicial apparatus to preserve and enhance their role as public institutions as much as they have been negatively impacted by these bodies.

Illustrative of the populist and often anti-party nature of state politics are the numerous initiatives (both to the voters and to the legislature) and referenda that have been filed over the years which have either had the intention or the consequence of regulating and restricting party activity. During the early days of the initiative process, a significant number of initiatives were filed, dealing with issues such as the nomination of candidates (attempting to modify the law of 1907), the primary elections (the creation of a blanket primary system), and non-partisan elections (the extension of non-partisan elections to statewide offices). By the 1930s, some of these measures were beginning to gain approval; for example, the blanket primary system was instituted by initiative (to the legislature) in 1934–35, and non-partisan school board elections were put into place by an initiative to the people in 1938.

In the 1960s and 1970s, many ballot measures appeared concerning campaign finance and party financing restrictions. In 1972 Initiative 276 (to the people) instituted a campaign finance and public disclosure regime, the first move into the regulation of party funding by the state. That initiative also created the Public Disclosure Commission, which will be discussed later. Term limits appeared in 1976 (although the attorney-general at the time declined to prepare a ballot for this, on constitutional grounds), and a ballot measure pertaining to reform of the presidential delegate selection system appeared in

1989. Limited term limits were passed in 1992 (I-573), and there were inter-mittent proposals for the limitation of campaign funding and party spending from the 1980s through the 1990s. Campaign finance restrictions were pro-posed in I-134 (to the legislature) and, when the legislature failed to act on the proposal, were passed in the general election of November 1992. In short, the initiative and referendum process, itself considered to be an anti-party device, has been used over time to restrict parties' margins of maneuver in Washington State.

Despite these anti-party measures, political parties have been neither insig-nificant in state history, nor have they withered away as a result of these re-forms. Previous studies have shown that parties have been quite active at the state level (Appleton and Deporter 1996; Nice 1992; Cotter et al. 1989; Mullen and Pierce 1985), and they have been an integral part of the politics of Wash-ington. While party identification among the electorate remains perhaps weaker than in other states—in large part due to the blanket primary to be discussed later—there is evidence to suggest that party loyalty in government has been on the increase (Nice 1992). As Aldrich (1995) observes, political parties have be-come the indispensable mechanism in American political life through which coalitions have become institutionalized, and the ambitions of political elites have been satisfied (Schlesinger 1966).

The Legal Framework

The Constitution. The constitution of the state of Washington neither mentions the right to party formation, nor guarantees political parties a central role in the political process. Article 1, Section 1 vests all political power in the people; Section Four mandates that "The right of...the people peaceably to assemble for the common good shall never be abridged," which obviously acknowledges the possibility of political parties. Where parties are in fact directly mentioned under the state constitution, it is mostly to provide replacements in the case of vacancies in partisan elected offices. In such cases, appointments should be made by the district committees of the same party as that of the vacating legislator or, failing that, by the governor from members of the same party.

Article 2, Section 43 prohibits elected officials of state parties from partici-pating in the legislative redistricting process, and extends the same prohibition to persons who have held state political party office within the previous two years. The same section also prohibits discrimination against political parties in the redistricting process, perhaps once again acknowledging the inevitability of party involvement in the politics of the state.

The Regulation of Parties. Although the state constitution does not make much reference to political parties, the same is not true of state laws. Starting from the earliest years of statehood, a growing web of legal requirements and restrictions have been placed on political party organizations and their operations.

Beck (1997, 67) characterizes Washington as being in the category of states that have moderate levels of party regulation (his categories being weak, moderate, and high), although it is in the upper tier of that middle group. Historically, three broad areas of party activity have been the subject of legal regulation: party organization, nominations, and financing. We will discuss each of these in turn.

Party Organization

The organization of political parties in the state of Washington is subject to a number of broad legal requirements. RCW 29.42 accords a political party "the right to make its own rules and regulations." However, the same chapter of the regulatory code then proceeds to present a detailed legal definition of party status and lay out a mandatory organizational structure and mechanism for the internal distribution of power and leadership selection. While no quantitative judgment can be made of the extent of the regulation of parties in Washington in comparison to other states, recent studies indicate that they are among the most tightly circumscribed by state law in the country.

RCW 29.01.090 provides a legal distinction between major and minor party status in Washington, a conceptual distinction which in its current form dates to 1977, although it was first conceived back in 1907. According to the chapter in question, "'Major political party' means a political party of which at least one nominee for president, vice president, United States senator, or a statewide office received at least five percent of the total vote cast at the last preceding state general election in an even-numbered year." The dichotomy between major and minor party status is most relevant to the procedures that are mandated for parties to nominate their candidates (more of which later). Some minor parties have criticized the existence of two separate legal regimes as tending to favor the interests of the major parties, although ballot access laws in Washington State have generally been regarded as among the more favorable to third parties in the nation (*Seattle Times,* May 14, 1996).

In 2003, eleven political organizations were recognized as minor parties, according to Secretary of State Sam Reed. These parties ranged from organizations that had some national prominence in recent years, such as the Reform Party and the Green Party, to others that are far less visible (e.g., the Constitution Party of Yakima, an offshoot of the Constitution Party of Washington). In the 2000 general election, the state's Libertarian Party qualified for major party status, joining the Democrats and Republicans as those party organizations bound by the provisions of the law relating to these types of parties.

State law also lays out the formal structure of party organization, including the procedures by which they select party leaders; this intervention in intra-party organization dates back to 1921. Major political parties are built upon a three-tiered structure embedded in the legal framework: precincts, county committees, and the state central committee. Any qualified member of a major party may be elected to the post of precinct committee officer, the election taking place during the general election in even-numbered years. RCW 29.42.050 includes a provision that the winning candidate must receive at least ten percent of the votes cast for a candidate of the same party winning the most votes in the precinct, a provision that is intended to prevent "insurgencies" within the party structure. From the standpoint of scholars, it is significant that the law includes both recognition of and a role for party membership, even though this is not classically considered a concept that carries much meaning in the United States. Notwithstanding, the same law provides no definition of party membership, instead requiring precinct chairs to certify lists of party members to the county chair. This practice is rarely performed, inasmuch as party members are somewhat thin on the ground level.[1]

The second tier of the party structure in the state is that of the county committee, which is composed of several precinct officers. RCW 29.42.030 stipulates that incoming county committees must meet within a period of about two months following the general election in even-numbered years to elect a chair, a vice chair, and a state committeeman and committeewoman. The chair and vice-chair must be of the opposite sex, a provision that was inserted during the era of national Democratic Party reform in the 1960s and 1970s when the Democrats were in ascendancy in Washington. The county chairs of major political parties in Washington have certain discretionary powers afforded to them; for example, they may choose to eliminate or add members to the lists provided by precinct officers when presenting the lists to the county auditor for certification. In the late 1960s, an amendment to these regulations mandated the appointment of legislative committees elected by precinct officers residing in state legislative districts in which a majority of precincts lie in counties populated by more than one million people.

The state central committee is composed of each county's two delegates. The central committee appoints the state chair and vice-chair, with a similar requirement that they be of the opposite sex. RCW 29.42.020 lays out the scope of the duties and activities of the state committees. While acknowledging the freedom that such organizations have to determine their political activities and participation in public life, the regulation specifically prohibits the state central committee from making rules and codes determining the procedural aspects of state party conventions.

To summarize, the legal framework in Washington State determines many aspects of party structure and the selection of party leadership. Though requiring that major parties compile certified membership lists, the state does not enforce compliance to that rarely implemented practice.

Party Nominating Procedures

One of the principal purposes of a political party, of course, is to nominate and present candidates for elected office. The history of political parties in Washington, as in other states, is tightly interwoven with state intervention in this arena; however, the unusual nature of its primary system, to be discussed below, has had a number of significant consequences for the major political parties bound by these statutory provisions.

Until 1907, political parties in Washington were free to adopt whatever nominating procedures they saw fit. However, in that year the state adopted, as part of the wave of Progressive Era reforms sweeping the nation, a direct primary system that applied to newly defined major political parties (those whose candidates had received at least ten percent of the vote for a statewide office in the previous election). Under this system, voters could opt which party primary they wished to participate in, but were constrained to vote only for candidates of that one party. This reform did not include a provision for partisan voter registration, a practice which did not exist in all areas of the state until 1934.

In 1934, two powerful interests in the state—the Grange and organized labor groups—drafted an initiative and gathered enough signatures to present it to the legislature on August 21. The key stipulation of the proposed legislation was that "…voters may vote for their choice at any primary…for any candidate for each office, regardless of political affiliation and without a declaration of political faith or adherence on the part of the voter." (RCW 29.18.200). What is now known as the "blanket primary" was adopted by the legislature in February 1935, and this statute has governed the nomination of candidates in Washington ever since.

Under this unique system,[2] there can be no partisan voter registration. Subsequent revisions of the state code do permit major parties to hold voluntary primaries for presidential nominations (which will be discussed below), but the state does not permit the official certification of such lists. For researchers, the consequence has been that the measurement of party identification in the state can only be done using survey-based (or reported) information; no observed data are available. More importantly, it has resulted in a sense that the political culture of the electorate in the Evergreen State is one of independence and split-ticket voting; in the words of Secretary of State Sam Reed, "Our voters fiercely and rightly defend their freedom to choose any candidate on the ballot."

The blanket primary was not to the liking of party elites, who wished to assert their right to organize—if not in caucuses and conventions—at the very least in closed, partisan primaries. Fearing the potential party-weakening effects, in 1936 they went to court to challenge the new system. In the decision handed down concerning *Anderson v. Millikin* in June 1936, the State Supreme Court upheld the constitutionality of the law establishing the blanket primary.

The court did so again in 1978 when the law was again challenged in *Heavey v. Chapman*. Neither the state Republican nor Democratic parties have ever embraced the blanket primary, and both have on occasion mounted vigorous attempts to institute partisan or closed primaries. In 1979, the state Senate went so far as to hold hearings on an alternative primary system, but these efforts did not result in any legislative proposals. An important supplement was added by an initiative to the legislature, I-99, submitted in 1988 and codified into law in 1989. I-99 instituted presidential preference primary elections for determining the composition of delegations to the national party conventions of the major parties.

However, the blanket primary system ran into apparent trouble in the late 1990s. In 1996, Proposition 198 was approved by California voters, which mandated that a blanket primary system be adopted. The major parties immediately appealed to the courts, and ultimately the U.S. Supreme Court determined it to be a constitutional violation of the rights of political parties to freely associate (*Jones v. California* 2000). In the wake of this 7-2 ruling, parties in both Washington and Alaska served notice that they intended to challenge the primary system in their own states. Although under much pressure from the governor, legislative leaders, and state officials to act cautiously, the state Democratic Party declared its intention to try to have the primary system changed before the general election in November 2000. At the time, however, even those urging restraint felt that the blanket primary was doomed (*The Columbian*, July 15, 2000).

The blanket primary system was used in the 2000 statewide primary for what many thought would be the last time after Secretary of State Ralph Munro refused to withdraw it unless ordered to do so by the courts. Federal District Judge Frank Burgess declined to issue such an order, and instead signed off on an agreement negotiated between Munro and the two major parties that would empower the legislature to resolve the issue during the next session. Even so, when the new legislature convened, both the Democratic and Republican caucuses sent "their state party organizations strongly worded letters asking them to back off their insistence that future primaries be limited to self-identified members of the parties" (*Associated Press*, January 22, 2001). Public opinion seemed to be firmly set against changing the system, with some observers claiming that as many as 95 percent of respondents supported the status quo (*The Columbian*, September 30, 2000). Notwithstanding, both state party chairs held firm in their view that the parties should have the right to organize their own closed primaries and that the state should implement a partisan registration system.

At least three bills were prepared in the course of the new session, one of which would have introduced a radical change through the adoption of Instant Run-off Voting (IRV). Meanwhile, both the Democratic and Republican state committees prepared their own proposals for reform; in an interesting twist, the Libertarian Party, newly qualified for major party status and thus bound by the same primary rules, announced that it too would seek to have the blanket primary eliminated. In a delicious irony, the Libertarians, who had previously argued that their exclusion from the blanket primary under the rules regulating minor parties had imposed heavier costs on them in terms of having to hold conventions and caucuses, now sought a return to a non-primary system.

Just as the deadline for resolving the lawsuit approached, the state House and Senate adopted two vastly different primary plans. The Senate plan opted for the so-called "Cajun primary," a two-round system where two members of the same party can face each other in the runoff. While this system retains the non-partisan registration features of the blanket primary, the majority opinion in *California Democratic Party v. Jones* (2000), written by U.S. Supreme Court Justice Scalia, seems to endorse the Louisiana primary system as avoiding the constitutional pitfalls of the Washington version. In contrast, the House bill envisaged a mixed system, by which those voters having registered with a party preference might vote solely for that party's candidates, while independents would be able to vote for any candidate. Parties would have the option of declaring at least six months before the primary whether they intended to include independent votes in determining the election outcome. This second version was much more palatable to state party leaders themselves, who seem to have been motivated as much by the possibility of getting access to new state-maintained records of party identifiers as anything else.

A compromise was abrogated when Governor Locke refused to accept either version, thus sending the matter back to the courts. Events took a strange turn in March 2002 when Judge Burgess unexpectedly and firmly rejected the original lawsuit, declaring the blanket primary to be in conformity with the First Amendment.[3] Interestingly, the judge cited the long history of the blanket primary in Washington as providing a compelling state interest based upon the manifest wishes of the voters. In his ruling the judge opined that, "The political parties' evidence that there is a burden on their constitutional right of association is, for the most part, incompetent and inadmissible, and, at best, it is insubstantial and speculative" (Modie and Galloway, *Seattle Post-Intelligencer,* March 28, 2002). The three major parties in the state immediately filed suit with the 9th Circuit Court of Appeals and, at the time of this writing, the suit is pending.

The controversy over the blanket primary only extends to major parties. Minor parties in the state have the option of organizing either caucuses or conventions to nominate their candidates. State law requires them to gather a specified number of signatures of registered voters (200 for statewide and presidential offices, 25 for others), and stipulates that any nominating convention must be attended by at least 25 registered voters from the jurisdiction in question.

Nominated candidates must then garner at least 1 percent of votes cast in the primary election in order to qualify for the general election ballot (although they are exempt from this requirement in the nomination of presidential candidates). However, these relatively light obligations define Washington as having one of the most open ballot-access situations in the country (*Seattle Times,* May 14, 1996). In addition, recent administrative rulings by state election officials have also allowed new parties to side-step the more onerous convention and nominating procedures if they wish to place a stand-in candidate on the ballot early in the election cycle (prior to formally designating their official candidate). Furthermore, legislation signed by Governor Locke in April 2001 pushed back the deadline for presidential nominations to just 70 days before the general election (*Ballot Access News* 17:2, May 2001).

Campaign Finance

Springing from an organization identifying itself as the Coalition for Open Government (COG), the state's Public Disclosure Commission (PDC) was created directly by a vote of the people in the 1972 election in the form of Initiative 276. While the proposed legislation and its reform-minded supporters had been defeated in the state's legislature, they won a resounding victory at the ballot box, carrying 72 percent of the statewide vote. The commission was created to gather, and place in the public domain, information on the financing of political campaigns and to ensure that spending restrictions were observed by candidates for public office. Thus, as an agency with a $1.9 million biennial budget, the PDC is charged with collecting, analyzing, and reporting contribution and spending reports provided by all state candidates, elected officials, political parties, political committees, lobbyists, and lobbyist employers.

The statute that created the five-member, bi-partisan citizen commission covers five areas related to the financing of political activity in the state. The first is personal financial affairs. Anyone holding or seeking a state elected office or holding a high level state appointed position is required to file a statement outlining their personal finances, including sources of income and gifts, real estate holdings, investments, creditors, and business ownership and the major customers of those businesses. The second area of agency purview is campaign finance. Both candidates and political groups raising and spending more than $3,500 must file frequent periodic reports indicating the names, addresses, occupations, and employers of their contributors; the total amount each has donated; and how those funds were spent. The PDC also oversees the regulations governing political advertising and ensures that individuals and groups paying for political ads clearly identify themselves as the sponsors. The fourth area of the PDC's oversight extends to collecting financial reports for traditional lobbying activity. The agency analyzes and makes public detailed monthly reports focusing on the compensation of lobbyists and their employers, the identities of persons entertained by lobbyists, and gifts and contributions to political campaigns. The intended "sunshine" mission of the commission is exercised in the creation of public records—the PDC's final and most purposeful area of action. The commission provides the bulk of information contained in the reports presented to the public on a Web site. In fact, for some advocates of campaign finance reform, Washington's on-line disclosure requirements have become a model for similar efforts around the country (Hoover Institution, 2002).

The PDC's most difficult task has been to ensure compliance with disclosure provisions, contribution limits, campaign practices, and other campaign finance laws. Since the PDC was created, the agency has been chronically underfunded and understaffed. It was only with the passage of voter Initiative 134 in 1992 that the agency received a much needed budget increase. However, Initiative 134 also gave the agency more oversight responsibilities with regard to campaign finance; it set fixed contribution limits for the commission to monitor and enforce.

This perhaps unintentional state of affairs has resulted in an agency becoming overwhelmed by its broad reporting duties. When Doug Ellis, the PDC's public spokesman, responded to news of approximately $11 million dollars worth of state party omissions uncovered by three watchdog groups, he observed, "We don't have the staff to monitor one political committee and every one of their filings" (*News Tribune*, Aug. 23, 2002). When the PDC does uncover violations of the statutes governing state campaign financing or disclosure, the commission is responsible for imposing penalties on groups, elected officials, or candidates. For example, during the fall of 2002 the Washington Republican Party was ordered to forfeit $6.6 million in contributions it did not report, which the party refused to do. Cases that cannot be settled within the hearings of the PDC are sent to the state's Attorney General, along with recommendations on the penalties to be assessed. In this instance, the PDC only elicited an admission of wrongdoing by the state party, but no fine was paid.

Party Trends

Historically, Washington cannot be considered to be a one-party dominated state, although there have been periods when one of the major parties has enjoyed a significant advantage in electoral terms (Appleton and Deporter 1996; Nice 1992; Mullen and Pierce 1985). In recent years, the picture has been one of near parity and a high degree of competitiveness (Beck 1997, 37). While the Democrats currently have the edge in state-wide offices, the Republicans now hold one of the legislative houses and it is unlikely that this pattern will change in the near future.

Evidence from the mid-1990s indicated that the GOP can be successful in the state when it displays a more moderate image; the party suffered when it appeared to voters that it was becoming hijacked by right-wing activists associated with the New Christian Right (Appleton and Buckley 1999). The election of Chris Vance to the post of state chair undoubtedly signals a more moderate stance within the party organization itself. The success of John McCain in the 2000 presidential primary was an additional indicator that Republican voters have become relatively moderate and independently minded after the turmoil of the 1990s.

However, in an interesting paradox, competitiveness as measured by outcomes has been accompanied by a decline in the number of contested races at the state legislative level. In the 2002 elections, 28 state House races were uncontested by the filing deadline, with a few more having just one major party contender. In 8 of 10 Senate races (over one third of those up for renewal), incumbents faced no contest, and only a minor party challenge in two others. By comparison, only 8 House seats and four Senate races were uncontested in 2000. Press reports cite state election officials and campaign strategists as suggesting that the state parties had decided to concentrate their resources on a number of selected competitive "swing seats" (*The Columbian,* July 30, 2002).

Furthermore, the number of districts in which incumbents face active challengers in primary elections also has waned; whereas 18 percent of incumbent members of the state Senate and 11 percent of the members of the state House faced primary challenges in the period 1990–92, these numbers had fallen to 11 percent and 9 percent correspondingly for 1994–2000 (New 2001, 5). There also has been a slight decline in the numbers of incumbents defeated, comparing the same two periods. Thus, the increasing party competitiveness of the overall election outcomes masks a drift towards less competitiveness in different areas of the state. Some studies have suggested that this is a consequence of campaign finance restrictions that force parties to choose where to concentrate their campaign money (New 2001), although an examination of money raising and spending by the state parties does not seem to indicate penury on their part.

Earlier studies have shown that Washington's state party organizations, while operating in what has historically been a relatively restrictive and anti-party environment, have in recent years become more professionalized and more centralized (Appleton and Deporter 1996; Nice 1992). Studies suggested that during the 1970s, state and county party organizations became stronger than the national average (Cotter et al. 1989), and recent evidence shows nothing to hint that this may have changed. While the strengthening of major parties at the state level is one clear consequence of the federal campaign finance regime, in Washington it has been facilitated even more by the state campaign finance laws already discussed; furthermore, where there have been attempts to apply the provisions of those laws in a restrictive manner *vis-à-vis* political parties, the parties have routinely prevailed in the courts.

Recently released campaign finance information demonstrates the central position that state party committees have come to play in the financing of political campaigns. Despite the existence of a web of regulations concerning political money at both the state and federal levels, there is a large discrepancy between figures provided by public bodies and independent monitoring groups. Washington State is considered to have some of the nation's toughest campaign finance restrictions and reporting requirements (the Center for Public Integrity ranked it second in the nation in 2000), but lack of enforcement has led to severe doubts about the effectiveness of this regime (Center for Public Integrity, 2002). Indeed, one report suggested that the bulk of money spent in state races is now simply unreported (*Seattle Times,* November 4, 1996). According to the state PDC, the money spent by state party committees declined through the 1990s (Washington State Public Disclosure Commission 2002). But the election of 2000 saw a marked reversal, with contributions and expenditures more than doubling over a four-year period since 1996; state Democrats raised $10.3 million, while Republicans had a slight edge with $12.7 million. Four out of every 5 dollars was in the form of unregulated contributions (soft money) in the Democratic camp, and the Republican Party reported 9 of every 10 dollars raised as unregulated contributions. The Washington Council for Fair Elections has cast doubt on whether the official state spending data captures all of the money spent. Executive Director Teresa Purcell was quoted in the *Political Finance and Lobby Reporter* (1997), suggesting that "Since Initiative 134 was passed…there has been a dramatic increase in the amount of money spent and much less disclosure."

Table 1

Expenditures in the 2000 Cycle for Washington State

Expenditure Type	Democrats Total	Republicans Total	Grand Total	Number of Expenditures
Overall Expenditures	$12,807,654	$14,280,716	$27,088,370	2938
By Party	$11,038,260	$13,152,739	$24,190,999	860
By Caucus	$1,769,394	$1,127,977	$2,897,370	2078

Source: The Center for Public Integrity.

The Center for Public Integrity estimates that the Republican and Democratic state parties spent a combined total of over $27 million in the 2000 election cycle (see Table 1).

Table 2

Detailed Expenditures in the 2000 Cycle for Washington State

Broad Category	Democrats Total	Republicans Total	Grand Total
Administrative	$801,593	$252,658	$1,054,250
Candidate Support	$1,980,025	$2,316,435	$4,296,460
Fundraising	$135,370	$193,244	$328,614
Media	$96,633	$65,065	$161,698
Political Contributions	$1,295,046	$2,109,158	$3,404,205
Transfers	$9,058,778	$9,741,559	$18,800,337
Undetermined	$4,609	$1,697	$6,306

Source: The Center for Public Integrity.

Table 2 shows how state party and caucus committees spent the money during the 2000 election cycle. Transfers in this table include money moved by a committee to its own federal account or to another party or caucus committee at the state, local, or national level.

According to these data, the state parties transferred approximately two-thirds of the total money spent to their federal campaign accounts. At the same time, the national parties are estimated to have transferred $12.5 million to the state parties in unregulated soft money contributions, with Washington receiving the seventh highest among all 50 states (and more than New York).

The practice of money transfers between national and state party organizations, the consequence of the hard–soft money distinction, has created what some have termed "the dispersion of disclosure." For example, the Washington State Republican Party failed to disclose donations it received from the Republican National Committee late in the 2000 election. Moreover, the Republican national party committees (RNC, RNCC, NRSC, NRCC) did not report those donations until a year after the fact. The Public Disclosure Commission demanded the forfeiture of about $6.6 million, $4.8 million of it from the RNC. The RNC contested the decision, arguing that it had complied with the intent if not the letter of the law, and the PDC agreed to a retroactive rule change that would exonerate both the party and their candidates (*Associated Press,* September 27, 2002).

The state Democratic Party engaged in similar practices. The party central committee reported to the PDC that it had received $705,040 in soft money transfers from the party's national committees in 2000. However, a comparison with Federal Election Commission records showed that a much larger amount—$6.6 million—had been reported by the national committees. According to the Center for Public Integrity, "[I]t was the biggest discrepancy between the amount of soft money any state had reported receiving from their national headquarters and how much the national offices told the federal government they disbursed" (Center for Public Integrity 2002). The state party filed 24 late reports documenting $2.8 million of the money in question, leaving $3.8 million remaining unaccounted for. Officially, the state central committee blamed the difficulties on new staffing and new technology for its failure to comply with state campaign finance law. As the CPI noted, "Whatever the cause, the Washington State Democratic Central Committee was able to avoid disclosure requirements that are among the most rigorous in the nation for nearly a year and a half" (Center for Public Integrity 2002). At the time of this writing, the official complaint filed by the PDC is pending.

These cases are relatively typical of what has been happening in the national context; the Center for Public Integrity, the National Institute for Money in State Politics, and the Center for Responsive Politics conducted a study resulting in the estimate that state parties left $16 million in soft money transfers unreported in 2000. A combination of federal and state loopholes, combined with the ability of party organizations to raise and spend unregulated soft money, has created a web of complex transactions that make exact documentation of spending patterns almost impossible. Although the PDC has had some limited successes in stemming the avalanche of such practices (e.g., Governor Locke, the state Democratic Party, and candidate organizations were forced to relinquish about $37,000 in contributions from two labor unions during the 2000 election), it has simply been overwhelmed by these shell-game type practices in recent years. Most observers agree that the restrictions on spending imposed by Initiative 134 either have been circumvented or outright subverted by state parties and campaign professionals flush with soft money resources.

The influx of soft money brought with it the possibility of party growth and professionalization. The state Democratic Party invested in new staff and technology; Table 2 shows that their reported administrative costs in the 2000 election cycle were almost four times higher than that of the Republicans. A rough gauge of how state parties have become more central in the campaign finance game is the amount of money flowing from the central committees in relation to other party committees. Table 3 shows the relative spending by the Democratic central committee and two key campaign committees in two presidential election years.

There has been a clear shift to the state central committee as the money pump for campaign financing; a similar trend is noticeable for the state Republican Central Committee, which made $1,266,327 in 149 contributions in the

Table 3

Relative Campaign Spending by the Democratic
Central Committee, 1992 and 2000

Committee	Total $ Disbursed (1992)	Number of Contributions	Total $ Disbursed (2000)	Number of Contributions
Central Committee	79,336	37	1,819,134	403
House Caucus Committee	134,139	45	640,341	219
Senate Caucus Committee	210,841	24	269,267	114

Source: Compiled by the authors from data provided by the Center for Public Integrity.

same year. In fact, the Washington Republican Party ended the 2000 election cycle with cash unspent; this was a fact that led to intra-party squabbling when the state chair, Don Benton, attempted to move the party into new party headquarters.

With federal campaign finance reform on the horizon in 2000, national parties and affiliated committees had redistributed soft money donations among the state parties. The McCain-Feingold reform law, which went into effect after the 2002 elections, has now banned unregulated and unlimited contributions to the national parties. It is too early to determine what the effects of the new campaign finance regime will be; however, the impact of McCain-Feingold at the state level will be a further strengthening of state parties. It is clear that during the era of campaign finance regulations since the mid 1970s, state political parties have become an indispensable node in the financing of political campaigns—and the Evergreen State is an exemplar in this regard.

Conclusion

Over the years, political parties have continued to be a major organizational presence in the state, despite the existence of a state culture distrustful of the partisan divisions of political life, and a state regulatory framework that has prescribed organizational processes and circumscribed elections and campaigning. Even though the state has attempted to implement some of the toughest and most open campaign finance rules, the influx of soft money from the federal level, and the increasing stakes in a period of intense party competitiveness, have resulted in an expanded role for the key organizational elements of the parties.

Party organizations have become highly adaptive, too. Whether in the arena of nominating, campaigning, or fundraising, the state parties have become more autonomous from both electorate and state institutions, and central in the election process. The trends noted by Cotter et al. (1989) appear to have continued, and the state party organization has emerged as a professional and potent player. Party strengthening, while in an anti-party environment in Washington, is indeed a noteworthy phenomenon.

More recently, scholars have identified the "cartel party" as part of the evolutionary cycle of political parties in democratic societies; that is, major parties which, in the face of dealignment and/or new competitors, strategically collude to restrict the threats and retain their collective dominance (Katz and Mair 1995). It would be a stretch to suggest that the state parties in Washington are highly collusive, yet the experience with both the blanket primary and the circumvention of recently-implemented state campaign finance laws shows that they are not immune to acting in concert to further their strategic interests. The legal distinction between major and minor parties, with the accompanying differences in legislated nominating and operating procedures, is a critical fault line in the organization of party political life in the state. The major party organizations have acquired the capacity and the professionalism to make themselves indispensable in the election process, and, by extension, in linking citizens to the institutions of the state.

Endnotes

1. In a communication from the Secretary of State's office, it was suggested that many of the formal provisions of Washington State law regarding party organization are poorly known and seldom applied at the precinct and county levels.
2. The only other states to have used the system are California and Alaska, which have since abandoned it in favor of a closed primary with voter registration. The so-called "Cajun primary" in Louisiana shares the feature of unrestricted voter participation across primaries for different offices, although it has a second round run-off for the top two candidates if one of them does not receive an outright majority of votes cast.
3. Although many state officials and observers were surprised by the ruling, those involved with the court proceedings also noted the poor quality of the arguments deployed by the plaintiffs and the lack of good expert testimony on their behalf.

References

Aldrich, John H. 1995. *Why Parties? The Origin and Transformation of Political Parties in America.* Chicago: University of Chicago Press.

Ammons, David. 2000. "On Politics: Voters Rage over Plan to Nix 'Blanket' Primary." *The Columbian* (Vancouver, Wash.) (30 September).

Ammons, David. 2001. "Party Leaders: Blanket Primary Is Doomed," *The Associated Press State and Local Wire* (January 22).

Ammons, David. 2000. "Primary Politics: Will Demos Rue Yanking Voter's Blanket?" *The Columbian* (July 15).

Ammons, David. 2002. "GOP Baking Crescent Solution to Election Woes." *The Columbian* (January 13).

Appleton, Andrew, and Anneka Deporter. 1996. "Washington." In *Comparing Parties in the Fifty States: Development, Organization, and Resources,* ed. A. Appleton and Daniel S. Ward. Washington, D.C.: Congressional Quarterly Press.

Appleton, Andrew, and Michael Buckley. 1999. "The Limits to Mobilization: New Right Activism in Washington in the 1998 Elections." In *God at the Grassroots,* Vol. 3, ed. Clyde Wilcox and Mark Rozell. New York: Rowman and Littlefield.

Ballot Access News. 2001. *Ballot Access News: May Newsletter* 17(2). http://www.ballot-access.org/.

Beck, Paul Allen. 1997. *Party Politics in America.* Eighth edition. New York: Longman.

Caston, Phillip. 2002. "Tough Disclosure Laws Still Fail to Catch Millions in Undisclosed Soft Money." Center for Public Integrity (Sept. 26). http://www. publicintegrity.org/.

Center for Public Integrity. 2002. "State Secrets: Washington." (Nov.). http://www. publicintegrity.org/

Cotter, Cornelius P., James Gibson, John Bibby, and Rob Huckshorn. 1989. *Party Organizations in American Politics.* University of Pittsburgh Press.

Galloway, Angela. 2002. "State Dems Deserve Spot in PDC Doghouse," *News Tribune* (Tacoma, Wash.) (Aug. 23).

Hoover Institution, Public Policy Inquiry. 2002. *Campaign Finance: State and Local Overview.* (Nov.). Stanford: California. http://www.campaignfinancesite.org/structure/states1.html.

Katz, Richard S., and Peter Mair. 1995. "Changing Models of Party Organization and Party Democracy: The Emergence of the Cartel Party." *Party Politics* 1: 5-28.

Modie, Niel, and Angela Galloway. 2002. "Blanket Primary Is Ruled Legal; Political Parties Expect to Appeal Judgment that Upholds Present System." *Seattle Post-Intelligencer* (March 28).

Mullen, William F., and John C. Pierce. 1985. "Political Parties." In *Political Life in Washington: Governing the Evergreen State,* ed. Thor Swanson, et al. Pullman: Washington State University Press.

New, Michael J. 2001. "Campaign Finance Regulation: Lessons from Washington State." *Cato Institute Briefing Paper No. 73.* Washington D.C.: Cato Institute.

Nice, David C. 1992. "Political Parties in Washington." In *Government and Politics in the Evergreen State,* ed. David Nice, John Pierce, and Charles Sheldon. Pullman: Washington State University Press.

Political Finance & Lobby Reporter. 1997. (Oct. 8).

Serrano, Barbara A., and Jim Simson. 1996. "Campaign Dollars Rerouted, Not Cut, since Law revised—Donations to Top Two Parties Quadruple." *Seattle Times* (Nov. 4).

Schlesinger, Joseph A. 1966. *Ambition and Politics: Political Careers in the United States.* Chicago: Rand McNally.

Varner, Lynne K. 1996. "Ballot-Access Laws in the Northwest Are among the Most Liberal in Nation." *Seattle Times* (May 14).

Washington State Public Disclosure Commission. 2002. *Washington, 2001.* http://www.pdc.wa.gov/.

Chapter Three

Interest Group Politics in Washington State: Emergent Urbanization and the Continuing Struggle for the Public Domain

Robert Herold and Jeff Gombosky

F ROM EARLY IN THE NINETEENTH CENTURY, when de Tocqueville wrote in *Democracy in America* (de Tocqueville, Lawrence and Mayer 1966) on the virtue of civic associations, to the time President Harry Truman campaigned against the influence of "special interests," on into LBJ's administration that saw the nation's capital experience an explosion of formal interest groups, through to the present, the efforts of organized groupings of citizens to advance a public issue or agenda has resulted in a checkered history of highs and lows in national, state, and local politics. The noted political commentator, Kevin Phillips, argued in a widely read book, *Arrogant Capital* (1994), that the explosive growth and geographic concentration of interest groups in the Washington, D.C., metropolitan area in the 1990s represented an unhealthy development for American democracy. Phillips observed the following in this regard:

> At some point, probably in the 1970's, the buildup of interest groups in Washington reached what we could call negative critical mass. So many had come to Washington or been forced to come that the city started turning into a special-interest battlefield, a competitive microcosm of interest-group America. When policy decisions were made, attendance would be taken, checks would be totaled, lobbyists would be judged, mail would be tabulated and if a group wasn't on hand to drive its vehicle through the Capitol Hill weighing station, that organization was out of luck. Few organizations could afford to stay away, and very few did. It is at this point that the institutions of politics and government—and of American democracy—began to bend under the burden. The pressure worsened as industries and groups of Americans began to worry that the tides of America's postwar economic zenith were beginning to recede, which only increased their need to hasten to Washington to try to prolong the good times for themselves, necessarily at others' expense.

Phillips noted that state capitals have undergone a similar experience, and Olympia is no exception to this rule. Yet, at almost the same time that Phillips was warning the country about the pernicious influence of interest groups in our national and state capitals, Harvard political science professor Robert Putnam sparked the interest of editorialists and opinion-makers in the national media with his argument that fewer people were joining grassroots civic associations and interacting with their friends and neighbors, and that this trend toward social isolation was fraying the fabric of community in America. Putnam writes in *Bowling Alone* (Putnam 2000):

> At the conclusion of the twentieth century, ordinary Americans shared this sense of civic malaise. We were reasonably content about our economic prospects, hardly a surprise after an expansion of unprecedented length, but we were not equally convinced that we were on the right track morally or culturally. Of baby boomers interviewed in 1987, 53 percent thought their parent's generation was better in terms of "being a concerned citizen, involved in helping others in the community," as compared with only 21 percent who thought their own generation was better. Fully 77 percent said the nation was worse off because of "less involvement in community activities" (Putnam 25).

The rise of formal interest groups may well reflect the vacuum created by this new reality; however, if Putnam is correct, the irony is that we may see an inverse relationship between the number and size of interest groups and actual civic involvement and public participation, a situation which adds further to the noteworthy concerns expressed by Phillips.

The new political reality aside, we can say that the issues, problems, and opportunities that derive from interest groups are of historical concern to Americans. Indeed, in *Federalist #10,* Founding Father James Madison argued that the union held the promise to "break and control the violence of faction." Writing in 1787, the term faction no doubt meant political party. Had he written *Federalist #10* even fifty years later, he most likely would have altered his view on the matter and, instead of parties, identified faction with what would be represented by the interest groups mentioned above (Cooke 1961).

De Tocqueville, as noted, took a somewhat more benign view of Americans' tendency to seek association than does Phillips and other critics of contemporary interest group politics. As de Tocqueville saw it, unlike in Europe where association certainly in the form of party presumed to represent the majority, in America the claims of association were typically far narrower. De Tocqueville writes: "In Europe associations regard themselves in a way as the legislative and executive council of the nation which cannot raise its own voice; starting from this conception, they act and command. In America, where everyone sees that they represent only a minority in the nation, they talk and petition" (de Tocqueville 1966, 195). De Tocqueville saw what we have come to term "narrow self interest" as being politically healthy, if for no other reason than it puts a brake on presumption; in any case, de Tocqueville reported, as a key finding, a young democratic nation fitted with associations, of every manner and sort.

Political scientists have sought to understand these interest groups ever since. By way of drawing an analytical distinction between interests groups and political parties, most students of the phenomenon have found it useful to note that parties seek to take control of the government through elections which fix accountability and responsibility, while interest groups seek to influence government without necessarily winning elections. Consequently, interest groups are considered inherently less accountable and less responsible than political parties. In the past, political parties were established for the primary purpose of winning elections, and they served as key mediating institutions providing ordinary Americans a voice and some influence over their government. As noted elsewhere in this book, the *blanket primary* in Washington significantly reduces the mediating role of organized political parties in the state, and interest groups have stepped in to fill the vacuum. Although Washington's political parties are far from moribund, the major work of the policy advocacy in the state has fallen to interest groups.

Types of Interest Groups in Washington State

Interest groups take many forms and emerge in any number of configurations. We find it quite useful to draw distinctions with reference to organization and cohesion. While some interest groups are "formal" in the sense that they have recognized leadership, feature official membership, and are located at a headquarters; many others are much less formal, such as "labor" or "the elderly." Cohesion refers to mission and purpose of the organization and the degree to which the membership can be counted upon to support both. The National Rifle Association would be an example of a formal, highly cohesive organization. The AFL-CIO is equally formal, but, as demonstrated by the election of Ronald Reagan in 1980, not nearly as cohesive as Democrats had always thought.

The interest group universe is forever changing as "potential groups" gain the necessary self-awareness to form associations. Women, for example, were primarily a statistical category in politics through most of our nation's history. Then, through the efforts of feminist writers and political organizers, women became highly sensitized to their mutual interests. Interest groups, such as the National Organization of Women, were established to translate women's issues into public policy preferences. Or consider the rise of the so-called "Moral Majority"—at first only empty political rhetoric, then a broadened sense of shared concern, and finally, a variety of formal interest groups organized to seek influence in government.

The Public Disclosure Commission (PDC) in Washington State groups political action committees (PACs) into the three categories (see Table 1): business, union, and issue PACs. Business PACs contribute more heavily to Republican than to Democratic candidates. Union PACs contribute more heavily to Democratic candidates, and Issue PACs contribute to those that tend to support their particular issue (e.g., environmental PACs tend to support Democrats). Upon closer scrutiny important distinctions among interest groups emerge.

Though most business PACs heavily favor GOP candidates, individual business interests may deviate from that general norm. The Washington Medical PAC is a case in point. During the 2000 election year, the Medical PAC gave $39,050 to Republican state house candidates and $36,210 to Democratic state house candidates. By comparison, the Realtors PAC gave $48,600 to Republican state legislative candidates and $16,350 to Democratic state house candidates. Every union interest group supported Democrats more generously than Republicans. For example, the Washington Federation of State Employees contributed $53,200 to Democratic state legislative candidates during the 2000 election year, compared to $6,250 for Republican candidates.

Among *issue* interest groups, those that were formed on behalf of trial lawyers represented the largest segment. For nearly all interest groups, incumbents enjoy a clear advantage overall in terms of receiving contributions from interest groups. Increasingly, so-called "soft money" contributions are becoming the resource of choice among interest groups. Soft money contributions are expenditures made on behalf of a candidate for office without the control (or often even the knowledge) of the candidate. In fact, if the candidate possesses advance knowledge of the independent expenditure it then must be reported by the candidate's campaign as a direct contribution and become subject to the limits with which all other contributions must comply. Independent expenditures are one of the results of the U.S. Supreme Court's decision in *Buckley v. Valeo*. That decision regarding federal campaign reporting and limitation statutes and regulations held that while individual contribution limits to campaigns were constitutional, overall spending limits for candidates were not. The State Public Disclosure Commission notes in this regard,

> …independent expenditures may not, constitutionally, be subject to any limit. Every citizen's and entity's right to free political speech means that they may spend as much as they choose to support or oppose candidates, so long as those expenditures are made independently of candidates and their campaigns. Expenditures that are made in conjunction with a candidate or candidate's campaign are considered contributions to that candidate. Contributions to legislative and other state office candidates are limited (PDC 2002, 154).

Independent expenditures are increasingly a favored method of action for PACs. During the year 2000 election, independent expenditures totaled $1,104,514

Table 1

50 Most Active Political Action Committees in 2000
From the Washington State Public Disclosure Commission

1.	Washington Education Assn. PAC	Union	$651,195
2.	United for Washington	Business	$568,017
3.	Washington Conservation Voters	Issue	$410,441
4.	Realtors PAC	Business	$383,218
5.	Washington State Labor Council	Union	$264,586
6.	Public School Employees of WA	Union	$246,732
7.	Washington Affordable Housing Council	Business	$237,388
8.	Washington Medical PAC	Business	$235,869
9.	Washington Restaurant Assn. PAC	Business	$234,153
10.	Washington Machinists Council	Union	$219,335
11.	Washington State Dental PAC	Business	$210,835
12.	SEIU State Council	Union	$166,570
13.	Washington State Auto Dealers PAC	Business	$151,422
14.	Council of County and City Employees	Union	$130,972
15.	Build Seattle	Business	$125,255
16.	Alliance for Responsible Leadership	Other	$117,086
17.	Washington Health Care Assn. PAC	Business	$113,235
18.	Washington Teamsters Legislative League	Union	$106,735
19.	Trucking Action Committee	Business	$98,309
20.	AASK PAC	Business	$98,036
21.	Victims Advocates	Issue	$96,508
22.	Eastside Business Roundtable	Other	$93,606
23.	Washington Public Employees PAC	Union	$93,457
24.	Certified Public Accountants PAC	Business	$93,071
25.	Brotherhood of Electrical Workers #77	Union	$90,327
26.	Chiropractic Trust	Business	$87,319
27.	PAC 48 of Washington	Union	$82,745
28.	Western Washington Trial Lawyers	Issue	$74,141
29.	Gun Owners Action League of Washington	Issue	$73,000
30.	Qwest Washington PAC	Business	$72,422
31.	Washington Soft Drink Assn. PAC	Business	$71,572
32.	District Council of Carpenters	Union	$70,400
33.	Affordable Housing Council	Business	$67,655
34.	Vote Tuesday November 7th	Business	$64,459
35.	City of Destiny PAC	Issue	$64,457
36.	Abraham Lincoln Memorial Society	Issue	$63,818
37.	Central WA Lawyers of Families	Issue	$62,839
38.	Beer and Wine Wholesalers PAC	Business	$60,468
39.	Citizens to End Lawsuit Abuse	Issue	$60,218
40.	Broadband Communications PAC	Business	$58,600
41.	Puget Sound Citizens for Responsibility	Issue	$57,809
42.	East King County Lawyers for Justice	Issue	$52,632
43.	Justice PAC	Issue	$50,930
44.	Education Excellence Coalition	Issue	$50,867
45.	Southeast Washingtonians	Business	$49,610
46.	Physicians EYEPAC	Business	$49,511
47.	WA Optometric PAC	Business	$46,088
48.	WA Thoroughbred Owners PAC	Business	$46,950
49.	WCV Green Voters Fund	Issue	$46,865
50.	Northern Attorneys PAC	Issue	$46,519

in Washington State. According to the state PDC, "independent expenditures usually take the form of political advertising: yard signs, brochures mailed to voters, radio and television ads, etc." Interest groups making independent expenditures for candidates tend to be the same ones that make regular contributions.

Interest groups are not, we need remind ourselves, created equally. For every well-funded, organized, and economically positioned formal group such as the Washington Education Association, the Boeing Corporation, and Washington Conservation Voters, there is a more loosely organized "movement" or "issue" group engaged in efforts to raise salient issues for public consideration. Groups such as The Children's Alliance, the Recreation Gaming Association, and the State Association of Evangelicals fall into this category. Grist for the mills of those who share Kevin Phillips' fear of the power and influence of "special interest groups" are the financial contributions made to candidates for public office by the larger, better-funded and organized groups and their PACs. As reported by the PDC, the ten most active political action committees in the year 2000, based on reported expenditures, were (in rank order): the Washington Education Association, United for Washington, Washington Conservation Voters, Realtors PAC, Washington State Labor Council, Public School Employees of Washington, Washington Affordable Housing Council, Washington Medical PAC, Washington Restaurant Association PAC, and the Washington Machinists Council.

But financial contributions, though the most important resource at an interest group's disposal, are only one aspect of their political influence. Large contributions raise the question: what did they buy? No doubt financial contributions buy a degree of access to decision-makers. But access that is not supported by cogent argument, analysis, pertinent data, and—most importantly— reliable information, may not amount to much. Legislators must be properly informed to perform their jobs, and smart lobbyists address that need. In Washington State, where legislating is considered only a part-time duty, and legislative staffs are rather sparse, the need for information is great indeed. The effective formal interest group turns access into an opportunity to influence public policy by producing a track record that gives the legislator confidence in the information provided by their lobbyist. Though information and analysis is frequently provided in broad view through testimony at public hearings, it nonetheless remains true that interest groups do have a voice behind the legislature's proverbial closed doors, exploiting the access paved by their campaign contributions.

Although it is obvious that campaign support buys political access to decision-makers, what impact do political contributions and direct lobbying have on outcomes? Evidence suggests that at the very least substantial contributions and lobbying, coupled with good organization, serve to protect the "fair share"

Table 2

Percentage of Groups Using Various Lobbying Techniques

TECHNIQUE	PERCENTAGE
Testifying at hearings	99
Contacting government officials directly to present a point of view	98
Engaging in informal contacts with officials-at conventions, over lunch, etc	95
Presenting research results or technical information	92
Sending letters to members of an organization to inform them about its activities	92
Entering into coalitions with other organizations	90
Attempting to shape implementation of policies	89
Talking with people from the press and the media	86
Consulting with government officials to plan legislative strategy	85
Helping to draft legislation	85
Inspiring letter-writing or telegram campaigns	84
Shaping the government's agenda by raising new issues and calling attention to previously ignored problems	84
Mounting grass-roots lobbying efforts	80
Having influential constituents contact their congressperson's office	80
Helping to draft regulations, rules or guidelines	78
Serving on advisory commissions and boards	76
Alerting members of Congress to the effects of a bill on their districts	75
Filing lawsuits or otherwise engaging in litigations	72
Making financial contributions to electoral campaigns	58
Doing favors for officials who need assistance	56
Attempting to influence appointments to public office	53
Publicizing candidate's voting records	44
Engaging in direct-mail fund raising	44
Running advertisements in the media about issues	31
Contributing work or personnel to electoral campaigns	24
Making public endorsements of candidates for office	22
Engaging in protests or demonstrations	20

Source: Kay L. Schlozman and John T. Tierney. 1986. *Organized Interests and American Democracy.* New York: Harper and Row.

of state resources accorded to a major interest. For example, even though K-12 education is assured of funding in the state by virtue of constitutional provision, the well funded and organized teacher's union, the Washington Education Association, spares no effort and expense to elect friendly candidates and to lobby the government for the sake of its own interests. It would appear that the association's efforts have been successful, because K-12 education is allocated nearly half of the state budget. In contrast, higher education does *not* appear among the state's fifty biggest special interest donors. Interestingly, state budget support for higher education has steadily declined as a percentage of the whole over the past decade. Granted, higher education is caught between the constitutionally mandated support of K-12 and an array of federally mandated matching programs. Nonetheless, it would tend to appear that there is correlation between special interest efforts and the financial allocation of state resources.

In a weak-party and weak-government state like Washington, the legislature tends to be besieged by special interest groups, while political influence is concentrated more in the office of the chief executive. Armed with a line-item veto, Washington's governor is in a position to have the last word on many issues and questions. Though the governor often doesn't have close ties with his party's leadership, his power derives more from his constituted position and public visibility than it does from his role as party leader. The governor is largely immune to the kinds of narrow lobbying efforts that typically beset legislators. Moreover, governors, occupied as they are with running the state bureaucracy, present to the interest group an institutional shield that is often difficult to penetrate.

What the statewide data on interest group lobbying and company contributions do not reveal is the erosion of discretionary power held by either the governor or the state legislature associated with the operation of American federalism. There has been a noteworthy shift of interest group activity to both the federal level and towards the use of methods of direct democracy. The former reflects the enormity of federal government presence in Washington State, as reflected in the vast extent of federal land ownership, the large scale of federal military and civilian operations, the wide range of grants and contracts, environmental mandates, etc. As this has been coupled with the crippling effects of direct democracy exercised through the state's permissive initiative process and a constitution which serves as a design for a weak government, state government has watched its scope of discretionary action shrink significantly. For example, less taxing authority is available than in the past, since the enactment of spending caps via the initiative process has restricted the state from building ample reserves when strong economic performance would make that possible. Plus, the earmarking of funds for specific purposes through passed initiatives has constrained choice over the use of remaining state resources. As a result, while there is less to fight over during the legislative sessions in Olympia than in the past, the fights generally have become more intense, because the stakes have gone up for many actors dependent upon state apportionment. There is less old-fashioned pork-barrel distribution taking place, and more redistribution of state benefits going on.

Interest Groups in Washington State: The Hypothesis

While the PDC's broad categories are generally informative, they do not answer the important questions for those seeking deeper understanding: Are there historical developments, patterns, and characteristics unique to the region that serve to explain interest group politics in Washington State? Or are we left only with an image of political cacophony described in terms of campaign contributions and the diverse activities of lobbyists?

Many studies have shown that, historically, interest group configurations in America do indeed take on distinctive regional characteristics (Litt 1965), reflecting, as political scientist V.O. Key (1956) observed, the effects of historical political cleavages and geographical locations that cannot be easily explained or engineered away. For example, in his classic study of politics in the South, Key argued that "Black Belt politics" (Key 1949) dominated the interest group politics in the South. Key wrote *Southern Politics* in the late 1940s, but his thesis remained insightful for another twenty years until the Civil Rights Movement took hold and southern urban areas became much more integrated into the national political culture and political interest group network.

Over the past two decades especially, information and transportation technologies have dramatically altered our concept of space and time. Measured in social, economic, and political terms, we have witnessed cultural homogenization that no doubt has served to diminish regional distinctiveness present in America from its beginning, emboldened by emigration patterns and frontier conditions (Turner 1893; Elazar 1984). Downtown Manhattan today plays home to the very same menu of national brand stores that one can find in Seattle or Spokane, Washington. The same movies open on the same day in cities across the country. Writers such as Joel Garreau do nonetheless find new cultural patterns emerging, patterns which lead to the *bi-coastal theory* of American cultural life (Garreau 1981). This theory holds that America has become a social fabric defined by two coasts and a midlands area. If this theory possesses merit, then Seattleites would have more in common with people in Boston than they do with those in Spokane, and people in Spokane would have more in common with the populace in Wichita than with Portlanders.

While the bi-coastal pattern cultural analysis is interesting, it likely oversimplifies a much richer taxonomy of political cultures. It ignores a reality fundamental to the study of interest group politics in Washington State (or in any other state)—namely, the effects of American federalism. The differing circumstances of American states, as Daniel Elazar and others have correctly noted, continue to matter in the study of public policy and civic affairs, regardless of cultural homogenization occasioned by technological innovation. Interest groups, we have noted, attempt to influence policy without accepting responsibility for governing. State governments, in contrast, continue to make important (if decidedly constrained) policy. Our reading of Washington's interest group political landscape suggests the following: the new political reality, cultural homogenization, and our ever smaller geo-economic world notwithstanding, interest group politics in Washington State have been largely defined by historically and geographically rooted forces similar in importance to what Key found in the South over a half century ago—namely, the *public domain* and *urbanization*.

The Public Domain

If for no other reason than that much of Washington is public owned land, interest group politics have historically revolved around matters relating to the ownership, uses, distribution, protection, and regulation of the state's public domain. The stakes go far beyond the nineteenth century issues of land grants— at that time often embroiled with railroad concerns—into the more immediate questions dealing with agriculture and timber. Public domain issues extend to natural resources in a broad sense and to quality-of-life factors. Whereas in the American South interest group politics could not escape race, interest group politics in Washington State have never been able to avoid issues pertaining to the public domain and what can be done with it (Herold 1981). Because the federal government has always been Washington State's largest land owner, federal authorities have historically played a dominant role in state politics, both as ultimate authority and through their many agencies and bureaus and their constellation of associated interest groups. The centrality of public domain issue politics for the Evergreen State is clearly evident in two particular areas: 1) the development of the Columbia River, and 2) the management of the state's ample forestland.

The Columbia River: Domain Interest Group Politics and Water Reclamation

The single most politically significant cause for controversies regarding the public domain came about through the construction of large dams on the great Columbia River, one of the mightiest flows of water in North America. Pulled downward from high elevations in Canada by gravity, the Columbia rushes southward into Washington. A few miles past the site of Grand Coulee Dam, the river takes a swing northward and then westward, where it rights itself, rushes southward and then, some miles downriver, careens around a stretch today known as the Hanford Reach. Now deemed a national monument, thanks to the Clinton Administration, this 50-mile stretch of river remains the only pristine section of the Mid-Columbia not altered by dams (Hardin 1996).

Next, some twenty or so more miles downstream, the Snake River adds its substantial waters to the Columbia. After this merger, the Columbia makes one more dramatic curve before pointing westward and flowing the remaining two hundred miles to the Pacific Ocean.

In the days before Franklin Roosevelt's "New Deal," the Mid-Columbia was navigable only at great risk. Stories are told of the intrepid steamboat captains who made their way upriver from Portland to what is now called the "Tri-Cities"—Richland, Kennewick, and Pasco. Beyond these small towns in southeastern Washington commercial access to the rapid-obstructed Columbia River was problematic.

Since the construction of the first large dams on the Columbia during the 1930s—Bonneville Dam (upriver from Portland), Rock Island Dam (below Wenatchee), and the remarkable Grand Coulee Dam (upstream from Wenatchee)—the river has served as a fountain of economic lifeblood. The Columbia and Snake dam complex has for decades given the entire state the cheapest electrical power in the United States. It also has served to irrigate the Columbia Basin Irrigation Project, covering a region the size of a small state. The Columbia's electric turbines spawned an aluminum industry which, in turn, enabled a small aircraft company called Boeing to become an industry leader building bombers and passenger aircraft, particularly beginning in World War II. Author Marc Reisner even suggests that it would not be too much of a claim to say that Grand Coulee's electrical power for aluminum plants, Boeing, and Hanford won World War II (Reisner 1986).

The locks on the Columbia's dams fostered a thriving barge industry as well. More to the political point, the dams made it possible for Lewiston, Idaho, and Clarkston, Washington—two towns positioned on opposite banks of the Snake River some 250 miles away from the Pacific Ocean, in the heart of agricultural territory—to become legitimate ports (Hardin 1996, 17; Cone and Ridington 1996, 106-108). The barge industry, an emerging interest group, initially allied with farmers who felt exploited by an earlier railroad monopoly. Ironically, today, that same barge industry has become a monopoly all of its own for the transportation of inland Northwest grain to Portland.

The Columbia River dams, now so essential to economic life in the Evergreen State, also largely destroyed the wild salmon runs on the Columbia and Snake rivers and their tributaries (Dietrich 1995). Indeed, because the U.S. Bureau of Reclamation did not construct fish ladders when building Grand Coulee Dam, no salmon of any sort—wild or hatchery alike—can be found upriver of Grand Coulee. The salmon issue has brought members of numerous Native American tribes together to form an interest group in an effort to save and increase wild salmon runs. One of the largest concentrations of the nation's Native American population once lived in the Pacific Northwest. During LBJ's "Great Society" era of the 1960s, the many tribes located west of the Cascades—most near salmon bearing waters—formed a loose conglomerate of a community action agency known as STOW (Small Tribes of Western Washington) (Hardin 1996). Over the past several decades, and certainly since the mid seventies when the last of the lower Snake River dams was completed, STOW has fought to save the salmon runs that represent a critical element of their cultural heritage. For assistance, this particular interest group turned not to the state, but to the real owner of the public domain; they took their case to the federal courts, and cited nineteenth-century treaty rights as the basis for their claims. In the now famous "Boldt" decision, U.S. District Court Judge George Boldt agreed with the tribes, holding that the U.S. government had promised to the tribes the right to take salmon "in the usual and accustomed places," and the court handed down a decision that has led to almost three decades of political infighting that has yet to been resolved (*U.S. v. Washington,* Phase 1,384 F supp.312.356,343 WD Wash 1974). The tribes want some of the dams removed, principally those on the lower Snake River that allow the towns of Lewiston, Idaho, and Clarkston, Washington, to be ports (Hudson 1999).

Forests, the Public Domain, and Interest Groups

The forested foothills west of the Cascade Range in Washington State extend down to Puget Sound. This rugged terrain denied to most early settlers the kind of Midwest-style farming that had come to typify Oregon's Willamette Valley by the middle of the nineteenth century. But in the Cascade Range, and to the west, there was a vast amount of virgin timber waiting to be felled. This seemingly inexhaustible abundance of timberland included the vast Olympic Peninsula across Puget Sound, as well.

Many transplanted Midwest and southern loggers migrated to Washington after the old growth timber in the Great Lakes region and the South had largely played out. And log they did, with active encouragement and assistance from the U.S. Forest Service (USFS). By the late 1940s and '50s, the USFS had evolved from a scientific management agency that sought to balance the claims for conservation and the extraction of natural resources to a more complex, entrepreneurial, and controversial agency. The "new" USFS was driven not so much by the directives of forestry science as by the excitement and influence associated with timber selling and road building in the national forests. Logging companies throughout the Pacific Northwest determined that large scale clear-cutting would be the harvest technique of choice, and with the acquiescence of the USFS the logging industry transformed public forestlands throughout the region. Today, however, only thirty years after the single largest annual cut in Washington State's history, logging has fallen below even the rates of historical hard times. The commercial logging of old-growth timber has ceased, for the most part. The forestry industry, once the dominant economic power in the state along with Boeing, today accounts for only a small percentage of Washington's economy. Georgia-Pacific, a major corporation in the wood products industry, has relocated back to the more productive southern pine forests, where the devastating clear-cuts of a half-century ago have been replaced by another crop of harvest-ready trees.

Why this dramatic turn of events resulting in such drastic effects to the state's economy? The central issues surrounding the decline in the timber industry will be discussed later in this chapter through a specific case study.

Defining Movements and Consequences: Populism and Progressivism

From the adoption of its constitution, written in the late nineteenth century, to its many electoral reforms and periods of labor and agrarian unrest, and on into its present reliance on direct democracy, Washington State government, and interest group politics, have been greatly influenced by the residue of two late-nineteenth-century national socio-political movements. These movements, Populism and Progressivism, were shaped by the emergent and continuing interest group cleavages of their time.

In other parts of the country, these movements were largely fueled by reaction to the consequences of rapid industrialization following the Civil War, and their advocates were primarily concerned with what writer Robert Wiebe termed "The Search for Order" (Wiebe 1967). In Washington State, however, the driving force was always public domain politics. Both social movements, in the context of Washington's history, can be viewed as a reaction to the way in which the federal government and large corporate interests had collaborated, often through the creation and support of state-subsidized monopolies, to distribute, exploit, develop, and otherwise make use of the public domain for the profit of the few. Both movements left in their respective wakes, however, a legacy of major unintended consequences.

The initial distribution and development of the public domain in the Evergreen State led to dramatic governmental action. Interest groups formed as a consequence of that action, and the primary beneficiaries—railroads, timber companies, banks, etc.—then were confronted by popular reaction to their extreme political influence and abuse of the resources over which they were permitted to govern in the public trust. In this context the calls for reform issued by Populists and Progressives found deep root among the state's citizenry. Interest groups formed and fought over timber issues—what to cut, how much to cut, where to cut, if to cut? In similar fashion, they have fought over the largess provided by the dams. Who gets the electricity? How much? At what cost? They have fought over the water itself. What to irrigate? At what cost? To whom? They have fought over the unintended consequences brought about by the dams, especially the demise of wild salmon stocks. The dams have been used by interest groups to counter railroad monopolies, only to eventually find themselves held hostage by a barge industry monopoly fostered by the dams. Interest groups, including federal agencies, have used the Columbia River to cool the Hanford nuclear plants that allowed the nation to build the atomic bomb dropped on

Nagasaki near the end of World War II. Along the way to building a "nuclear deterrent" in the Cold War, agencies of the federal government also spewed radioactive material into the region's air and dumped nuclear waste into land-fills that continue to threaten the Columbia River itself (Hardin 1996).

As designed and executed, the original U.S. government land grant acts had brought about the unintended result that interest group politics in Washington Territory—and then Washington State—would emerge. The homestead land grants of the nineteenth century, for example, were doomed to often fail in the American West, because the progam was framed by legislators with the typical rich Ohio Valley farm in mind, and based upon Jefferson's ideals of the yeoman farmer. A homestead typically encompassed 160 acres; in reality, to survive west of the Rocky Mountains, farmers often needed to work much more land than this. People and organizations with access to capital were typically those who eventually acquired sufficient land. Left largely behind in the process were the small farmers for whom the land grant legislation was originally intended. Throughout the American West, the land grant acts resulted in both the aggre-gation of capital and land, and the acquisition of concentrated political power and influence by a few. In reaction to this trend, Populists pushed for the state regulation of political parties, while Progressive reformers pushed for direct de-mocracy, as in the establishment of popular initiatives as described in other chapters in this book. The state of Washington proved to be particularly fertile ground for both Populist and Progressive reformers.

Consider, for example, the societal outcomes associated with the relatively recent development of the Columbia Basin irrigation protects. As Blaine Hardin and others have discussed (Hardin 1996; Dietrich 1995), the water projects that the New Dealers believed would help the small family farmer resulted in yet another unintended consequence—the creation of large agribusinesses (and highly subsidized agribusiness, at that). Consider as well the land grant acts that provided for railroad development. Huge tracks of land were deeded to the railroads, especially the Northern Pacific (now part of Burlington Northern Santa Fe), in exchange for the promise to lay track across the continent. States and cities courted, connived, and contrived to bring in railroads. In coopera-tion with the U.S. Congress—which distributed the land grants—they sought the commercial life's blood that the railroads promised. But in the wake of all that deal-making came monopolies that ultimately were protected in the terri-torial legislative chambers. This same process occurred throughout the western states. (It was at one time "suspected" that the Southern Pacific Railroad, con-trolled by Leland Stanford, "owned" all but one or two state representatives in the California State Assembly.) Eventually, those who felt the stranglehold of the railroads' monopolies reacted—sometimes vehemently. Consequently, Popu-lism arose by the 1890s, the national agrarian reform movement that until the presidential election of 1896 threatened the very existence of the Democratic

Party as the nation's second major party (Hicks 1961). Populism, too, with its ties to organized labor, helped spawn several decades of radical movements in Washington State, the Industrial Workers of the World (IWW)[1] being the most notorious.

Following on the heels of the Populists came the Progressives. These turn-of-the-century civic reformers sought to sanitize the very same issues that defined the earlier Populists' goals by ending "corruption" in political parties and bringing professional "scientific management" into government (Bledstein 1976; Skowronek 1982). Progressives actually took the earlier Populist reform proposals several steps further in the direction of popular constraint over the elite elements of society. Whereas Populists sought to control party bosses through closed primary nominating, Progressives—in many western states, and most definitely in Washington—did not stop there. They reasoned that if primaries were a good idea, why not adopt a blanket primary wherein voters could pick and choose candidates from either party? Parties would be reduced to little more than advertising agencies. And, if the adoption of referenda were a good means of controlling legislative bodies, why not introduce initiatives for the public as well?

Central to the turn-of-the-century reformers' agenda was the creation of what they termed "open, and honest government." From the early laws instituting various forms of direct democracy, to more recent open-meeting legislation, Washington State has continued to see "good government" interest groups working to hinder any perceived efforts of large-scale commercial entities (such as railroad and timber interests) to control elected officials behind closed doors as they once did. The reformers believed (and most still do) that out of "open and honest" government would come "efficient government."

The ultimate result of these reforms has been a weakening of the elected governing structure in Washington. Governance vacuums, however, have been filled with an array of interest groups competing for state and federal resources. Thus, increased political influence by interest groups has become the unintended result of reform politics in Washington.

In recent years, the workings of direct democracy have served to increasingly diminish the effectiveness of even locally elected government officials. Another unintended consequence of accommodation to diverse interests is particularly apparent today; in the life cycle of interest group politics, Washington State often seems mired in inaction.

Thus, in recent years, the workings of direct democracy have served to increasingly diminish the effectiveness of deliberative government in the state. In addition, it provides a perfect alibi for irresponsible governing by some elected representatives. For example, if the tax base and spending levels are set through direct democratic means, what does that leave for elected officials to do? And even if most representatives understand the problem, the effects of direct democracy give them the perfect political out. Why take a stand for tax reform, for example, if you can duck the issue entirely simply by going along with the dictates of the voters? We suspect that founding father James Madison, prime advocate for the republican form of representative government, would roll over in his grave were he to be aware of the present nature of political life in the Evergreen State.

Because of the centrality of public domain politics in Washington State, the most influential constellation of interest groups are involved with federal government connections. Over time, federal agencies have become active participants in the state's interest group politics. In fact, interest group politics in Washington cannot be understood apart from an understanding of the many federal agencies controlling the vast amounts of public land present in the state.

Long indeed is the list of agencies with a major presence in Washington: the Bureau of Land Management, the Bonneville Power Administration, the Bureau of Indian Affairs, the Bureau of Reclamation, the U.S. Forest Service, the U.S. Department of Agriculture, the Army Corps of Engineers, the U.S. Department of Transportation, the National Marine Fisheries, the Nuclear Regulatory Agency, the Bureau of Mines, the U.S. Department of Interior, and the National Oceanic and Atmospheric Administration—not to mention all the other usual federal interest groups such as the Army, Navy, Air Force, Veterans Administration, HUD, Health and Human Services. Some—most notably those that have worked, shaped, developed, and controlled vast areas of public land in the state—have long been actively involved in influencing Washington government at both the state and local levels.

Critical Outcomes and Trends: To Illustrate the Hypothesis

What critical outcomes and trends emerge through these historically developed patterns of interest-group configuration and influence? We would expect to find three particular trends to be of continuing or emerging importance:

1. As reform movements expand in influence, we would expect to see an explosion of direct democracy—with resulting diminishment of power in the state legislature and possibly even the executive branch.

2. While formal interest groups historically have had overwhelming influence on state politics and government, we would expect that they too would lose influence in the rise of direct democracy.

3. As public-domain politics continue to be a driving force, we would expect that federal governmental agencies would play an active role in the state, both in the form of participating interest groups and in the role of governing authority.

The following case studies are representative of these three trends.

Case Study #1—Tim Eyman and Direct Democracy

A fraternity watch salesman from the suburbs of south Snohomish County, Tim Eyman represents a new type of actor in Washington's political history. While citizens have mounted successful initiative campaigns in the past, Eyman has capitalized on his success with I-695 to form an interest group called Permanent Offense. This organization has no interest in advocating for public policy changes at the legislative or executive level in state government; rather, it exists entirely to advance specific government-weakening changes to public policy through the initiative process. Permanent Offense has not always been successful; two of its initiatives that were successful with voters were thrown out by the State Supreme Court, and another, related to transportation funding, went down to resounding defeat at the polls. However, Eyman has received generous local and national media attention and has built a solid statewide network of activists, which has made the once daunting task of advancing a proposal to the ballot much easier to accomplish. Tim Eyman is arguably the state's first postmodern political actor. He has mastered the media with glib sound bites and cultivated conservative radio talk show hosts as allies. Technologically savvy, Eyman uses the Internet to communicate with allies state-wide and maintains a Web site to provide information and make initiative petitions easily accessible to supporters. Eyman is non-ideological, never arguing that particular government efforts should stop, but asserts that government has plenty of money at its disposal if it would simply act more efficiently. Through his efforts, Eyman has effectively turned the tools of initiative and referendum into the fourth branch of government in Washington State. Legislative leaders now anticipate Eyman's action as a part of their legislative agenda, and have even met with him to ask how Permanent Offense will respond to certain proposals. Tim Eyman did lose some of his luster in early 2002 when he disclosed that he lied about deriving personal income from contributions made to Permanent Offense. This led to an investigation into his campaign activities by the State PDC, and a great deal of negative press coverage. Despite these problems, however, he remains a powerful force in state politics.

We describe Eyman as a postmodern political actor because of his unconventional methods and approach to politics, and because of how his use of the initiative process changes the accountability of our system to what *Washington Post* writer David Broder calls "laws without government" (Broder 2000). Broder quotes former Oregon Supreme Court Justice Hans A. Linde to make the point that responsibility under government dominated by initiatives is elusive. Judge Linde argues that "individual voters are under no obligation to vote on any particular ballot measure, or to vote at all... An act of 'the people' is always the act of some changing fraction of the people, often a small fraction" (Broder 2000). Feminist activists of the 1970s were known for the slogan "the personal is political." Judge Linde argues that the triumph of the initiative process brings that slogan to its extreme conclusion:

> Linde argued that the initiative process, far from promoting the public interest, was inherently tailored to private, personal interests. "There is a difference between deciding to reduce taxes on one's constituents and deciding to reduce taxes on oneself," he said. "In lawmaking by plebiscite, no retired homeowner is obliged to weigh the needs of, or to represent, the children who live in the next block; no urban weekend camper needs to consider the jobs of loggers; no logger, those of fishermen. Indeed the arguments made to the voters, especially on fiscal ballot measures, explicitly urge them to weigh their personal costs and benefits, complete with charts of taxes saved or services reduced… No lobbyist's testimony could appeal to the personal (as distinct from the electoral) self-interest of legislative committee members in the crass and simplistic terms routinely addressed to the voter as personal lawmaker" (Broder 2000).

Postmodernism challenges the notion of any claim to a "public good" or "common good." Ideologies that make claim to a public good are decried to represent a mask for some powerful interest. According to postmodern critics such as the University of Montana's Albert Borgmann, "universalism has been dethroned in almost every field of contemporary culture" (Borgmann 1992). Tim Eyman's postmodern approach is more obvious when contrasted with the actions of former Congresswoman Linda Smith. The successful advocate of two initiatives in the early 1990s—Initiative 134 in 1992, which placed more stringent restrictions on the ability of public employees' unions to raise and spend funds on political efforts, and Initiative 601, which established a state spending limit and restricted the legislature's authority to raise taxes—Smith developed her own political organization for running conventional electoral campaigns. Unlike Eyman, Smith used her success with these initiatives as a springboard for campaigns for higher office, succeeding in 1994 as a write-in candidate for the U.S. House of Representatives, but failing in 1998 in an attempt at the U.S. Senate. Smith was clearly ideological, generally aligning herself with the Christian Coalition and the conservative faction of the Republican Party. Clearly, she believed in a common good, and that a political party should govern in accord with a philosophy directed toward the attainment of the public welfare. In contrast, Eyman thus far has steered clear of political issues outside of taxes and tax-related transportation funding.

Since the late 1990s, other interest groups have joined Tim Eyman's direct-democracy act. During the 2000 election year, frustrated at their failure with the state legislature, the Washington Education Association fronted two initiatives, I-728 and I-732, which dedicated funding for reducing class size in K-12 education and mandated a yearly cost-of-living increase for teachers and other education professionals based on the Consumer Price Index for Seattle. No new source of revenue for either initiative was specified in either initiative. The state's voters, having been promised smaller classes for kids and better pay for teachers at no personal expense, passed both measurers by wide margins. When Washington's economy went into a deep recession in 2001, the WEA balked at any discussion of modifying the forms of the two initiatives. As an interest group, the WEA still lobbies the state legislature, the governor, the Superintendent of Public Instruction, and other policy makers. By going to the ballot with their own issues, the WEA has shown that teachers and school administrators are adept at taking a page out of Eyman's book when their advocacy falls on deaf ears.

Case Study #2—The Once and Former Overwhelmingly Formidable Boeing

What the business downturn of the late 1960s and early '70s did not do to Boeing's gradual diminishment as a preeminent interest group in the state, direct democracy à la Tim Eyman later did. The beginning dropoff in Boeing's influence was in evidence from its failure to bring about tax reform in the '70s, and its later failure to influence the state to address a range of urban transportation problems in the Puget Sound area where the firm maintained its headquarters and manufacturing facilities. Most recently, voters have defeated Referendum 52, which was intended to provide funds necessary to expand western Washington's very crowded highways through a gasoline tax. Boeing had made this issue one of critical importance to its continued prominence in the state economy. Not only did the measure lose statewide, it even lost in the Puget Sound area. As if washing its hands of further efforts to influence the state in its favor, in the spring of 2001 Boeing moved its corporate headquarters to Chicago. Before leaving Washington, the firm made public a list of complaints about the state's poor business environment. For observers, this signified that the political clout the company had once taken for granted had diminished.

This state of affairs reflected a dramatic change. For decades Boeing ruled the interest-group roost in Washington State. The clout of the state's famed aircraft manufacturer was summed up when former U.S. Senator Henry "Scoop" Jackson was referred to as "the Senator from Boeing." A look at public policy in Washington State reveals the influence of the company in many ways. The state maintains a sales tax exemption on aircraft and on machinery and equipment purchased by manufacturers. The state's emphasis on "outcome-based education," and the creation in 2001 of the Governor's Council on Competitiveness both strongly bear the influence of the Boeing Company in some measure. Despite its tremendous influence, however, Boeing did not always get its way, and, another telling example of the firm's declining influence surfaced during the 1997 state legislative session. Boeing advocated a proposal that year to modify a Washington State Supreme Court decision, *Birklid v. Boeing*. That Court's unanimous decision had held that Boeing was liable to pay workers compensation for using a product during manufacturing that caused workers to become ill. After losing in the Supreme Court, Boeing asked that the legislature change the standard by statute. While the Republican-controlled state Senate approved the measure drafted by Boeing lobbyists, the legislation failed in the Republican-controlled state House when seven Republicans joined with the chamber's forty-two Democrats to defeat the bill. Not surprisingly, the measure was opposed by organized labor and trial lawyers—viewed as perennial adversaries of business interests.

Paradoxically, by the end of the 1990s, Boeing was finding that some traditional legislative adversaries were increasingly becoming its allies. The announcement of the departure of Boeing's headquarters added fuel to the rhetorical fire of politicians of various political stripes. Governor Gary Locke,[2] a Democrat, responded to the announcement by creating and immediately convening the Governor's Council on Competitiveness. The council was charged to make recommendations on how to improve Washington State's business climate. One of the council's chairs was Boeing's Chief Operating Officer, Alan Mulally. The council developed a list of recommendations that became part of the governor's legislative agenda during the 2002 legislative session. An article in the Tacoma *News Tribune* reported on the impact of Boeing's move:

> Helping business in Washington has weighed heavily on legislators' minds recently. Boeing relocated its headquarters from Seattle to Chicago last year, a big blow to the state. Boeing Commercial Airplanes CEO Alan Mulally visited Olympia earlier this year and told lawmakers that of all the places the airplane manufacturer does business, Washington state is the worst. In a letter to House Speaker Frank Chopp (D-Seattle), Mulally said unemployment taxation and transportation were the company's main concerns (Cook 2002).

The two issues cited by Mulally placed Boeing against interest groups that were their allies in other areas. The reform that Boeing requested in the state's unemployment insurance system took the form of House Bill 2901 during the 2001 legislative session. The bill attempted to remedy, as Boeing argued, an inequity in the state's existing unemployment insurance system. The complaint read that steady employers—such as Boeing and other manufacturers, as well as retailers, restaurants, utilities, and other businesses—paid significantly more into a system than their workforce ever took advantage of as beneficiaries. On the other hand, seasonal employers—such as builders, contractors, farmers, and those in natural resource-based industries—contributed less than what their workforce received in unemployment insurance. The proposal attempted to strike a more equitable balance in terms of taxation. Farmers and those in agriculturally-based industries were exempted by the proposal. The Building Industry Association of Washington (BIAW) vociferously opposed the measure. Because the proposal split the business community and enjoyed the support of organized labor, in particular the Aerospace Machinists (Boeing's organized workforce), the measure passed both houses of a Democratically controlled legislature and was signed by the governor. At that point, however, the populist tradition of Washington State came running to the aid of those on the short end of the stick of the unemployment insurance fight. The BIAW organized a petition drive to make the measure subject to a public referendum. As Edward Seeberger perceptively noted,

> A referendum must be held on any measure passed by the Legislature if the signatures of a number of voters equal to four percent of those voting in the last gubernatorial election are submitted within 90 days adjournment of the legislative session in which the measure was enacted. The measure goes on the ballot at the next general election (Seeberger 1989).

During the 2000 election year Boeing contributed a total of $22,740 to Democratic candidates and their affiliated committees and PACs, and $218,450 to Republican candidates and their affiliated committees and PACs. During the same election year, the BIAW contributed a total of $6,500 to Democratic candidates and their affiliated committees and PACs, and $170,275 to Republican candidates and their affiliated committees and PACs. So, despite similarities in support of political candidates, business interests can vie significantly with each other over differences in public policy.

The other important legislative concern cited by Boeing focused on funding for transportation improvements. Transportation monies, however, were greatly reduced in 1999 when the citizens of Washington approved Initiative 695, sponsored by Tim Eyman, which reduced the State's Motor Vehicle Excise Tax (MVET) to $30 per passenger vehicle. The State Supreme Court subsequently found the initiative to be unconstitutional, but, fearing the wrath of the voters in the 2000 election year, the legislature and governor moved quickly to adopt the policy on the MVET prescribed by I-695. The result was a loss of $1.1 billion in the remainder of the 1999–2001 biennium, and a loss of $1.6 billion in the 2001–2003 biennium. The largest portion of the lost revenue had been dedicated to transportation funding. Boeing, which had opposed I-695, advocated an increase in the gasoline tax in subsequent legislative sessions to replace the lost transportation revenue. Interestingly, at that time, the Republican Party, whose candidates had received generous support from Boeing, broke ranks with the state's largest private-sector employer on I-695 and on subsequent legislative efforts to find alternative funding for transportation.

Case Study #3—The Continuing Battle over the Public Domain: "The Final Forest"

The Olympic Peninsula, home to most of the "last great trees of the Pacific Northwest"—old-growth timber—is what author William Dietrich has described as "The Final Forest" (Dietrich 1992).

A century ago, the U.S. government owned practically all of the Olympic Peninsula, itself the size of a small state. After the late-nineteenth century, when land-grant and other transcontinental and regional railroads were built, railways and state and federal agencies facilitated the growth of timber companies and other logging-related industries (e.g., wood-products processing plants, pulp mills, trucking companies, etc.) in Washington. In the early 1970s, the timber industry on the Olympic Peninsula still was operating at full throttle, and the cutting of old-growth forest continued unhindered. Forks, Washington, advertised itself as "The Logging Capital of America." Mills were running around the clock. New forest roads were cut, and the logging trucks rumbled. Bert Cole, the Washington State Land Commissioner who hailed from the area, was the loggers' best friend (Dietrich 1992). The U.S. Forest Service played its accustomed cooperative role on public lands, and large scale clear-cutting was carried out on both public (state and federal) and private lands in the area.

Environmental groups nationwide were just beginning to weigh in on forest management issues in the 1970s, with some impact on the national level. The establishment of Washington's North Cascades National Park attested to the environmental movement's growing momentum. That park was created following local reaction to a giant timber sale that would have denuded the mountains framing Lake Chelan, a sixty-six mile fiord that is the second deepest body of water in the lower 48 states. In addition, adjacent to the national park, Congress had established giant wilderness areas extending all the way to the Canadian border (McConnell 1975). It was only a matter of time before the environmental backlash reached the Olympic Peninsula and focused on its old-growth trees.

The interest groups that have fought over, divided up, exploited, preserved, and sought to regulate or otherwise impose political will on the Olympic Peninsula number in the dozens. Major players, in addition to the USFS and the Washington State Lands Commissioner, include the U.S. Bureau of Land Management, U.S. Fish and Wildlife Service, and the Washington State Department of Natural Resources.

It is important to parenthetically note that these government agencies are considered here both as authorities and as interest groups. It was political scientist Theodore Lowi who first advanced the concept of "interest group liberalism" in his book by the same name (Lowi 1969). Lowi argued persuasively in this influential "polemic" (his word) that during the twentieth century, and especially from FDR's New Deal on, the line that we presume separates government and private interest has all but vanished, replaced by notions of "cooperation" and "partnership." When this happens on a broad scale, the public is subjected to the downside of pluralism. The largest, most well organized interest

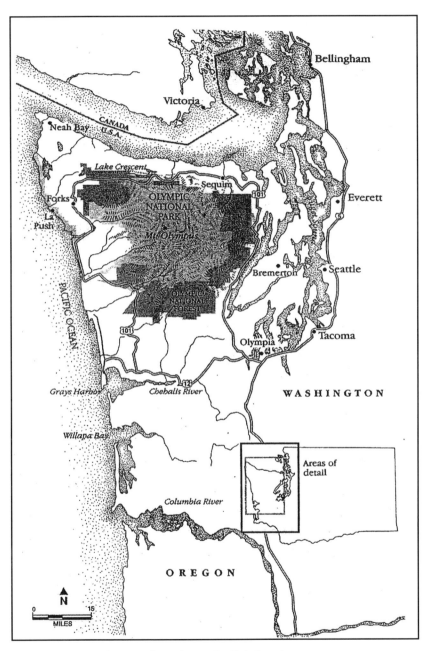

Source: William Dietrich. 1992. *The Final Forest*. New York: Penguin.

groups, now armed with preferred access to authority, will almost always achieve their private interest. Add to these interest groups the liberalism dynamic of the nineteenth-century land grants—framed to benefit the many, but in reality leading to an ever greater aggregation of land resources—and government becomes more a facilitator for concentrated capital formation than it does for the egalitarian development of the American West. In light of this concept, the USFS should, for much of its history, be viewed less as a governmental authority charged with managing forests than as a facilitator of forest resource harvest in league with major timber companies (Lowi 1969; McConnell 1966).

The boom years for logging in Washington State extended well into the 1980s. The timber industry ranked second to Boeing as the state's most important economic engine. Today, however, less than two decades later, logging of old growth timber on the Olympic Peninsula has all but come to a halt—because of the spotted owl (Dietrich 1992). The effort to protect this endangered species illustrates the continued influence and scope of authority that the federal government exerts over interest group politics in the state. The owl also serves to demonstrate the continued importance of the public domain to interest-group politics in the Evergreen State. And, finally, the spotted owl case underscores what Lowi sees as an antidote to "interest group liberalism"—namely, "juridical democracy," meaning statutes written so as to limit the bureaucratic discretion that tends to be exercised in favor of the best organized interest groups.

Certainly, in the peninsula's "Final Forest"—until the issue turned to the protection of the northern spotted owl and away from interest groups doing deals—the primary paradigm at work was interest-group liberalism, both in the state's Department of Natural Resources and the USFS. Ironically, the established environmental interests were almost dragged into the issue of spotted owl protection as an appropriate antidote to interest group liberalism. They shied away from the owl as an advocacy issue at first because they saw the enormity of the implications of such an action and had doubts that such a frontal assault on the timber industry would succeed. It was actually wildlife biologists who discovered and outlined the problem. For a number of years in both Oregon and Washington, scientists had been considering the question of habitat as it relates to the survival of this predatory bird. The evidence they collected strongly suggested that the owl needed both a broad area and canopy in order to locate food necessary for its survival. Second-growth forests provided for neither element of critical habitat. Neither did tree farms, planted with Douglas-fir, produce the wildlife complexity necessary for the owl's food supply.

In due time, the USFS was forced to take action on this issue. The politically charged task of studying the problem and making policy recommendations fell to Jack Ward Thomas, a field biologist stationed in Le Grande, Oregon. After working day and night for sixty days, his committee of knowledgeable wildlife experts concluded that 7.1 million acres of prime, old-growth forestlands had to be declared off-limits to logging if the spotted owl were to survive. Despite being assailed by the congregate of logging interests and their supporters in Congress, the team's work held up under close scrutiny. (Indeed, shortly after the issue came to a head, it began to appear to the lumber industry that Thomas's solution was the lesser of two evils after the Fish and Wildlife Service produced its own study concluding that the number of acres needed for the owl's habitat was closer to 11.6 million acres [Dietrich 1992, 259; Thomas 1998]).

When Thomas completed his study and considered the consequences of its conclusions, he understood the enormous ramifications of his work. He realized that life in the Pacific Northwest "would no longer be the same again." This single issue in the use of the public domain forever impacted life and livelihood in the state (Thomas, 1998).

Conclusion

Underscoring the far-reaching influence of public-domain politics, Thomas went beyond habitat concerns and urged consideration of a far more probing question. *How to manage the ecosystem,* said Thomas, was the *right* question to ask. That same question, in the state where the public domain has dominated politics since the start of political time, will serve to raise the stakes as interest groups continue to grapple over Washington's resources. As battle lines form again and again to fight over "who gets what, when, and how," the state's most defining political resources will continue to relate to the public domain and the natural resources lying therein. Whether the issue be growth management, saving the Pacific salmon, updating transportation systems, or providing for renewable sources of energy, the dynamics of ongoing urbanization and public domain management will engage the energies and talents of a broad range of experienced and resourceful interest groups.

Endnotes

1. It was President Franklin Delano Roosevelt's Postmaster General, James Parley, who, during the presidential campaign of 1936, described the United States as being made up of forty seven states and "the Soviet of Washington." He was referring to the active presence in the Evergreen State of radical labor groups epitomized by the Industrial Workers of the World (IWW) [Wobblies], who were unabashed communists. The IWW can be viewed as a particularly virulent manifestation of a deep-seated *populist* sentiment that has defined Washington State politics for over a century. This movement is to be understood with reference to the politics of public land and its distribution and ultimate uses that fueled the state's principal political protest movements of the 1930s and 1940s.

2. By early 2004, the governor's pro-Boeing efforts would result in a series of proposed special concessions for the airplane manufacturer.

References

Bledstein, Burton. 1976. *The Culture of Professionalism.* Cambridge, Mass.: MIT Press .

Borgmann, Albert. 1992. *Crossing the Postmodern Divide.* Chicago: University of Chicago Press.

Broder, David. 2000. *Democracy Derailed: Initiative Campaigns and the Power of Money.* New York: Harcourt, Inc.

Cone, Joseph, and Sandy Ridington. 1996. *The Northwest Salmon Crisis.* Corvallis: Oregon State University Press.

Cook, Rebecca. 2002. "House OKs Unemployment Changes." *News Tribune* (Tacoma, Wash.) (12 March). p. B2-6.

Cooke, Jacob, ed. 1961. *The Federalist.* Middletown, Conn.: Wesleyan University Press.

Dahl, Robert. 1960. *Who Governs.* New Haven, Conn.: Yale University Press.

de Tocqueville, Alexis. 1966. *Democracy in America.* Edited by J.P. Mayer. Translated by George Lawrence. New York: Harper and Row.

Dewey, John. 1927. *The Public and Its Problems.* New York: Holt and Co.

Dietrich, William. 1995. *Northwest Passage.* Seattle: University of Washington Press.

_____. 1992. *The Final Forest.* New York: Penguin.

Elazar, Daniel. 1984. *American Federalism.* New York: Harper and Row.

Garreau, Joel. 1991. *Edge City.* New York: Doubleday.

_____. 1981. *The Nine Nations of North America.* New York: Avon Press.

Gottdiener, M. 1987. *The Decline of Urban Politics.* Beverly Hills: Sage.

Hardin, Blaine. 1996. *A River Lost.* New York: Norton.

Herold, Robert. 1981. "On Thinking About National Ocean Concerns." Rockville, Md.: National Ocean Survey. Available in the Archives of the National Oceanic and Atmospheric Administration.

Hicks, John. 1959. *The Populist Revolt.* Lincoln: University of Nebraska Press.

Hudson, Chuck (Columbia River Intertribal Fish Commission). 1999. Eastern Washington University Public Affairs: Symposium: "Salmon Recovery in the Columbia Basin," Spokane, Wash.: KSPS Public Television.

Kaufman, Herbert, 1960. *The Forest Ranger.* Baltimore: Johns Hopkins University Press.

Key, V.O., Jr. 1956. *American State Politics.* New York: Knopf.

_____. 1949. *Southern Politics.* New York: Vintage Books.

Levy, Frank, Arnold Meltsner, and Aaron Wildavsky. 1974. *Urban Outcomes.* Berkeley: University of California Press.

Litt, Edgar. 1965. *The Political Cultures of Massachusetts.* Cambridge, Mass.: MIT Press.

Lowi, Theodore. 1969. *The End of Liberalism.* New York: W.W. Norton Press.

McConnell, Grant. 1966. *Private Power and American Democracy.* New York: Alfred Knopf.

_____. 1975. Interview with Robert Herold. Stehekin, Wash.

Peterson, Paul. 1981. *City Limits.* Chicago: University of Chicago Press.

_____. 1985. *The New Urban Reality.* Washington, D.C.: Brookings Institution.

Phillips, Kevin. 1994. *Arrogant Capital.* Boston: Little, Brown and Company.

Putnam, Robert. 2000. *Bowling Alone.* New York: Simon and Schuster.

Reisner, Marc. 1986. *Cadillac Desert.* New York: Penguin Books.

Richmond, Peter. 1993. *Ballpark.* New York: Simon and Schuster.

Rourke, Francis. 1978. *Bureaucratic Power in National Politics.* Boston: Little, Brown.

Seeberger, Edward. 1989. *Sine Die.* Seattle: University of Washington Press.

Skowronek, Stephen. 1982. *Building a New American State*. Cambridge: Cambridge University Press.

Thomas, Jack Ward. 1998. Speech on the Occasion of Earth Day in Portland, Oregon.

Turner, Frederick Jackson. 1893. *The Significance of the Frontier in American History*. Ann Arbor: University Microfilms.

U.S. v. Washington, Phase 1, 384 F supp-312.356,343 WD Wash 1974.

Washington State Public Disclosure Commission. 2000. *Election Financing Fact Book 2000*. Olympia, Wash.: Washington State Department of Printing.

Wiebe, Robert. 1967. *The Search for Order, 1877–1920*. New York: Hill and Wang.

Youngs, William. 1995. *Fair at the Falls*. Spokane: Eastern Washington University Press.

Chapter Four

Direct Democracy in Washington

Carolyn N. Long

Introduction

T HE INITIATIVE AND REFERENDUM came to the United States in the late nineteenth and early twentieth century as an outgrowth of Populist and Progressive movements in the United States. Popular support for the initiative and referendum initially came from the left; the Socialist Labor Party was the first to endorse it, and next the People's Party, later known as the Populist Party (which included the Grangers, Farmers' Alliance, labor, and single-taxers) (Cronin 1989). Comprised primarily of political outsiders located in the West and Midwest, Populists generally believed the major political parties were beholden to elite, monied interests and were unsympathetic to the needs of the common person. Because they were concerned with the centralization of power in state legislatures, Populists viewed direct democracy as a means to circumvent the traditional legislative process and engage in self-governance. As one advocate noted, direct popular legislation would "break the crushing and stifling power of our great party machines, and give freer play to the political ideas, aspirations and opinions and feelings of the people. It will tend to release us from the dominance of partisan passions, and have an elevating and educative influence upon voters."[1] The goal was to supplant rather than support representative institutions with direct democracy mechanisms such as the initiative and referendum.

Although Populism was on the wane by the turn of the century, direct democracy found new support, although for different reasons, as the Progressive movement gained momentum (Zimmerman 1999). Like the Populists,

Progressives were disillusioned by the corruption that had taken hold of many elected officials and political institutions. However, Progressivism was a much broader political movement that sought to address the ills of industrialization along with achieving institutional reforms in government. Progressives viewed the initiative and referendum as among several tools—including nonpartisan elections, the direct primary, civil-service reform, and campaign finance reform —available to expand citizen participation and reform the political process. And, unlike the Populists, Progressives viewed direct democracy as a means to improve rather than to displace the legislative process. As Woodrow Wilson noted, these participatory devices would ensure that legislators would be "bound in duty and in mere policy to…represent the sovereign people to whom they profess to serve and not the private interests which creep into their counsels by way of machine orders and committee conferences."[2]

The Populist and Progressive reform movements centered primarily in the American West, and by 1918 the initiative and/or the referendum had been adopted in 19 states in western and central regions of the country. Five states would later incorporate mechanisms for direct democracy between 1959 and 1970; Mississippi was the last in 1992. Maine and Rhode Island came close to adding the initiative and referendum to their state constitutions in the 1980s (Cronin 1989). The initiative and referendum process does not exist at the national level, although members of the Congress explored the idea in the 1970s.

Direct Democracy in Washington State

Early support for direct democracy in Washington came from the Socialist Labor Party in 1895, then later from labor organizations, the Grange, Progressives, and Democrats. However, the movement to amend the state constitution to include the initiative and referendum did not begin in earnest until 1910 when a coalition of labor, farmers, and urban progressives came together to find an alternative to the recalcitrant legislature of the period. In 1910 several organizations, including the Direct Legislation League of Washington, the State Federation of Labor, the State Grange, and the Farmers' Union, formed the Joint Legislative Committee to lobby the state legislature to amend the constitution to provide for the initiative and referendum and to later secure adoption of the institutional amendment. Despite initial resistance from members of the Republican Party, which controlled the legislature, the amendment moved fairly quickly through both houses. According to one observer, "the majority of members knew little about the amendment and cared less."[3] When the constitutional amendment came before the voters in the November election of 1912, the issue did not capture the attention of a majority of voters. Many of the state's newspapers paid little attention to the effort and those that did—primarily the larger newspapers—opposed the amendment. The few newspapers that favored adoption were from rural areas. In the end, however, Washingtonians passed the amendment in 1912 by over a 2–1 margin, with the constitutional amendment passing in every county in the state.

In Washington State, voters can use one of four avenues to participate directly in the lawmaking process: the direct initiative, the indirect initiative, the popular referendum, and the voluntary referendum. With the direct initiative, or "initiative to the people," 8 percent of the electorate voting in the previous gubernatorial election must sign a petition proposing a statute, which is then submitted directly to voters for approval or rejection at the next general election.[4] Washington is one of only nine states offering the indirect initiative, or "initiative to the legislature," which also requires a petition signed by 8 percent of the electorate who had voted in the preceding election.[5] The indirect initiative is first submitted to the state legislature at its next regular session. The legislature then has the option to enact the initiative into law without a vote of the people, to reject or refuse to act on the initiative, or to amend the initiative. If the legislature rejects or refuses to act on the initiative, it is then placed on the ballot in the next general election. If the legislature amends the initiative or proposes an alternative, the amended or substitute measures are placed on the ballot along with the original initiative at the next general election.[6]

The referendum allows voters to accept or reject laws proposed or enacted by the legislature. Popular referenda, or referendum measures, are laws enacted by the legislature that are placed on the ballot because 4 percent of the voters in the previous gubernatorial election have petitioned to have the measure subject to a vote of the electorate. Voluntary referenda, or referendum bills, are bills recently enacted by the legislature that have been referred to the electorate by the legislature for a popular vote. A simple majority of voters must approve direct or indirect initiatives and referenda in order for them to become law, with the exception of gambling or lottery measures, which require 60 percent approval.[7]

The scope of the people's initiative and referendum power in Washington is indeed broad; however, there are several significant restrictions. For example, initiatives can only be used to create a new state law or to amend or repeal an existing law. The subject must also be legislative in nature; the process cannot be used for administrative matters. Moreover, unlike the practice in many initiative states, the process cannot be used to amend the state constitution. And, the state constitution excludes from the referendum process "such laws as may be necessary for the immediate preservation of the public peace, health or safety, support of the state government, and its existing public institutions."[8] Also, no law approved by the people can be amended or repealed by the legislature in the two-year period following enactment, except by a vote of two-thirds in both houses.[9] After this period, initiatives can be amended or repealed like ordinary legislation by a simple majority in each house and with the governor's signature.

Participating in direct government in Washington is straightforward and is governed by a procedural framework set up by the state legislature. The intention of these rules is to facilitate the right of Washingtonians to engage in direct democracy. In 1914, on its first occasion to evaluate the legitimacy of legislation governing the process, the Washington Supreme Court reasoned that the powers of the initiative and referendum should be liberally construed, and that legislation governing the process be interpreted in light of this principle.[10] Any registered voter in the state with five dollars can propose an initiative or referendum measure, and the overall process involves minimal intrusion by the state. Most of the rules address relevant deadlines and procedures for preparing petitions for the solicitation of signatures.

The process begins when an individual files a proposed measure with the secretary of state.[11] Direct and indirect initiatives must be filed within ten months prior to the next state general election, and a referendum measure may be filed any time after the bill to be referred to a vote has been signed by the governor. After the proposed initiatives have been filed, a copy is provided to the code reviser who reviews the measure for "matters of form and style, and such matters of substantive import as may be agreeable to the petitioner, and shall recommend to the petitioner such revision or alteration of the measure as may be deemed necessary and appropriate."[12] However, any advice given is advisory. The petition is then given a number and forwarded to the attorney general for formulation of the ballot title and ballot summary. Individuals dissatisfied with the attorney general's actions can appeal to the Superior Court and request it amend the title or summary.[13] The process for proposing a referendum is similar; in lieu of a ballot measure, the referendum sponsor instead provides a copy of the act or part of the act for the referendum.[14] After the title and summary have been finalized, initiative and referendum measure sponsors have a limited amount of time to gather the requisite number of signatures to meet the signature threshold; signatures for direct elections must be filed four months before the upcoming general election and signatures for indirect initiatives must be filed at least ten days before the next regular session of the legislature.[15] Signatures for referendum measures must be filed within ninety days after the final adjournment of the legislative session at which the act was passed.[16] There are various rules governing the collection of signatures, such as the format of the petition, the number of signatures allowed on a petition, and the inclusion of a "warning statement" alerting people that falsely signing the petition is punishable under the law.[17] After the signatures have been gathered, the secretary of state checks a petition for validity, and if a sufficient number of signatures have been gathered, the measure is placed on the ballot and put to a popular vote.

A number of state and federal court cases have interpreted the restrictions put on signature gathering. One of the most contentious issues concerns whether petitions for initiative and referendum measures can be circulated on private property. Several Washington Supreme Court decisions have shed light on this issue; the extent of access to private property for the distribution of initiative and referendum petitions has been decided on a case-by-case basis. Generally, when evaluating whether signature-gatherers can solicit on private property, the court balances the nature and use of the property, the scope of the invitation the owner of the property has extended to the public, and the impact the case will have on the initiative process.[18] In *Alderwood Assoc. v. Washington Environmental*, a sharply divided Washington Supreme Court ruled that initiative and referendum sponsors could gather signatures in a privately owned shopping mall, even if the owners or managers of the mall objected to such actions, because the mall constituted a public forum. In the words of the court, the mall represented the "functional equivalent of a town center or community business block."[19] This right was limited, however, in that signature-gatherers could not do so in a manner that unreasonably restricted the rights of the private property owners.[20]

Later, in *Southcenter Joint Venture v. National Democratic Policy Comm.*, the Washington Supreme Court limited the right of a private political organization to solicit contributions and sell literature in a privately owned shopping mall.[21] And, more recently in 1999, in *Waremart v. Progressive Campaigns, Inc.*, when evaluating whether a private signature-gathering business could solicit signatures in front of a supermarket, the court set restrictions in a manner more protective of the private property owner's rights.[22] It ruled that Progressive Campaigns, an independent political group, did not have a constitutionally protected right to solicit initiative petitions in front of the supermarket, and that forcing the supermarket to do so would violate its First, Fifth, and Fourteenth amendment constitutional rights. Of note in this decision was the difference in the property upon which the signature gathering would take place. In *Waremart*, the court did not equate the front of the store with a public forum. Hence, while the court did not determine that the front of a supermarket constituted a public forum, it did affirm its earlier ruling in *Alderwood* upholding the constitutionality of gathering signatures in a shopping center that "bears the earmarks of a town square or public forum."[23] Restrictions on signature-gathering in private areas will likely continue to be an issue in the future, and as the resolutions in these three cases suggest, the outcome of challenges to such restrictions is largely reliant upon the specific facts of the case.

One area that has received little attention by scholars interested in direct legislation is the use of the initiative and referendum by local governments. Most states, including Washington, do not constitutionally provide for direct legislation at the local level. However, the initiative and referendum is available, and is used by Washingtonians in municipalities and those counties featuring home rule charters. According to the state's revised code, in "code" cities, also known as "statutory home rule cities," the general signature requirement for initiatives and referendum at the municipal level is a petition signed by at least 25 percent of the voters in the previous mayoral election.[24] Once the signatures have been authorized by the municipal clerk, the municipality has the option to pass the ordinance without alteration within 20 days, or to call a special election where the initiative will be subject to a vote of the people.[25] The signature requirement for referenda at the municipal level is the same. Both initiatives and referenda, if enacted, are subject to judicial review.[26] Moreover, municipalities with home rule charters have considerable latitude over the structure and functions of their government and have the authority to impose their own requirements for direct legislation, and several have done so. For instance, the City of Spokane requires only a 15 percent mayoral vote threshold for initiatives and referenda, and the City of Seattle requires 10 percent for city ordinances and 8 percent for referenda.

The five Washington counties that have enacted home rule charters have all included provisions for the initiative and referendum. The most notable difference between the counties is the percentage of signatures needed to certify a ballot measure. Snohomish County has the lowest signature threshold; only 7 percent of voters in the previous gubernatorial election are required for initiative petitions, and only 5 percent for referendum petitions. Whatcom County has the highest requirement, with both initiative and referendum petitions requiring 15 percent of the voters in the last gubernatorial election. Pierce and King counties each require 10 percent for initiatives and 8 percent for referendum and in Clallam County the percentage requirement is 10 percent in the previous gubernatorial election.[27] Each county also provides for a "mini-initiative" with only a 3 percent signature threshold in the previous gubernatorial election. After the signatures for a mini-initiative have been certified, it goes directly to the county for action before later being submitted to the voters. King County is the only county in the state that allows an "institutional initiative" whereby any city can propose an ordinance of countywide significance if it is able to secure the approval of at least half of the cities in the county.

Significantly, most municipalities and county charters featuring the initiative and referendum impose significant restrictions on their subject matter; for instance, they cannot affect the compensation or working conditions of employees, authorize or repeal taxes, or appropriate funds without specifying the new source of income. As a result, the power of the initiative and referendum, while available to cities and home rule charter counties, is considerably more limited than at the state level.

Extent of Use

At the national level, the use of the initiative and referendum has fluctuated considerably over time; some of the most intensive use of direct democracy occurred in the first two decades of their adoption. From 1910 to 1920, for instance, state ballots contained 250 measures; and, this rate was duplicated in the following decade. Use of direct legislation then declined significantly between 1940 and 1960, before increasing in use again since 1970. This past decade has seen the most initiative activity in history. Between 1990 and 2000, voters considered 458 initiatives.[28] The lion's share of these initiatives came from several "high use" initiative states located in the West. For example, 60 percent of all initiatives between 1990 and 2000 came from Arizona, California, Colorado, North Dakota, Oregon, and Washington. In absolute terms, Washington state ranks fifth in the number of direct and indirect initiatives adopted. Only Oregon, California, Colorado, and North Carolina have enacted more. Nationally, voters enact approximately two-thirds of all referenda and defeat two-thirds of all initiatives, although there is considerable variation between the states in this regard.[29]

Table 1 lists a summary, by decade, of the number of direct initiatives, indirect initiatives, referenda by petition, and referenda by the legislature that have been filed and certified in Washington over the last 88 years. The table also indicates whether the voters approved the measures in question. The first thing one will notice is that while a large number of both direct and indirect initiatives are filed each decade, especially since 1970, only a small percentage are actually certified and put forward to a vote of the people. Many measures never make it past the signature collection phase, most likely because of the large number of signatures required for certification. It is also clear that initiative proponents favor the direct initiative over the indirect initiative. One possible reason for this is because there is little incentive to propose an indirect initiative, as the signature requirement is the same as that of the direct initiative.

Once certified, however, initiatives have a rather good prospect of adoption. Washington voters approve direct initiatives slightly less than half the time, and indirect initiatives are approved a little over half the time. The approval rate for initiatives has been fairly consistent over time, particularly between 1960 and 1999. However, this pattern of outcome may be changing. More direct and indirect measures are being certified, and the number of them being approved is increasing. This change began between 1990 and 1999 when twenty-three direct initiatives were put forward to the electorate, which approved eight, while three of six indirect initiatives passed. Then, between 2000 and 2002, eleven direct initiatives were put forward to the voters, who approved nine. It appears as if the use of the direct initiative has increased significantly over recent years; and, the number of direct initiatives being certified and their approval rate have both increased dramatically in recent years.

The referendum by petition, and referendum by the legislature, are used significantly less frequently than initiatives, although—as with the initiative—the process of direct legislation has increased over time, with the most activity

Table 1
Initiative and Referendum in Washington by Decade

Date	Measure	Filed	Certified	Passed	Failed
1914-	Direct initiative	34	8	2	6
1919	Indirect initiative	1	1	0	1
	Referendum by petition	14	10	1	9
	Referendum by legislature	1	1	0	1
1920-	Direct initiative	21	5	1	4
1929	Indirect initiative	1	1	1	0
	Referendum by petition	6	5	0	5
	Referendum by legislature	2	2	1	1
1930-	Direct initiative	83	15	11	4
1939	Indirect initiative	8	0*	0	0
	Referendum by petition	4	1	1	0
	Referendum by legislature	2	2	2	0
1940-	Direct initiative	35	9	4	5
1949	Indirect initiative	8	2*	0	1
	Referendum by petition	8	7	1	6
	Referendum by legislature	4	4	3	1
1950-	Direct initiative	30	12	4	8
1959	Indirect initiative	8	2	2	0
	Referendum by petition	2	1	0	1
	Referendum by legislature	1	1	1	0
1960-	Direct initiative	42	11	8	3
1969	Indirect initiative	9	1	0	1
	Referendum by petition	4	4	1	3
	Referendum by legislature	9	9	9	0
1970-	Direct initiative	126	14	6	8
1979	Indirect initiative	38	6	5	1
	Referendum by petition	5	3	0	3
	Referendum by legislature	18	18	13	5
1980-	Direct initiative	126	14	6	8
1989	Indirect initiative	45	4*	1	3
	Referendum by petition	5	0	0	0
	Referendum by legislature	4	4	4	0
1990-	Direct initiative	177	23	8	15
1999	Indirect initiative	114	6*	3	3
	Referendum by petition	4	1	0	1
	Referendum by legislature	8	6	6	0
2000-	Direct initiative	66	11	9	3
2002	Indirect initiative	30	0	0	0
	Referendum by petition	1	1	0	1
	Referendum by legislature	1	1	0	1

*In each of these years, and twice between 1990-1999, the indirect initiative, after being presented to the legislature, was enacted. In all other years, the legislature either rejected the initiative or placed an alternative on the ballot, which was then presented to the voters at the next general election. Only those numbers are represented in the total number of indirect initiatives certified and considered by the electorate.

occurring between 1970–79. Also notable is the fact that referenda by the legislature enjoy a high approval rate. Direct legislation measures are more likely to be approved by the voters, while referenda by petition is the type of measure less likely to be approved.

Initiative Subject Matter

The subject matter of initiatives and referenda, and their relative success in gaining approval by voters, has varied over time. Table 2 lists a summary of the subject matter and success rates of initiatives presented to the people by decade. During the first four-and-a-half decades, the subject matter of initiatives covered a rather limited range of concerns. Most involved government regulation and reform, including legislative redistricting and creating or abolishing state offices. A number of tax reform measures were also presented to the voters, including the repeal of the poll tax and limitation of taxes on real and personal property. There were several measures involving public morality, including alcohol prohibition and later the regulation of liquor advertising and sales. Only two initiatives concerning the environment—both fishing regulations—were presented to the voters, with mixed results. Overall, when reviewing the subject matter of initiatives from 1914 to 1958, one notices that government reform initiatives were most likely to be approved by voters, reflecting the state's Progressive roots. Also popular with voters were minor tax reforms. Initiatives not approved by voters covered a similar, limited range.

Beginning in the 1960s, at the same time Washingtonians were utilizing the process of direct democracy more frequently, initiatives became more diverse. As in previous decades, however, government reform initiatives—including public disclosure measures, increases in the minimum wage, and increases in salaries for public officials and schoolteachers—still remained popular, with many measures being approved by voters. Tax reform initiatives—including abolishing the inheritance tax, limiting the motor vehicle excise tax, exempting goods from certain taxes, and limiting tax expenditures without voter approval—also increased in popularity over time, particularly over the last fifteen years. Their success rate has increased as well. Public morality initiatives, including measures addressing obscenity, abortion, and the introduction of gaming on Indian lands, were consistently presented to voters since the 1960s; however, unlike in previous years, morality measures were more likely to be rejected.

It is noteworthy that the last four decades have seen an increase in the number of measures seeking to protect the environment and wildlife, including bottle refund bills and restrictions on hunting. Also interesting is the introduction of several measures involving criminal justice, such as mandatory sentencing, as well as initiatives addressing civil rights and liberties, including a measure prohibiting discrimination based on sexual orientation. Washingtonians also appear

Table 2
Subject Matter of Direct Initiatives in Washington, by Decade

Time Period	Subject Matter	Approved	Rejected
1914-1918	Government Reform/Regulation	1	0
	Tax Reform	0	0
	Criminal Justice	0	0
	Environment/Wildlife	0	0
	Civil Rights and Liberties	0	0
	Public Morality	1	0
	Miscellaneous	0	0
1920-1928	Government Reform/Regulation	0	3
	Tax Reform	1	1
	Criminal Justice	0	0
	Environment/Wildlife	0	0
	Civil Rights and Liberties	0	0
	Public Morality	0	0
	Miscellaneous	0	0
1930-1938	Government Reform/Regulation	4	4
	Tax Reform	5	0
	Criminal Justice	0	0
	Environment/Wildlife	1	0
	Civil Rights and Liberties	0	0
	Public Morality	1	0
	Miscellaneous	0	0
1940-1948	Government Reform/Regulation	3	5
	Tax Reform	0	0
	Criminal Justice	0	0
	Environment/Wildlife	0	1
	Civil Rights and Liberties	0	0
	Public Morality	1	0
	Miscellaneous	0	0
1950-1958	Government Reform/Regulation	3	5
	Tax Reform	0	0
	Criminal Justice	0	0
	Environment/Wildlife	0	1
	Civil Rights and Liberties	0	0
	Public Morality	0	1
	Miscellaneous	1	1
1960-1968	Government Reform/Regulation	2	1
	Tax Reform	1	1
	Criminal Justice	1	0
	Environment/Wildlife	1	0
	Civil Rights and Liberties	0	0
	Public Morality	0	0
	Miscellaneous	3	0

Time Period	Subject Matter	Approved	Rejected
1970-1978	Government Reform/Regulation	2	0
	Tax Reform	1	3
	Criminal Justice	1	0
	Environment/Wildlife	0	2
	Civil Rights and Liberties	1	0
	Public Morality	1	2
	Miscellaneous	0	1
1980-1988	Government Reform/Regulation	2	0
	Tax Reform	1	1
	Criminal Justice	0	0
	Environment/Wildlife	2	1
	Civil Rights and Liberties	0	0
	Public Morality	0	1
	Miscellaneous	0	0
1990-1999	Government Reform/Regulation	2	3
	Tax Reform	2	2
	Criminal Justice	1	1
	Environment/Wildlife	1	3
	Civil Rights and Liberties	0	1
	Public Morality	1	3
	Miscellaneous	1	2
2000-2002	Government Reform/Regulation	2	1
	Tax Reform	6	1
	Criminal Justice	0	0
	Environment/Wildlife	1	0
	Civil Rights and Liberties	0	0
	Public Morality	0	0
	Miscellaneous	0	0

more likely to use the direct initiative for miscellaneous matters, such as measures regarding daylight savings time, prohibiting fluoridation in public water, and the licensing of denturists. The approval rate of initiatives in these three subject areas is mixed.

When reviewing initiatives in Washington, the most significant trend over the last several decades has been a greater diversity in the type of initiatives presented to voters. Even more significant in terms of impact has been the increase over the last fifteen years in the number of initiatives that reformed the state's tax structure, which has decreased elected officials' discretion in state budgetary decisions. As Lance T. LeLoup and Christina Herzog demonstrate in their chapter on "Budgeting and Public Finance in Washington," the effect of this "ballot-box budgeting" in the state has been dramatic. Complicating the situation further is the fact that voters occasionally will approve initiatives that cost the state money, such as increasing public school teacher salaries and limiting classroom size, while at the same time approving initiatives that restrict the amount of revenue that can be collected to pay for such measures. While some applaud the overall effect of voter-approved initiatives—that it has limited the growth of state expenditures—the fiscal ramifications of such actions are only now becoming apparent as the state faces record deficits, forcing elected officials to make difficult policy choices.

The Role of the Courts in Evaluating Initiatives

Unlike traditional lawmaking in state institutions where, in order to become law, bills must pass through numerous procedural obstacles, the only institutional checks on the direct initiative in most states, including Washington, are the courts. The indirect initiative, which must be presented to the legislature before being enacted, and referendum bills and referendum measures, which likewise already have been through the legislative process before being presented to the voters, differ from the direct initiative in this respect, as they are checked through the lawmaking process. Because of its importance as an institutional check, the role of the courts in judging ballot initiatives, and the implications of this judicial review, deserves close attention.

Many disputes involving initiatives and referenda concern procedural rules governing the initiative process. State courts are called upon to address issues involving signature collection and verification, appropriate ballot titles, and questions regarding subject matter (Magleby 1998). As noted previously, the state plays a rather minimal role in overseeing the process, and in Washington, as is the practice in most states, rules governing the initiative process are generally interpreted liberally (Zimmerman 1999).

Questions about the constitutionality of initiatives and referenda, however, are another matter. If the voters approve direct legislation, it is likely that the measure in question will be challenged in state or federal court, and more likely than not, the voter-approved initiative will be struck down as unconstitutional (Miller 2001). Moreover, it appears as if the role of the courts as an institutional check may be changing, and that the courts are becoming more aggressive in invalidating initiatives or referenda for violating the state or federal constitution. While some critics of the initiative favor this development, others find it a dangerous limitation on the people's right to engage in direct democracy.

In fact, recent empirical analysis into the role of the state and federal judiciary in evaluating the constitutionality of ballot initiatives reveals that courts are increasingly invalidating initiatives.[30] In his study of four high-use initiative states (California, Oregon, Washington, and Colorado) between 1960 and 1999, Kenneth Miller found that in a majority of cases voter-approved initiatives are challenged in court and that roughly half of all challenged initiatives are invalidated either in part or in their entirety.[31] Looking specifically at Washington

State, Miller found that fifteen of the thirty-six initiatives passed in the period 1960-1999 were challenged in court (42%), a rate similar to Oregon (nineteen of forty-three, 44%) and Colorado (fourteen of twenty-nine, 48%), but a little lower than California (thirty-six of fifty-five, 65%). Miller concluded from his research that: "In all of these high-use initiative states, including Washington, the sheer number of challenges and the crucial policy significance of many of the cases have now fully established the courts as an important component of the initiative process."[32]

Also of note in the Miller study was the pattern of outcomes of these cases. Eight of the fifteen Washington State initiatives challenged in the courts (53%) were ruled unconstitutional in whole or in part.[33] He also found that initiatives challenged in federal court had a higher likelihood of being struck down than initiatives challenged in state court, particularly in Washington. Between 1960 and 1999, four of the twelve initiatives challenged in state court were invalidated in whole or in part, and all five challenged in federal court were invalidated in whole or in part.[34] One possible reason for this, he notes, is that the life-time appointments of federal judges may contribute to a greater feeling of insulation when compared to state judges—particularly in the West where judicial terms are subject to a popular vote.

The high rate at which courts strike down initiatives in Washington leads one to speculate why this is occurring, especially given the fact that in many states initiatives enacted by the voters are presumed to be constitutional and are reviewed by the court in the same manner as legislatively enacted bills. To answer this question, Miller suggests that a judge's particular orientation toward initiatives plays an important role in determining whether a judge will be more or less likely to strike down initiatives.

In his article, "Courts as Watchdogs of the Washington State Initiative Process," Miller divides judges into two categories depending upon their judicial orientation toward initiatives.[35] In the first category are "juris-populists," who believe courts should give greater deference to initiatives because they represent a more "pure form of democracy."[36] Found in the second category are those judges embracing the "initiative watchdog" perspective, who do not believe initiatives should be evaluated in the same manner as bills enacted by the legislature. Initiative watchdogs maintain that courts should give less deference to initiatives because of problems inherent in the initiative process; they believe that "courts need to be more vigilant, not less, when reviewing laws enacted thorough the initiative's unfiltered majoritarian process."[37]

Using a recent Washington State Supreme Court decision which invalidated a popular initiative, Miller suggests that a majority of the justices on the current Washington Supreme Court fall into the initiative watchdog category, and have "shifted discernibly from granting deference to initiatives toward applying tougher scrutiny."[38] The case, *Amalgamated Transit Union Local 587 v.*

State of Washington,[39] involved a challenge to I-695 (which was summarized in this fashion when approved by voters: "Shall Voter Approval be Required for Any Tax Increase, License Tab Fees Be $30 Per Year for Motor Vehicles, and Existing Taxes Be Repealed?") The citizen-passed initiative was struck down by a King County Superior Court judge, a ruling later affirmed by the Washington Supreme Court for violating four state requirements for initiative lawmaking, most notably the state's "single subject rule" specified in the state constitution. The rule, "No bill shall embrace more than one subject, and that shall be expressed in the title"[40] is similar to single subject requirements in fifteen of the twenty-four states using the initiative.[41] In 1995 the Washington Supreme Court first applied this rule in *Washington Federation of State Employees v. State of Washington,* although it ultimately ruled that the initiative at issue in that case did not violate the single subject rule.[42] The two subjects in I-695 were the limitation of the license fee tabs and the requirement of voter approval of all future state and local tax increases. Because both were in the title and body of the initiative, the entire initiative was invalidated.

After reviewing the case, and researching previous state Supreme Court decisions involving the single subject rule, Miller concluded that the Washington court was acting in the "initiative watchdog" mold when it struck down I-695, because courts have a degree of latitude when interpreting the single subject requirement. In this case the court applied the standard more rigidly than it had been applied in the past. He notes that this may be part of a larger trend in several states with a high frequency of initiatives where the courts "are more strictly applying technical state constitutional restrictions on initiative lawmaking, such as single subject rules and ballot title requirements, invalidating numerous initiatives on these grounds."[43] However, this may ultimately be risky for judges who must face voters in elections. According to Miller, "The same populist impulse…that drives initiative campaigns can be enlisted to defeat watchdog judges. If the court becomes more politicized, its legitimacy, independence, and capacity to protect representative government, minority interests, and individual rights may erode. At that point, the Populist ideal of the unmediated power of the people will have moved a step closer to realization. Populism will have undermined not only the legislature, but the courts as well."[44]

Current Controversies: The Initiative Industry and the Professionalization of Signature-gathering

Proponents of direct legislation praise the initiative and referendum as useful mechanisms that democratize the political process. However, as the use of the initiative and referendum has increased over the years there has been a growth in the *initiative industry.* This is a form of business enterprise that assists groups in obtaining necessary petition signatures, manages initiative campaigns, and defends the enacted measures in court (Magleby 1998). The growth in this industry has changed the manner in which initiative and referendum campaigns are being conducted in the states, including Washington, and may have implications regarding whether the use of direct democracy is fulfilling its Populist and Progressive ideal.

Over the last several decades, initiative and referendum campaigns have become increasingly professionalized, and critics note that this development has impinged on the purity of the process by falling victim to the same ills that might plague regular elections and the legislative process (Ellis 2001; Magleby 1998). Much of the criticism centers on the use of paid petition circulators, who gather signatures to certify measures on the ballot. Because all states have signature requirements to qualify measures for the ballot (the average range is five to ten percent) and only a set amount of time in which to gather signatures (generally 90-120 days), it has become necessary for initiative advocates to move beyond the old days when efforts were powered by volunteers. As one critic noted, gathering signatures has become a profitable business, and like any other business it is run primarily for profit as opposed to the promotion of ideals. The great majority of the people sitting behind petition tables are not idealistic volunteers, but rather represent "interested mercenaries and bounty hunters who are paid by the signature and remain largely indifferent to the substance of the petition."[45]

Washington State provides an interesting case study regarding signature gathering. Prior to 1976, eight states, including Washington, statutorily restricted or prohibited the paying of petition circulators (Zimmerman 1999, 40). In 1913, shortly after Washingtonians amended the constitution to include the initiative and referendum, the governor asked the state to pass legislation regulating the initiative process. The legislature responded later that year by overwhelmingly passing a law that included a ban on the use of paid signature gatherers. The law made it a gross misdemeanor for any person who "gives or offers any consideration or gratuity to any person…to solicit or procure signatures upon an initiative."[46] The law went unchallenged for many years, until in 1973, when some individuals who were prosecuted for the solicitation of signatures for an initiative challenged it as an illegitimate use of the state's police power, and a violation of the first and fourteenth amendments' right to freedom of speech and assembly under the U.S. Constitution. In *State v. Conifer Enterprises* the Washington Supreme Court affirmed the constitutionality of the law, noting that it was a valid exercise of the state's police power and necessary to protect the integrity of the electoral process.[47] The court also dismissed the first amendment claim, noting in so doing that "the state did not make it unlawful for respondents to solicit signatures on an initiative petition…[it] only makes it unlawful for the respondent to pay (or offer to pay) other persons to solicit signatures."[48]

Fifteen years later, however, the Washington Supreme Court's ruling was effectively overturned, when a unanimous U.S. Supreme Court ruled that a similar Colorado law unconstitutionally restricted the respondents' right to engage in political speech in violation of the first and fourteenth amendments.[49] In *Meyer v. Grant* the U.S. Supreme Court determined that Colorado had failed to illustrate that the law was necessary to protect the integrity of the initiative process, and that petition circulation represented "core political speech," subject to the highest level of judicial scrutiny. The Court ruled that the Colorado state law burdened speech in two ways: first, it restricted the number of voices that would convey a message, and therefore limited the audience that could be reached, and secondly, it also made it less likely that enough signatures could be gathered, thus limiting the opportunity to make a matter the focus of statewide discussion.[50]

The Washington State legislature responded to *Meyer* several years later when it decided to outlaw signature-gathering on a per-signature basis, while still allowing petition-gatherers to be paid on an hourly basis. It amended the previous rule, making it a gross misdemeanor for "soliciting or procuring signatures on an initiative or referendum petition if any part of the consideration is based upon the number of signatures solicited or procured..."[51] The constitutionality of the law was then considered in federal court in 1993 after Sherry Bockwinkel, who headed a signature-gathering firm called Washington Initiatives Now (WIN), purposely violated the law by paying her signature gatherers on a per-signature rather than hourly basis. Interestingly, the campaign Bockwinkel was working on, an initiative that would allow the makers of dentures to sell directly to the public, was the only initiative campaign out of nine that year to qualify for the ballot.[52] In *LIMIT v. Maleng,* U.S. District Court Judge Barbara Rothstein, relying on *Meyer,* struck down the law as a violation of freedom of political speech guaranteed by the first and fourteenth amendments. She was unpersuaded by the state's argument that the law was justified because paying individuals on a per signature basis encouraged the introduction of fraud into the process "by providing an incentive for misrepresenting the nature or effect of a ballot measure."[53] The state has not yet responded to this ruling, and as a result, there currently are no restrictions on the use of paid petition circulators in Washington.

One critic of the initiative process has observed that the introduction of paid signature gatherers has changed the use of direct legislation in Washington dramatically. Over the last decade, the use of professional signature-gathering firms has significantly increased the chances for initiatives to reach the ballot booth. Between 1992, the first year paid signature circulators were used in the state, and the year 2000, twenty-four of the thirty direct initiatives certified made it to the ballot with the assistance of paid signature gatherers.[54] The measures certified without the use of a paid firm included: I-655, criminalizing the hunting of bears and cougars with bait or dogs; I-688, increasing the state minimum wage; I-694, making partial-birth abortions a felony; I-695, repealing the state's motor vehicle excise tax and requiring voter approval for all tax increases; and I-713, outlawing body-gripping animal traps and certain poisons. Based on this list, it appears that volunteer efforts will result in the requisite number of signatures only if a measure involves a hot-button issue that is of interest to most voters.

It does not look as if this trend will abate in the future. Most likely, initiative and referendum proponents will have to continue to adopt plans to raise money to finance campaigns for state-wide measures if they want to reach the ballot box successfully. While this is a typical strategy for candidates running for political office and for political parties and special interest groups contributing to political campaigns, one wonders about the broader implications of these developments. How would the Populists and Progressives who brought direct legislation to the Evergreen State regard this evolution in direct democracy?

Conclusion

Each year, dozens of Washingtonians willing to spend five dollars will file the necessary paperwork with the secretary of state, proposing a direct or indirect initiative measure. Much less frequently, legislation enacted by the state is subject to a popular vote through referendum by petition and referendum by the legislature. Washington is one of several "high initiative states" in the American West, where voters frequently resort to the ballot box to influence public policy. The direct and indirect initiative processes are the most favored methods of direct democracy in the state, and, if placed before the voters, an initiative measure has approximately a 50 percent chance of approval. Over the last fifteen years there has been a dramatic increase in the number of initiatives considered and approved by voters. While the subject matter of initiatives has become more diverse, the most frequent focus deals with reforming and regulating government or reforming tax policy. Initiatives altering the state's ability to collect revenue have had a dramatic effect on budgeting and public financing. As initiatives have become a more frequent feature of voting in Washington, and as the stakes have grown in terms of impact on policy, judicial review of voter-approved initiatives has grown in importance. Remarkably, a large percentage of duly enacted initiatives will be invalidated by either state or federal judges.

As the use of the initiative and referendum process has grown in popularity, so too has the growth of the "initiative industry." The use of paid signature-gatherers to help sponsors meet the arduous task of qualifying a measure for the ballot box has expanded greatly over the past decade. Initiative and referendum campaigns have become increasingly professionalized as state and federal courts have struck down restrictions on paying for the gathering of voter signatures.

While this may be a positive development for individuals and groups with the resources to fund a ballot measure campaign, to others it is evidence that the initiative and referendum process now resembles the unseemly side of traditional political campaigns—where money and influence rule. It appears that the lofty ideals that brought direct democracy to the state in the first place are being pushed aside.

Endnotes

1. Woodrow Wilson, "The Issue of Reform," in William B. Munro, ed., *The Initiative, Referendum, and Recall* (New York: D. Appelton and Company, 1912), p. 87.
2. Thomas E. Cronin, *Direct Democracy: The Politics of Initiative, Referendum, and Recall* (Massachusetts: Harvard University Press, 1989), pp. 47-48.
3. Claudius O. Johnson, "The Initiative and Referendum in Washington," *Pacific Northwest Quarterly* XXXVI (January, 1945), p. 31.
4. Office of the Secretary of State, State of Washington, "Initiatives to the People," www.secstate.wa.gov.
5. Joseph F. Zimmerman, *The Initiative: Citizen Law-Making* (Westport: Praeger, 1999) p. 7. The other states include: Alaska, Maine, Michigan, Mississippi, Nevada, Ohio, Utah, and Wyoming.
6. Office of the Secretary of State, State of Washington, "Initiatives to the Legislature," www.secstate.wa.gov.
7. Wash. Const., Article II, Section 1.
8. Wash. Const., Article II, Section 1(b).
9. Wash. Const. Art. II, Section 1(c). Before 1952, initiatives could not be amended or repealed under any circumstances; but this was changed with adoption of the 26th Amendment.
10. *State ex. Rel. Case v. Superior Court* 81 Wash. 623, 632, 143 P. 461, 464 (1914).
11. RCW 29.79.010.
12. RCW 29.79.015.
13. RCW 29.79.040—29.79.060 (1993).
14. RCW 29.79.010.
15. Office of the Secretary of State, State of Washington.
16. Office of the Secretary of State, State of Washington.
17. RCW 29.79.080—29.79.115.
18. *Waremart v. Progressive Campaigns, Inc.* 139 Wash. 2d 623, 641, 989 P. 2d 524 (1999).
19. *Alderwood Assoc. v. Washington Environmental Council* 96 Wash. 2d 230, 246, 635 P.2d 108, 117 (1981).
20. *Alderwood* at 246.
21. *Southcenter Joint Venture v. National Democratic Policy Comm.* 113 Wash. 2d 413, 433, 780 P 2d 1282, 1292 (1989).
22. *Waremart* at 641.
23. *Ibid.*
24. RCW 35.17.260.
25. Meredith Newman and Nicholas Lovrich, "Washington" in Dale Krane, Platon N. Rigos, and Melvin B. Hill, Jr., *Home Rule in America, A Fifty State Handbook* (Washington DC: Congressional Quarterly Press, 2001), p. 443.
26. *Ibid.*

27. Information collected from the Clallam County Home Rule Charter, the King County Home Rule Charter, the Pierce County Home Rule Charter, the Pierce County Home Rule Charter, and the Whatcom County Home Rule Charter.
28. Richard J. Ellis, *Democratic Delusions: The Initiative Process in America* (Lawrence: University Press of Kansas, 2001), p. 35.
29. David B. Magleby, "Ballot Initiatives and Intergovernmental Relations in the United States," 28 *Publius* (Winter, 1998), p. 149
30. *Citizens for Rent Control Coalition for Fair Housing v. City of Berkeley* 454 US 290, 295 (1981). The Washington State Supreme Court ruled as early as 1933 that initiatives were subject to constitutional mandates in *Culliton v. Chase* 1974 Wash. 363, 25 P.2d 81 (1933).
31. Kenneth Miller, "Judging Ballot Initiatives: A Unique Role for Courts." Paper delivered at the Western Political Science Association Annual Meeting, 2000, p. 4.
32. Kenneth Miller, "Courts as Watchdogs of the Washington State Initiative Process," 24 *Seattle University Law Review* (2001), p. 1057.
33. *Ibid.*, pp. 1056-7.
34. Note: two initiatives were challenged in both state and federal court and were double counted for purposes of this comparison. See Miller, "Judging Ballot Initiatives," p. 12.
35. Miller, "Courts as Watchdogs," pp. 1070-1071.
36. *Ibid.*, p. 1072.
37. *Ibid.*, pp. 1073-4. The 1977 anti-porn initiative and 1992 term limits initiative were challenged in both state and federal court.
38. *Ibid.*, 1055.
39. *Amalgamated 587 v. State* 142 Wash. 2d at 191-192, 11P3d at 773 (2000).
40. Wash. Const. Art II, Section 19.
41. Zimmerman, op. cit. p. 68.
42. *Washington Federation of State Employees v. State of Washington* 901 P.2d 1028 (1995).
43. Miller, "Courts as Watchdogs," p. 1055.
44. *Ibid.*, p. 1085.
45. Ellis, op. cit., p. 44.
46. RCW 29.79.490(4)
47. *State v. Conifer Enterprises* 82 Wash. 2d 94; 508 P.2d 1949 (1973).
48. *Ibid.*, at 98.
49. *Meyer v. Grant* 486 US 414 1988, at 420-428.
50. *Ibid.*, at 420-425.
51. RCW 29.79.490(2).
52. Ellis, op. cit., p. 51.
53. *LIMIT v. Maleng* 874 F. Supp 1138 (1994).
54. Ellis, op. cit., p. 52.

References

Bowler, Shaun, and Todd Donovan. 2003. "Direct Democracy in the American States." In *Politics in the American States: A Comparatve Analysis,* eighth edition, ed. V. Gray and R. Hanson. Washington, DC: CQ Press.

Cronin, Thomas E. 1989. *Direct Democracy: The Politics of Initiative, Referendum, and Recall.* Cambridge, Mass.: Harvard University Press.

Ellis, Richard J. 2001 *Democratic Delusions: The Initiative Process in America.* Lawrence: University Press of Kansas.

Johnson, Claudius O. 1945. "The Initiative and Referendum in Washington." *Pacific Northwest Quarterly* XXXVI (January).

Magelby, David B. 1998. "Ballot Initiatives and Intergovernmental Relations in the United States," *Publius* 28 (Winter).

Miller, Kenneth. 2000. "Judging Ballot Initiatives: A Unique Role for Courts." Paper delivered at the Western Political Science Association Annual Meeting.

Miller, Kenneth. 2001. "Courts as Watchdogs of the Washington State Initiative Process." *Seattle University Law Review* 24.

Newman, Meredith A., and Nicholas Lovrich. 2001. "Washington." In *Home Rule in America, A Fifty State Handbook,* ed. Dale Krane, Platon N. Rigos, and Melvin B. Hill, Jr. Washington, DC: Congressional Quarterly Press.

Office of the Secretary of State, State of Washington, "Initiatives to the Legislature," www.secstate.wa.gov.

Office of the Secretary of State, State of Washington, "Initiatives to the People," www.secstate.wa.gov.

Wilson, Woodrow. 1912. "The Issue of Reform." In *The Initiative, Referendum, and Recall,* ed. William B. Munro. New York: D. Appelton and Company.

Zimmerman, Joseph F. 1999. *The Initiative: Citizen Law-Making.* Westport, Conn.: Praeger.

Cases Cited

Alderwood Assoc. v. Washington Environmental Council 96 Wash. 2d 230, 246, 635 P.2d 108, 117 (1981).

Amalgamated 587 v. State 142 Wash. 2d at 191-192, 11P3d at 773 (2000).

Citizens for Rent Control Coalition for Fair Housing v. City of Berkeley 454 US 290, 295 (1981).

LIMIT v. Maleng 874 F. Supp 1138 (1994).

Meyer v. Grant 486 US 414 1988, at 420-428.

Southcenter Joint Venture v. National Democratic Policy Comm., 113 Wash. 2d 413, 433, 780 P 2d 1282, 1292 (1989).

State v. Conifer Enterprises 82 Wash. 2d 94; 508 P.2d 1949 (1973).

State ex. Rel. Case v. Superior Court 81 Wash. 623, 632, 143 P. 461, 464 (1914).

Waremart v. Progressive Campaigns, Inc. 139 Wash. 2d 623, 641, 989 P. 2d 524 (1999).

Washington Federation of State Employees v. State of Washington 901 P.2d 1028 (1995).

Chapter Five

Washington's Constitution: History and the Politics of State Constitutional Jurisprudence

Cornell W. Clayton and Stephen Meyer

Introduction

CONSTITUTIONS SERVE BOTH descriptive and normative functions. On the one hand, they describe the nature and structure of government—defining its institutions and their respective powers and relationships to one another. On the other hand, constitutions establish political goals or aspirations for the community to lived up to—creating general welfare, establishing justice, or protecting individual rights. Understanding a political community thus begins with understanding its constitution and how it has changed over time.

The United States has always been a system of dual constitutionalism. State constitutions preexisted the federal document and were the primary instruments for distributing and limiting government power during most of the nineteenth century. Despite this long history of constitutional dualism, Americans are today largely ignorant about state constitutions and state constitutional law. Leading constitutional commentaries and texts focus exclusively on the federal constitution, and many Americans do not even realize that their state has a constitution.[1] This undoubtedly is the result of the nationalization of American politics following the New Deal, a period capped-off by the Warren Court's expansion of federal constitutional power into seemingly every aspect of American life. It would be a mistake, however, to think that state constitutions are today unimportant or that they simply mirror their federal counterpart. State constitutions differ in important ways from the federal document. They have their own histories, their own concerns, and authorize and restrict government power in wholly different ways.

In recent years state constitutions also have taken on new importance. As the Rehnquist Court has retrenched judicial protection of federal constitutional rights, many state high courts have begun turning to their own state constitutions to expand individual rights and to limit governmental powers (Tarr 1997). Not surprisingly, this "new judicial federalism" has engendered a growing controversy about the legitimacy of using state constitutional law in this manner (see Gardner 1992; Kahn 1996). Washington's Supreme Court has been a leader in this movement, and its development of an independent constitutional jurisprudence also has become the subject of intense debate (Clayton 2002; Spitzer 1998; Utter 1992). Studying the state constitution and recent developments in state constitutional law should therefore tell us not only much about Washington's political system but also about the promise and problems of a system of dual constitutionalism in the twenty-first century.

Washington's Constitutional History and the Concerns of the Framers

Efforts to make Washington a state began immediately following the Civil War. Measures calling for a state constitutional convention began appearing on territorial ballots in 1869 and one finally passed in 1876. The first convention was held in Walla Walla in June 1878. After forty days the 15 delegates to the convention (plus one nonvoting delegate representing the panhandle region of northern Idaho) produced a lengthy draft constitutional document (Beckett 1968). Statehood, however, would be stalled for another decade.

Throughout much of the 1870s and 1880s, Congress was unwilling to admit new states into the Union out of a concern about how it might effect the delicate balance of party politics. Democrats, who controlled the House, were reluctant to admit new states that were perceived to be Republican (including Washington), while Republicans, who maintained precarious control of the Senate, refused to acquiesce to states that might elect Democrats to their chamber. The impasse finally broke in 1888, when Republicans gained control of both houses of Congress and the presidency. On February 22, 1889, Congress passed statehood-enabling legislation for Washington, Montana, and North and South Dakota.

A second constitutional convention convened in Olympia on July 4, 1889. The seventy-five delegates in Olympia were selected by a special election; two-thirds were Republican and one-third Democrat. The constitution they drafted was approved by a special election on October 1, 1889, by a vote of 40,152 to 11,879 (Beckett 1968). On November 11, 1889, President Benjamin Harrison proclaimed Washington admitted to the Union as the forty-second state.

Although a transcriber was hired to take detailed notes of the convention debates, the person was never paid and the notes were lost or destroyed.

Nevertheless contemporaneous news accounts and other historical documents shed some light on the attitudes and views of those at the convention.[2] The debates in Olympia echoed those made in other state conventions during this period. Indeed, late-nineteenth-century state constitution makers operated self-consciously in a context of constitutional pluralism and experimentation. Delegates were of course familiar with the federal constitution, and its influence on both the structure and language of the state document was ubiquitous. Not only did they copy structural features such as a separation of powers into three branches and a bicameral legislature, but several provisions of the state constitution, such as article I, section 3 ("No person shall be deprived of life, liberty, or property, without due process of law"), are copied nearly verbatim from the federal document (see U.S. Const., amendment 5).

Even more important, however, was the influence of other state constitutions. Delegates at these late-nineteenth-century constitutional conventions engaged in systematic analysis of other state constitutions and borrowed freely from the provisions they thought had been successful elsewhere (Fritz 1994; Utter and Spitzer 2002, 9-10). This spirit of comparative constitutional construction clearly infected the delegates in Olympia. Scarcely any of the provisions in Washington's constitution can claim originality. Perhaps one of the more obvious examples is article IV, establishing the state judicial system, which is taken nearly entirely from California's constitution of 1879. But nearly all the other provisions too—from the various provisions of rights found in article I, to the restrictions placed on corporations under article XII, to the design of the executive branch and the titles given various state officers in article III—had appeared in other states' constitutions before their adoption in Olympia. In fact, prior to the convention a former territorial judge, W. Lair Hill, drafted a model constitution which was distributed to delegates at the convention (Knapp 1913). Drawing heavily on California's constitution, Hill's draft eventually provided the exact wording for fifty-one sections and similar wording for forty-one sections of Washington's constitution. In all, the constitution of California provided complete wording for at least forty-five provisions, Oregon's constitution accounted for twenty-three provisions, Wisconsin's for twenty-seven, and Indiana's for seven (Clayton 2002).

In addition, the basic structural features of Washington's constitution were all borrowed from other constitutions. They provided for a bicameral legislature: the House would consist of between 63-99 members, each serving two-year terms (art. I, sec. 2); the Senate would be from one-third to one-half this size, and senators would serve four year terms, with half the seats selected every two years (art. I, sec. 6). Regular legislative sessions would be biennial, in odd-numbered years, and limited to 60 days (art. I, sec. 12). The convention also decided to disperse the executive authority among the office of governor, elected to a four-year term, who would serve as chief executive (art. III, sec. 2), and seven other independently elected officers—the lieutenant governor, secretary of state, treasurer, auditor, attorney general, superintendent of public instruction, and the commissioner of public lands (art. III, sec. 1).

There was lively debate about giving the governor the veto power. In the end, the convention granted the governor a broad power to veto any bill or even a single item of any bill, and required a two-thirds vote of those present in both legislative houses to override (art. II, sec. 12). The court system, again drawing on the California model, was to consist of a supreme court of five members (later expanded to nine) and lower superior courts (art. IV). Supreme Court justices were to be elected to six-year terms and superior court judges to four-year terms (art. IV, secs. 3 and 5).

The general attitudes and concerns of late-nineteenth-century America influenced the Olympia convention in many other ways as well. Two contentious issues of the period, women's suffrage and the prohibition of alcohol, were debated at the convention. In the end, the convention offered voters two separate articles dealing with these issues. Neither passed; the article for women's suffrage was defeated by a state-wide vote of 16,527 to 34,513, while prohibition was defeated 19,546 to 31,487 (Beckett 1968).

Other social and political attitudes of the period, however, did find their way into the constitution. In general, late-nineteenth-century America was an era of wrenching social and economic change. The nation was shifting from an agrarian economy to industrial capitalism and the period was marked by rapidly increasing concentrations of wealth, rising corporate power, and government corruption. In response to these problems, Progressive third parties had sprung up throughout the United States, and Washington was no exception. State chapters of the Grange, the Farmers Alliance, and the Knights of Labor were all established in territorial Washington and their ideas animated much of the debate at the Olympia convention (Crawford 1939; Schwantes 1982).

Influenced by the Progressive-era attitudes, the delegates in Olympia had very different concerns about the operation of democratic institutions and their relationship to private power than did the framers of the federal constitution one hundred years earlier (Airey 1945; Avery 1962; Dolliver 1992; Fitts 1951). In particular, while the federalists had been influenced by the ideas of civic republicanism and a fear of populist majorities, the framers of Washington's constitution were strong advocates of popular sovereignty and more direct forms of democracy. They feared concentrations of power in government, especially the legislature, but the tyranny they feared most was not *the tyranny of the majority* but the *tyranny of corporate power and special interests* who might capture or corrupt governing institutions. Liberty, they believed, would be best secured through an open, democratic government that was capable of strong regulation and controlling private concentrations of power (Dolliver 1989; Dolliver 1992; Snure 1992). Similar to other Western states adopting constitutions at this time, delegates in Olympia thus sought to balance their desire to encourage economic development in the state with their desire to protect citizens against concentrations of private power and corporate tyranny (Bakken 1987; Fritz 1994; Johnson 1992: Tarr and Williams 1998).

Understanding this historical milieu and the progressive political culture of the era can help make sense out of several otherwise disparate provisions of Washington's constitution. To secure popular, democratic government and protect against corporate corruption, while simultaneously protecting individual rights, the framers concentrated on four priorities:

1) Rights. The framers made rights their first concern. Article I of the constitution is a broadly phrased declaration listing 27 individual liberties that range from traditional legislative prohibitions on bills of attainder and ex post facto laws (sec. 23), to specific proclamations of individual liberties, including a right to assemble (sec. 4), a right to speak freely (sec. 5), a right to religious freedom (sec. 11), a right to trial by jury and other due process restrictions (sec. 3, 21, 22, 26), a right to bear arms (sec. 24), and a right to privacy (sec. 7). Unlike the federal bill of rights, most of these provisions are phrased as broad affirmations of rights and are therefore limitations, at least in text, against both government and private intrusion.

2) Restricting the Legislature. The framers attempted to restrict the legislative branch so that it would not become the tool of corporate or special interests. For example, the legislature was constitutionally prohibited from lending public money or credit to private companies (art. XII, sec. 9 and art. VIII, sec. 5), from contracting out convict labor (art. II, sec. 29), from authorizing lotteries or granting divorces (art. II, sec. 24), or from passing "private or special" legislation involving taxes, highways, mortgages, corporate privileges, deeds and wills, interest rates, fines and penalties, adoptions, or civil and criminal actions (art. II, sec. 28). Moreover, the constitution imposed structural restrictions on the legislative process, such as an openness provision requiring open meetings (art. II, sec. 11), an anti-log-rolling provision that prohibits bills from embracing more than one subject (art. II, sec. 19), and specific prescriptions against bribery and corruption of government officials (art. II, sec. 30, and sec. 39).

3) Enhancing Democracy. The framers of Washington's constitution provided for direct democratic control of all three branches of government. This included the direct election of both houses of the legislature (art. II, sec. 4 and 6), the popular election of judges (art. 4, sec. 3 and 5), and the separate election of all major offices in the executive branch (art. III, sec. 1). Democratic control of government was further enhanced by amendments 7 and 8 in 1912, which allowed the people to directly legislate through the initiative and referendum processes (art. II, sec. 1), and made all state-wide elected officials, except judges, subject to popular recall after their election (art. I, sec. 23).

4) Restricting Private and Corporate Power. Finally, the framers adopted an entire article (art. XII) and several separate provisions directly restricting private corporations. These included: barring the formation of monopolies and trusts (sec. 22), prohibiting companies from discriminating in the rates that they charge customers (sec. 15), prohibiting railroads from consolidating lines (sec. 16), requiring stockholders to assume liability for corporate debts (sec. 4 and 11), prohibiting companies from receiving public subsidies or credit (sec. 9), and prohibiting the use of the government's eminent domain powers on behalf of private corporations (art. I, sec. 16). And in one of the more unique provisions in a state constitution, the framers also prohibited corporations from "organizing, maintaining or employing an armed body of men" (art. I, sec. 24). This last restriction was the result of an event in 1888 when mining companies in Cle Elum and Roslyn employed armed strikebreakers to resolve a labor dispute (Dolliver 1992).

Differences Between the State and Federal Constitutions

In addition to reflecting a distinct history and attitude of its framers, Washington's constitution, because it is a state constitution, differs from the federal document in several structural respects as well. Understanding these differences is crucial to understanding constitutional politics at the state level.

1) Restricting or Empowering Government. Constitutions can either be *sources* of political power or *limitations* on political power. It is well-known that the federal constitution was thought to establish a government of enumerated powers, so that when Congress wants to regulate an area it must find a specific grant of constitutional authority to do so.[3] The opposite is true of state constitutions. State governments possess plenary legislative authority—that is, all power not specifically removed by the federal constitution (Grad 1968). This is where the idea of "state police powers" comes from (powers not possessed by the federal government). The framers of Washington's constitution understood this difference quite well, which is one reason why the state constitution is more detailed in its restrictions on legislative authority (Utter 1985). Members of Washington's Supreme Court realize this, too, as former Justice Andersen observed:

> As this court has often observed, the United States Constitution is a grant of limited power authorizing the federal government to exercise only those constitutionally enumerated powers expressly delegated to it by the states, whereas our state constitution imposes limitations on the otherwise plenary power of the state to do anything not expressly forbidden by the state constitution or federal law (*State v. Gunwall* [1986], 815).

Because of this structural difference, when the constitutionality of legislative enactments in Washington are challenged, the object of judicial inquiry is not whether the statute is authorized by the constitution, but whether it is specifically prohibited. Thus, in contrast to federal jurisprudence, at the state level the burden falls squarely on those challenging a statute to find specific restrictions on state governmental authority (Grad 1968). Secondly, unlike the federal level where judges interpret grants of government authority expansively (such as the Supreme Court's modern commerce clause jurisprudence), constitutional specifications of authority at the state level often act as limitations on what the government may do. In a constitution of plenary authority, an authorization to pursue one course of action may by negative implication preclude others that were otherwise available in the absence of the "grant" or specification (Tarr 1998, 6-9; Utter 1985). This structural difference also forces interpreters to think differently about individual rights provisions of the federal and state constitutions. In the federal constitutional tradition, the absence of a specific grant of government authority usually acts as an implicit protection of individual liberty. At the state level, however, protection from legislative power is found solely in positive constitutional affirmations of individual liberties.

2) Positive Rights. At the federal level rights are often thought of as "trumps" against the exercise of governmental power. This is because the rights found in the federal Bill of Rights are generally "negative" rights, or rights that *prohibit* government from taking certain actions (Congress shall make no law...). State constitutions, by contrast, often contain positive affirmations of rights as well as provisions that *require* government to act (Hershkoff 1999).

Of the 35 sections in Washington's Declaration of Rights, only three were expressed in the negative, as limitations on the power of government (art I, sec. 8, 12, 23). The others are phrased as general affirmations that the state must act to enforce and not simply refrain from breaching. Moreover, in contrast to the federal document, the Washington constitution contains several provisions that expressly confer rights to some form of governmental resource. For example, article II, section 35, provides: "The legislature *shall* pass necessary laws for the protection of persons working in mines, factories and other employments dangerous to life or deleterious to health..." Article XIII, section 1, provides that educational, reformatory and penal institutions, as well as state mental hospitals "shall be fostered and supported by the state." While article IX, section 1 declares: "It is the paramount duty of the state to make ample provision for the education of all children residing within its borders..."

What do such rights provisions mean for the role of courts in Washington? In a landmark case, *Seattle School District No. 1 v. State* (1978), the Washington Supreme Court held that the state had breached its constitutional duty to ensure a "basic education" to Washington students under article IX when it under-funded education. It then required the legislature to appropriate more money for public schools. In general, however, Washington courts have been reluctant to enforce the positive rights provisions of the state's charter, usually premising their reluctance upon doctrines of judicial restraint (Talmadge 1999). Whether such doctrines, which are grounded in separation of powers concerns, are appropriate within the Washington constitutional context is debatable. Unlike at the federal level, when Washington courts enforce such positive rights provisions they can rely upon clear textual support in the constitution, as well as the fact they are themselves democratically elected to enforce the constitution, and the knowledge that the power of judicial review was a firmly entrenched constitutional doctrine in 1889 and an accepted feature of the state's constitution (see Clayton 2002).

3) Length and Fluidity. Washington's constitution is much longer, more detailed, and more diverse in the concerns it addresses than is the federal constitution. The state document contains thirty-two articles and ninety-one amendments, as compared to seven articles and twenty-seven amendments in the federal document. It runs to nearly 40,000 words, compared to approximately 6,000 in the federal constitution. Its provisions range from relatively clear and specific commands (such as article III, section 14, which set the governor's salary at $4,000), to extremely open textured clauses that require pure political judgement to interpret (such as article I, section 32, requiring a "frequent recurrence to fundamental principles" in order to secure "individual rights and the perpetuity of free government").

Even more troubling for interpreters of Washington's constitution is its fluidity and frequent amendment—91 times since its adoption. The federal constitution, by contrast, has been amended a mere 12 times during this same period of time. As with the provisions of the original constitution itself, the amendments vary in detail and subject matter. The subject area calling forth the most amendments is public expenditure and finance, with more than 23 separate amendments. Other areas in which there have been multiple amendments include: courts and judges (10); local governments (8); compensation of public officials (5); voter qualifications (5); filling vacancies in elective offices (4); and alien land ownership (3). In all, 78 of the constitution's 247 original sections—nearly one-third of the entire document—have been altered by amendment, and 26 of these amendments were themselves subsequently amended or repealed (Clayton 2002).

Moreover there is no pattern of tectonic constitutional change or periods of major constitutional reconstruction in Washington history. At the federal level one can identify periods of political coherence or what have been called "constitution moments," such as the Civil War or New Deal, when the entire architecture of the constitution was realigned by sweeping amendments or judicial decisions (Ackerman 1991). But it is impossible to identify any such periods of coherence in changes made to Washington's constitution. There have been several unsuccessful political efforts to fundamentally alter the state constitution. In 1918, the legislature recommended calling a constitutional convention, but the proposal narrowly failed in a state-wide vote. Later, in the 1930s, Governor Clarence Martin created an Advisory Constitutional Revision Commission, which recommended nine sweeping reforms, including a move to a unicameral legislature. But none of the reforms were enacted. In 1965, the legislature created a Constitutional Advisory Council, which again made a series of proposals. Still no action was taken. Finally, Governor Daniel Evans, a strong advocate of constitutional reform, created constitutional revision committees in 1967, 1968, and 1975. But none of these efforts bore fruit either (Beckett and Peterson 1985).

The ninety-one amendments to the Washington constitution thus stand as individual, haphazard alterations. Some parts of the constitution have remained unchanged since 1889, while others have been altered on a regular basis (for example, article II has been amended 24 separate times). While some portions of the existing document may embody a principled and coherent constitutional perspective, others—as a result of continual amendment—reflect inconsistent constitutional perspectives and values. A judge or a lawyer seeking constitutional coherence in interpreting portions of the constitution may thus confront the task of *construction* rather than *discovery*. Moreover, to the extent the state constitutional provisions do not embody a single or consistent set of political perspectives, an interpreter cannot always look to the whole to illuminate the meaning of its various parts. Thus, unlike at the federal level, state constitutional interpreters are often forced to adopt a "clause-bound" interpretive approach, where each provision must be interpreted in isolation rather than applying a uniform interpretive process (Tarr 1998, 189-94).

The Politics of Developing an Independent State Constitutional Jurisprudence

Recent interest in state constitutions dates back to a speech delivered by former U.S. Supreme Court Justice William Brennan in 1977, in which he urged state judges to look past the rights protections of the federal constitution and toward those lying dormant in their own state charters (Brennan 1977). Brennan's call ushered in a renaissance in state constitutional law as one state high court after another began plumbing the language and history of their constitutions to discover new rights (Tarr 1997; Williams 1996).

Washington was an early leader in this movement. In 1983, former Justice Robert Utter addressed a state judicial conference and urged state judges to begin developing an independent state constitutional jurisprudence in Washington (Utter 1984). Even before this, Washington's Supreme Court had begun interpreting provisions of the state constitution so as to confer greater individual rights on Washington citizens. In *Alderwood v. Washington Environmental Council* (1981), for example, the Court held that the free speech clause of article 1, section 5, of Washington's constitution required owners of a private shopping center to accommodate free expression rights of political activists even though the federal First Amendment (which only guards against government suppression of speech) would not have provided such protection. Writing for the court, Justice Utter rejected the importation of the so-called "state action requirement" of the federal constitution into the state's free speech provision: "The United States Constitution…only establishes the minimum degree of protection that a state may not abridge." State courts "are obliged to [independently] determine the scope of their state constitutions due to the structure of our government" (113). In another prominent case, *State v. Chrisman* (1980), the Washington high court reversed a narcotics conviction of a university student when it excluded evidence from trial under article I, section 7 of Washington's constitution, even though the evidence was permitted under the Fourth Amendment of the federal constitution.

Not only did the court set out to establish an independent state constitutional jurisprudence in these early cases, but it also began to assert the primacy of state constitutional protections. In *State v. Coe* (1984), for example, the Court used the free speech provisions of article I, section 5, to bar a trial judge's gag order in a highly publicized murder trial. Writing for the Court, Justice Utter articulated several reasons why the case should be treated first under Washington's constitution rather than the federal First Amendment:

> First, state courts have a duty to independently interpret and apply their state constitutions that stems from the very nature of our federal system… Second, the histories of the United States and Washington Constitutions clearly demonstrate that the protection of the fundamental rights of Washington citizens was intended to be and remains a separate and important function of our state constitution… By turning to our own constitution first we grant the proper respect to our own legal foundations and fulfill our sovereign duties. Third, by turning first to our own constitution we can develop a body of independent jurisprudence… Fourth, we will be able to assist other states that have similar constitutional provisions develop a principled, responsible body of law… Finally, to apply the federal constitution before the Washington Constitution would be as improper and premature as deciding a case on state constitutional grounds when statutory grounds would have sufficed, and for essentially the same reasons (359).

From the very beginning, the revived interest in state constitutions had distinct political overtones. Justice Brennan's call was viewed by many as part of a liberal agenda to use state law to expand liberal rights in the face of the conservative drift of federal jurisprudence under the Burger and Rehnquist courts. Many conservatives, both on and off state courts, thus began to complain bitterly that the new state constitutional jurisprudence was "unprincipled" and simply "result-oriented" (Clayton 2002, 49-51).

Washington's high court was not exempt from such criticism. In *State vs. Ringer* (1983), for example, the Court held that a warrantless search of a vehicle, based only on an aroma of marijuana, was impermissible under article I, section 7, of Washington's constitution (even though a similar search would be permissible under the federal Fourth Amendment). In dissent, Justice Dimmick chided the majority for its "sudden leap to the sanctuary of our own state constitution." Complaining of the confusion that would be created by developing two separate sets of constitutional rights, Dimmick wrote: "Once again we confound the constabulary and, by picking and choosing between state and federal constitutions, change the rules after the game has been played in good faith..." (1250-51).

Washington's Supreme Court attempted to ensure critics that its new constitutional jurisprudence was principled and not simply political. The year after *Ringer* the court used two cases, *State v. Coe* (1984) and *State v. Williams* (1984), to settle rights disputes under the state constitution, but it emphasized that its decisions were consistent with federal constitutional jurisprudence and therefore not an effort to circumvent the latter. Still, criticism of the court continued and eventually turned into legislative efforts to curb the court's power of judicial review. Although bills to strip the court's authority failed to pass, they nevertheless sent clear signals to members of the state's judiciary (Talmadge 1999). More importantly, cases such as *Alderwood, Ringer* and *Coe* generated public controversy that became fodder in future elections to the court and changes in its personnel (Sheldon 1988, 183-187; Sheldon 1990, 8-10).

By the mid-1980s the court was thus on the defensive. In a pair of 1986 cases, it began retreating from its expansion of state constitutional rights in the area of police searches and seizures (see *State v. Stroud* [1986] and *State v. Kennedy* [1986]). Three years later, in *Southcenter Joint Venture v. National Democratic Policy Committee* (1989), the court also revisited its free speech jurisprudence. Appealing to "general principles of constitutionalism" the court abandoned its *Alderwood* decision and applied a federal-style "state action" requirement to article I, section 5, removing any state protection against private efforts to suppress free expression.

More importantly, to stem criticism that its constitutional jurisprudence was unprincipled, the court adopted a set of criteria to justify any future deviations from federal constitutional standards. In *State vs. Gunwall* (1986), Justice Andersen articulated "six neutral and nonexclusive criteria" that the court would look to when deciding whether to move from the federal to the state constitutions when adjudicating rights claims. The *Gunwall* factors include: 1) The textual language of the state constitution; 2) differences in the texts of parallel provisions of the two constitutions; 3) differences in state constitutional and common law history; 4) differences in preexisting state law; 5) differences in structure between the two constitutions; and 6) differences that may emerge from matters of particular state interest or local concern (12 13).

Two years later, in *State v. Wethered* (1988), the court made clear that briefing the *Gunwall* factors was mandatory before the court would even consider a state constitutional rights claim. In refusing to consider a claim under the self-incrimination provisions of article I, section 9 of Washington's constitution, Justice Utter reminded the bar that *Gunwall* imposed a procedural obligation: "By failing to discuss at a minimum the six criteria mentioned in *Gunwall*, (the defendant) requests us to develop without benefit of argument or citation of authority the 'adequate and independent state grounds' to support his assertions. We decline to do so…" (p. 800-01).

Post-*Gunwall*: Principled or Political Jurisprudence?

Gunwall was a calculated effort to reassure critics that the court's constitutional jurisprudence was "articulable, reasonable, and reasoned," not political (Utter 1992, 810). Nevertheless, the application and meaning of *Gunwall* has itself become controversial. Supporters of *Gunwall* argue that its requirement for structured analysis will ensure that the court acts in a principled way when moving beyond federal constitutional guarantees. Critics, on the other hand, contend that *Gunwall* has actually prevented the development of an independent state constitutional jurisprudence (Spitzer 1998).

Not surprisingly, this debate has been most evident on the court itself. At an aggregate level, the lack of consensus on the court over *Gunwall* can be gauged by how fragmented its decisions have become. Table I provides data on cases where members of the court cited *Gunwall* between 1986 and 2002. The data indicate, that for the entire 16-year period, cases in which *Gunwall* was cited produced 154 majority opinions. However, those same cases also produced 157 separate opinions (111 dissents and 46 concurrences). Moreover, conflict over *Gunwall* appears to be growing rather than diminishing, as the total number of dissenting and concurring opinions has been increasing as a percentage of the total.

Beyond *Gunwall's* failure to produce consensus on the court lies the substantive debate about whether it has advanced or hindered the development of state constitutional jurisprudence. A study examining the first decade of the court's decisions under *Gunwall* found that in 62 of the 108 cases where the court cited it as precedent, it did so only to point out that the parties had improperly briefed the criteria and thus refused to even reach the state constitutional claim at issue (Spitzer 1998). More importantly, the study concluded that in only 8 of the 108 cases (7.4%) did the court eventually analyze the state constitutional claims and reach a result different from the what the federal constitution would have required (1197-1200).[4]

Table 1

Gunwall Cases 1986-2002

Year	Total Majority Opinions	Concurring Opinions	Dissenting Opinions	Total Separate Opinions	Percentage of Separate Opinions
1986	2	1	0	1	33%
1987	2	0	2	2	50%
1988	10	5	6	11	52%
1989	12	4	7	11	48%
1990	9	1	3	4	31%
1991	11	2	6	8	42%
1992	12	5	7	12	50%
1993	14	6	3	9	39%
1994	12	3	6	9	43%
1995	6	1	7	8	57%
1996	15	6	10	16	52%
1997	12	4	15	19	61%
1998	10	1	11	12	55%
1999	8	3	9	12	60%
2000	9	2	8	10	53%
2001	7	2	7	9	56%
2002*	3	0	4	4	57%
Total	154	46	111	157	50.5%

* Through October 2002.

A more recent examination of the court's decisions under *Gunwall* yields nearly identical results.[5] Table II indicates that, between 1997-2002, the Court cited *Gunwall* in 39 cases. In only 14 of these (35.9%) did the Court agree to independently apply the state constitution. Moreover in only three of those fourteen cases (7.7%) did an independent state constitutional analysis yield a different result from what the federal constitution would have required.

The barrier that *Gunwall* presents to developing a state constitutional juris-prudence is quite clear. During the five years examined, the court continued to refuse to reach state constitutional arguments on procedural grounds, expressly invoking its briefing requirements to altogether preclude an analysis of the state constitution fully in 13 of the 39 cases (33.3%) citing *Gunwall*. Critics contend that this rigid requirement for briefing only ensconces process at the expense of substance (Spitzer 1998). When in 1996 the court refused to reach a state criminal due process claim because of improper *Gunwall* briefing, Justice Madsen

Table 2
Published Cases Citing Gunwall*

Cases citing Gunwall	Interpreted State Const.	Result Similar	Result Different	Result Unclear	Refusal to Interpet	Gunwall Analysis Conducted	Inadequate Briefing	Percentage Vote Against State Const.
39 (total Cases)**	14 (35.9%)	6 (15.4%)	3 (7.7%)	5 (12.8%)	23 (59%)	10 (25.6%)	13 (33.3%)	
Individual Justices								
Alexander	8	3	3	2	14	5	9	64%
Bridge	3	1	1	1	10	4	6	77%
Doliver	6	1	2	3	11	6	5	65%
Durham	4	2	1	1	6	2	4	60%
Guy	9	5	1	3	17	6	11	65%
Ireland	5	3	1	1	11	4	7	69%
Johnson	8	3	2	3	14	6	8	64%
Madsen	9	4	1	4	16	9	7	64%
Sanders	7	1	2	4	10	5	5	59%
Smith	11	4	3	4	22	10	12	67%
Talmadge	7	3	1	3	13	6	7	65%

* Over the past five years; the votes of individual justices represent those cases in which the justice joined the majority opinion. With fewer than five total votes, justices Chambers and Owens are not represented.
** Of the 39 cases citing Gunwall, 37 contained a discussion of the Gunwall factors and/or analysis.

castigated the majority for "…elevat(ing) form over substance (so as) to un-justly deny the defendant the protections he deserves as a Washington state citizen" (*State v. Thorne* [1996], 537). Indeed, the court has even imposed this procedural hurdle to deny a state constitutional analysis in death penalty cases (see *State v. Davis* [2000]).

Critics also argue that the *Gunwall* criteria force the court into a mode of analysis in which it must compare and contrast state constitutional provisions with analogous federal provisions. The consequence is that state constitutional interpretation is made overly rigid and contingent on developments in federal constitutional law (Atkins 1987; Clayton 2002). In the words of Justice Madsen, this compare-and-contrast requirement of *Gunwall* has left "independent state constitutional analysis…lost somewhere in the ever-shifting shadow of the fed-eral courts which are no less political and perhaps more so than our own state courts" (*State v. Glocken* [1995], 1274-75).

In addition to preventing state constitutional claims even from being con-sidered, *Gunwall* has not been effective at allaying concerns that the court's use of state constitutional provisions is unprincipled and political. Indeed, *Gunwall's* "structured analysis" is sufficiently malleable to allow inconsistent results in the hands of different justices. To take just one example, in several recent cases the court has addressed the relationship between the privileges and immunities clause of the state constitution (art. I, section 12) and the equal protection clause of the federal constitution (Fourteenth Amendment). In *Gossett v. Farmers Inc.* (1997), *DeYoung v. Providence Medical Center* (1998), and *In Re Detention of Turay* (1999), the court conducted a *Gunwall* analysis and then expressly held that the state provided no greater protection against discrimination than did the federal equal protection clause. Then, in the 2002 case of *Fire Protection District v. City of Moses Lake*, the court changed directions. After conducting a *Gunwall* analysis, the court decided to strike down a city's annexation process on the theory that it violated the state's privilege and immunity clause even though it did not run afoul of the federal constitution. Attempting to explain this discrepancy, Justice Bridge stated: "Although in recent cases we have held that the privileges and immunities clause is substantially similar to the equal protection clause [cites omitted], we have also left open the possibility that article I, section 12 could provide greater protection than the federal equal protection clause" (725). In dissent, Justice Madsen, also citing *Gunwall*, complained:

> The predictable, and unfortunate, result [of the court's decision] is that courts will have license to make what are essentially ad hoc determinations of consti-tutionality under article I, section 12… With this in mind, I believe it is essen-tial that the court adhere to a principled analysis… An important starting point is that a *Gunwall* analysis is intended to identify those situations where a state constitutional provision requires a separate and independent constitu-tional analysis (736-37).

In addition to using *Gunwall* to reach inconsistent results, the court's threshold determination of whether to even engage in a *Gunwall* analysis has been equally unpredictable. For example, in *Gallwey v. Grimm* (2002), the court upheld a state program that provided tuition assistance to place-bound students at certain public and private universities. Concluding that the program violated neither state nor federal constitutional prohibitions on public assistance to religious organizations, Justice Madsen's majority opinion contains no reference to *Gunwall* at all. Nevertheless, Justice Johnson's concurring opinion in *Grimm* contained a detailed *Gunwall* analysis. Thus the justices themselves appear uncertain as to when a *Gunwall* analysis is both necessary and appropriate.

Finally, reviewing the voting patterns of individual justices in cases that cite *Gunwall* also leads to the conclusion that it is being applied in a selective, result-oriented manner. As noted in Table II, the votes for and against an independent state constitutional analysis are fairly evenly distributed among the justices across the ideological spectrum. In other words, "conservatives" on the court appear equally willing to selectively favor or oppose an independent state constitutional analysis under *Gunwall* as do "liberals"—its structure for analysis appears to have provided no constraint. This suggests that Justice Madsen's dissent in *Fire Protection District* is right, that reliance on *Gunwall* does not guarantee a principled outcome and in fact appears to lead to the very sort of *ad hoc*, result-oriented jurisprudence it was designed to prevent.

Conclusion

The great constitutional historian Edward Corwin observed some time ago that "one of the greatest lures to the westward movement of population was the possibility which federalism held out to the advancing settlers of establishing their own undictated political institutions..." (Corwin 1950, 22). Washington's constitution has a distinct history. Its structure and purposes differ in important respects from the federal constitution. This is as it should be in a federal system.

The great promise of dual constitutionalism is that states can learn from each other and from the federal experience and act as "laboratories of democracy." Former Justice Utter recognized this promise in *Southcenter* when he noted that federal constitutional jurisprudence is "fraught with contradictions" and pitfalls that the state need not adopt. Federalism, he argued, "allows the states to operate as laboratories for more workable solutions to legal and constitutional problems. As part of our obligation to interpret our State's constitution, we have the opportunity to develop a jurisprudence more appropriate to our own constitutional language" (1303-06).

Washington's effort to develop an independent constitutional rights juris-prudence, however, also indicates the problems attendant with dual constitu-tionalism. At the national level, commitments to federalism principles are no-toriously political and strategic. Conservatives, for example, favor federalism when it comes to abortion rights or welfare policy, but favor strong national government when it comes to the war on drugs or in preventing doctor assisted suicide. Liberals, of course, hold the opposite views. There is no reason to sup-pose that such result-oriented commitments to constitutional federalism do not also apply to constitutional politics at the state level, leading both liberals and conservatives to favor state constitutionalism only when it advances their respective agendas. In Washington, the court's resort to the *Gunwall* criteria does not seem to have allayed these fears.

Nevertheless, interest in state constitutions and the new judicial federalism is here to stay. As with other constitutional developments its life is linked to broader political and economic changes in America that have forced Americans to rethink the locus and forms of governmental power. As in the past, this challenge will require new generations of Washington citizens to define them-selves and give voice to their political goals and aspirations. That voice, as in the past, will continue to be reflected in the state's constitution and discourse about its meaning.

Endnotes

1. Advisory Commission on Intergovernmental Relations, *Changing Public Attitudes on Gov-ernment and Taxes* (1991), 14. 52 percent of Americans surveyed knew their state had a constitution, 11 percent believed that it did not, 37 percent did not know.
2. Perhaps the best general discussions of the convention and prevailing attitudes of the day are found in two unpublished sources: James Leonard Fitts, *The Washington Constitu-tional Convention of 1889* (1951) (unpublished Master's Thesis, University of Washing-ton); Wilfred J. Airey, *A History of the Constitution and Government of Washington Terri-tory* (1945) (unpublished Ph.D. dissertation, University of Washington). See also Dolliver, supra note 97. For views of three delegates to the convention see John R. Kinnear, "Notes on the Constitutional Convention," 4 *Washington Historical Quarterly* 276 (1913); T.L. Stiles, "The Constitutional Convention of the State and Its Effects upon Public Inter-ests," 4 *Washington Historical Quarterly* 281 (1913); and Edmond S. Meany, *History of the State of Washington* (1937). For an account of the conventions day-to-day actions see Beverly Rosenow, *Journal of the Washington State Constitutional Convention*, 1869 (1962).
3. The literature on this aspect of the federal constitution is vast, but some of the more interesting discussions include: Kathryn Abrams, "On Reading and Using the Tenth Amendment," 93 *Yale Law Journal* 723 (1984); A.E. Dick Howard, "The States and the Supreme Court," 31 *Catholic University Law Review* 380 (1982); Lawrence Lessig, "Trans-lating Federalism: United States v. Lopez," 1995 *Supreme Court Review* 125 (1958).
4. The cases include: *Seattle v. McCready*, 868 P.2 134 (1994) (Wash. Const., art. I, 7); *First Covenant Church v. Seattle*, 840 P.2d 174 (1992) (Wash. Const., art. I, 11); *State v. Boland*, 800 P.2d 1112 (1990) (Wash. Const., art. I, 7); *Bedford v. Sugarman*, 772 P.2d 486 (1989) (Wash. Const., art. I, 7); *Sofie v. Fibreboard Corp.*, 771 P.2d 711 (1989) (Wash. Const.,

art. I, 21); *Witters v. State Comm'n for Blind*, 771 P.2d 1119 (1989) (Wash. Const., art. I, 11); *Seattle v. Mesiani*, 755 P.2d 775 (1988) (Wash. Const., art. I, 7); *State v. Stroud*, 720 P.2d 436 (1986) (Wash. Const., art. I, 7).

5. The sample of cases for the present study was compiled from an electronic search of all Washington State Supreme Court cases containing the term *"Gunwall"* during the past five years. The search yielded a list of thirty-nine published cases. Based upon a content analysis of the thirty-nine majority opinions, each case was categorized reflecting the court's *Gunwall* analysis and conclusions. Initially, the cases were divided into two groups: those in which the court concluded that the state constitutional provision at issue should be interpreted independently of its federal counterpart, and those in which the court refused to independently interpret or apply the relevant state constitutional provision. Cases involving an independent interpretation of the state constitution were further sub-divided into one of three categories: those in which an independent state constitutional analysis did not result in a final disposition different than that under the Federal Constitution; those in which the final disposition was different under the state constitution as opposed to the federal; and those in which it was unclear whether the outcome would have differed pursuant to a state or federal constitutional analysis. Similarly, the cases in which the court refused to independently apply the state constitution were subdivided into one of two categories: those in which the court rejected an independent interpretation of the state constitution based upon a *Gunwall* analysis, and those in which the court refused to independently interpret the state constitution because the *Gunwall* factors were not adequately briefed. Finally, for each of the thirty-nine cases contained in the sample, the votes of individual justices joining the majority opinion were recorded and classified pursuant to the previously discussed criteria.

References

Ackerman, Bruce. 1991. *We The People: Foundations.* Cambridge, Mass.: Harvard University Press.

Airey, Wilfred J. 1945. "A History of the Constitution and Government of Washington Territory." Unpublished Ph.D. dissertation, University of Washington.

Atkins, Linda White. 1987. "Note, Federalism, Uniformity, and the State Constitution— State v. Gunwall." *University of Washington Law Review* 62: 569.

Avery, Mary W. 1962. *History and Government of the State of Washington.* Seattle: University of Washington Press.

Bakken, Gordon Morris. 1987. *Rocky Mountain Constitution Making: 1850-1912.* New York: Greenwood Press.

Beckett, Paul. 1968. *From Wilderness to Enabling Act: The Evolution of a State of Washington.* Pullman: Washington State University Press.

Beckett, Paul, and Walfred H. Peterson. 1985. "The Constitutional Framework." In *Political Life in Washington: Governing the Evergreen State,* ed. Thor Swanson et al. Pullman: Washington State University Press.

Brennan, William J. 1977. "State Constitutions and the Protection of Individual Rights." *Harvard Law Review* 90: 489.

Clayton, Cornell W. 2001/02. "Toward a Theory of the Washington Constitution." *Gonzaga Law Review* 37: 1.

Corwin, Edward S. 1950. "The Passing of Dual Federalism." *Virginia Law Review* 36: 1.

Crawford, Harriet. 1939. "Grange Attitudes in Washington, 1889-1900." *Pacific Northwest Quarterly* 30: 243.

Dolliver, James M. 1989. "Condemnation, Credit, and Corporations in Washington: 100 Years of Judicial Decisions—Have the Framers' Views Been Followed?" *University of Puget Sound Law Review* 12: 163.

_____. 1992. "The Mind of the Founders: An Assessment of the Washington Constitutions of 1889." In *Washington Comes of Age: The State in the National Experience*, ed. David Stratton. Pullman: Washington State University Press.

Dworkin, Ronald. 1977. *Taking Rights Seriously*. Cambridge, Mass.: Harvard University Press.

Elazar, Daniel. 1993. "A Response: James Gardner's 'Failed Discourse of State Constitutionalism.'" *Rutgers Law Journal* 24: 975.

Fitts, James Leonard. 1951. "The Washington Constitutional Convention of 1889." Unpublished Master's Thesis, University of Washington.

Fritz, Christian G. 1994. "The American Constitutional Tradition Revisited: Preliminary Observations on State Constitution-Making in the Nineteenth-Century West." *Rutgers Law Journal* 25: 945.

Gardner, James A. 1992. "The Failed Discourse of State Constitutionalism." *Michigan Law Review* 90: 761.

Grad, Frank P. 1968. "The State Constitution: Its Function and Form for Our Time." *Virginia Law Review* 54: 928.

Hershkoff, Helen. 1999. "Positive Rights and State Constitutions: The Limits of Federal Rationality Review." *Harvard Law Review* 112: 1131.

Johnson, David A. 1992. *Founding the Far West: California, Oregon, and Nevada, 1840-1890*. Berkeley: University of California Press.

Kahn, Paul. 1996. "State Constitutionalism and the Problems of Fairness." *Valparaiso University Law Review* 30: 459.

Knapp, Lebbus J. 1913. "Origins of the Constitution of the State of Washington." *Washington Historical Quarterly* 4: 253.

Lunch, William M. 1988. *The Nationalization of American Politics*. Berkeley: University of California Press.

Schwantes, Carlos A. 1982. "Protest in a Promised Land: Unemployment, Disinheritance and the Origin of Labor Militancy in the Pacific Northwest, 1885-1886." *Washington Historical Quarterly* 73: 373.

Sheldon, Charles H. 1988. *A Century of Judging: A Political History of the Washington Supreme Court*. Seattle: University of Washington Press.

_____. 1990. "'All Sail and No Anchor' in New Federalism Cases." *State Constitutional Commentary and Notes* 1990: 10.

Snure, Brian. 1992. "Comment: A Frequent Recurrence to Fundamental Principles: Individual Rights, Free Government, and the Washington State Constitution." *University of Washington Law Review* 67: 669.

Spitzer, Hugh D. 1998. "Which Constitution? Eleven Years of Gunwall in Washington." *University of Washington Law Review* 75: 495.

Talmadge, Philip A. 1999. "Understanding the Limits of Power: Judicial Restraint in General Jurisdiction Court Systems." *Seattle University Law Review* 22: 695.

Tarr, G. Alan. 1998. *Understanding State Constitutions*. Princeton University Press.

_____. 1997. "The New Judicial Federalism in Perspective." *Notre Dame Law Review* 72: 1097.

Tarr, G. Alan, and Robert F. Williams. 1998. "Forward: Western State Constitutions in the American Constitutional Tradition." *New Mexico Law Review* 28: 191.

Utter, Robert F. 1984. "Freedom and Diversity in a Federal System: Perspectives on State Constitutions and the Washington Declaration of Rights." *University of Puget Sound Law Review* 7: 491.

_____ 1985. "Swimming in the Jaws of the Crocodile: State Court Comment on Federal Constitutional Issues When Disposing of Cases on State Constitutional Grounds." *Texas Law Review* 63: 1025.

_____ 1992. "The Practice of Principled Decision-Making in State Constitutionalism: Washington's Experience." *Temple Law Review* 65: 1169.

Utter, Robert F., and Hugh Spitzer, 2002. *The Washington State Constitution: A Reference Guide*. Westport, Conn.: Greenwood Press.

Williams, Robert F. 1996. "Looking Back at the New Judicial Federalism's First Generation." *Valparaiso Law Review* 30: xiii.

Williams, Robert F. 1997. "In the Glare of the Supreme Court: Continuing Methodological and Legitimacy Problems in Independent State Constitutional Rights Adjudication." *Notre Dame Law Review* 72: 115.

Cases Cited

Alderwood Associates v. Washington Environmental Council, 635 P.2d 108 (1981).
Seattle School Dist. No. 1 v. State, 90 P.2d 71 (1978).
DeYoung v. Providence Medical Center, 136 Wn.2d 136 (1998).
Fire Prot. Dist. v. City of Moses Lake, 145 Wn.2d 702 (2002).
Gallwey v. Grimm, 146 Wn.2d 445 (2002).
Gossett v. Farmers Inc., 133 Wn.2d 954 (1997).
In Re Detention of Turay, 139 Wn.2d 379 (1999).
Open Door Baptists Church v. Clark County, 140 Wn.2d 143 (2000).
Southcenter Joint Venture v. Nat. Democratic Policy Committee, 780 P.2d 1282 (Wash.1989).
State v. Chrisman, 619 P.2d 971 (Wash. 1980).
State v. Clark, 124 Wn.2d 90 (1997) (overruled by State v. Catlet. 1997. 133 Wn.2d 355).
State v. Coe, 679 P.2d 353 (Wash. 1984).
State v. Davis, 141 Wn.2d 798 (2000).
State v. Fire, 145 Wn.2d 561 (2002).
State v. Foster, 135 Wn.2d 441 (1998).
State v. Glocken, 896 P.2d 1269 (Wash. 1995).
State v. Gunwall, 720 P.2d 808, 815 (Wash. 1986).
State v. Kennedy, 726 P.2d 445 (Wash. 1986).
State v. Parker, 139 Wn.2d 486 (1999)
State v. Ringer, 674 P2d 1240 (Wash. 1983).
State v. Roberts, 142 Wn.2d 471 (2000).
State v. Stroud, 720 P.2d 436 (Wash. 1986).
State v. Thorne, 921 P.2d 514 (1996).
State v. Walker, 136 Wn.2d 678 (1998).
State v. Wethered, 755 P.2d 797 (Wash. 1988).
State v. Williams, 689 P.2d 1065 (Wash. 1984).

Chapter Six

The Washington State Court System

David May

Introduction

MANY CITIZENS PROBABLY CONSIDER it the primary function of the judicial branch to resolve disputes. They might further suppose that in the interests of fairness, judges must be isolated from the pressures of public opinion and ideological bias, and that, ideally, judges should simply declare the law without imbuing it with any particular political content. This view, which supposes that judges act as mere oracles of the law, represents one of the many, often polar positions held in American society concerning the role of judges and law in this country. While it may be appealing to imagine that judges are apolitical sages of the law, in reality they frequently are significant political actors, making important public policy choices.

Although law and politics may be conceptually distinct in the minds of many, they actually share many practical similarities. Washington State judges exercise broad powers of judicial review, and, in courts with discretionary jurisdiction, the selection and denial of cases is a politically charged process. Moreover, for the vast majority of judges in the state who are elected, the process of their selection and retention requires that they be, to some degree at least, political creatures. Thus, this chapter examines the factors that influence Washington judges' interpretation of the law and the exercise of their judicial role in the state.

Some of the factors that influence the role of Washington judges include: the structural components of the system, i.e., how the courts of Washington are organized; how judges are selected and courts are administered; and, perhaps most importantly, how courts interact with other political and social institutions, such as the state's executive and legislative branches and powerful interest groups and professional organizations. How these and other factors combine to create the context in which judges are either more or less likely to act in a policy-making manner, and how such action impacts law and public policy in the state of Washington, is the subject of this chapter.

Structure of the System

Judicial Administration

Composed of courts arrayed in a hierarchically ordered, four-tiered configuration, the Washington court system is comprised of trial courts and appellate courts, including the Supreme Court of the State of Washington in Olympia. These courts involve more than 400 judges. In addition, there are hundreds of attorneys and thousands of citizens who are involved in cases or the process of jury service. All of these people and activities require administrative support, which is provided by support agencies and personnel totalling about 3,000 people. Judicial administration in Washington includes everything from reform efforts and research requests to creating and maintaining court calendars. Records and documents produced must be carefully catalogued, filed, and archived by court clerks, county clerks, the reporter of decisions, court reporters, bailiffs, and law librarians. The court administrator oversees the entire process.[1] Although the administration, organization, and maintenance of the state's judicial system is a monumental task, it is undertaken for very little cost to the state. The entire budget for the judicial system, which has remained relatively consistent over time, is less the 0.3 percent of the total state budget. Certainly there are additional costs borne by local governments for the courts in their jurisdictions, but the statewide administration of justice is still a very good value for the dollar.

In addition to the macro-administrative needs of the system, individual judges at all levels require on-site administrative help. Law clerks, court reporters, court commissioners, visiting judges, law librarians, administrative assistants, and legal interns provide much needed administrative assistance to judges. Finally, to assure that sufficient judicial independence is maintained and that ethical standards are observed, the Task Force on Canons of Judicial Ethics and the Commission on Judicial Conduct oversee the conduct of judges and lawyers in the state. The Commission on Judicial Conduct is perhaps the more important of the two.[2] It was established by constitutional amendment in 1980 to oversee the ethical behavior of judges without having to utilize drastic measures of impeachment or other avenues of removal through the legislature. The commission investigates complaints and, in its administrative and oversight capacity, recommends to the Supreme Court the censure, suspension, or dismissal of judges. The commission can also recommend the removal of a judge for serious disabilities that prevent him or her from performing the duties of office.

Trial and Appellate Courts

As in most other judicial systems, Washington's courts can be divided into *trial* and *appellate* levels. To understand the judiciary, one must understand the important differences between these types of courts and something of their internal workings.

Trial and appellate courts generally perform very different functions in a judicial system. In simple terms, trial courts try fact. They are concerned with what events can be shown to have happened and who might have caused them. In most trial courtrooms, a single judge presides. He or she is the final say in what happens in that courtroom. A trial judge must be able to think quickly and make crucial decisions about evidence, legal motions and the law. For minor affairs—traffic cases for example—the judge alone may be in the position of deciding guilt and innocence and assigning a penalty. In more important matters, juries are selected to sift through competing versions of the facts and judges act as impartial overseers of the process. Trial courts are the most familar to the general public, thanks in part to television and cinema.

Everyone who loses a case in a trial court has a right of initial appeal, meaning that they can request an appellate level court review of the trial proceedings. However, the appellate review will not likely be concerned with the facts brought forth in the original trial. Appellate courts and judges are relatively unconcerned with ascertaining facts and usually rely on the facts established in the preceding trial court. Rather, appellate courts deal almost exclusively with questions of law and its application and constitutional analysis and precedents. These courts determine if all participants in the trial court followed the rules in making their case and if the judge applied the law correctly. Appellate courts do not involve juries, nor do they view evidence or make inquiries of witnesses. Instead, the cases they review turn on arguments about the meaning of the law. In written and oral arguments, the two sides present their interpretations of the meaning of the law and how it should be applied to the matter at hand to a panel of appellate judges. In Washington State, appellate courts consist of from three to nine judges who act in concert, collegially, to determine the outcome of disputes.

After the record has been reviewed and the arguments heard, the appellate court retires to deliberate and eventually produce a written opinion. Written opinions are usually required when decisions are rendered, although a written opinion is not mandated in relatively unimportant cases at the court of appeals level. If appellate courts find an error in the application of the law, they may simply reverse the lower court decision and dismiss the case or remand it to the trial court for further consideration. These decisions are reached and the opinions are written in a very different environment than the trial court. Because there is considerably less time pressure on appellate courts to resolve cases quickly, they may deliberate at length on each case before them.

As appeals rise through the judicial hierarchy, the decisions made become increasingly significant. Higher-level decisions are binding on the courts below. If a case reaches the state's Supreme Court, the decision rendered by that court establishes a precedent to which all other courts in the state must adhere.

Trial Courts

Trial courts populate the bottom tier of Washington's judicial system. At the lowest level of this tier are *courts of limited jurisdiction.* Included in this category in the state are *municipal* and *district courts.* Municipal courts, established by cities or municipalities, include both professional and lay judges and include traffic violations bureaus (traffic court). District courts represent county-level judicial bodies. Hearing the bulk of the state's cases, these lowest-level courts perform a vital judicial function. From these initial trial courts there is a right of appeal to the next level, the *superior courts.* The superior courts each oversee one of thirty-one state-mandated judicial districts. These courts function as both trial courts for large cases and as courts of appeal for cases arising from courts of limited jurisdiction.

Washington's courts of limited jurisdiction employ approximately 150 professional judges, each of whom has obtained a law degree and has passed the Washington State bar exam. Approximately 100 professional judges work in district courts, and the remainder preside over municipal courts. These judges are elected to four-year terms, through non-partisan elections within the geographic jurisdiction of the courts on which they will serve. In addition to the ranks of professional judges, there are also non-professional or lay judges serving in the state. There are approximately thirty such judges (or commissioners, as they are known in some municipal courts), who primarily oversee traffic court cases. These judges may be elected, but are most frequently appointed by city councils or county commissioners. Courts with non-professional or lay judges operate as courts of no record, meaning that they do not produce a written record of the proceedings.

Altogether, the total staffing level for courts of limited jurisdiction, including lay and professional judges, is about 180 judges. The subject jurisdiction of these courts is broad, extending to both civil and criminal cases for misdemeanors, gross misdemeanors, criminal traffic cases (e.i., DUI cases), and preliminary hearings in felony cases. The civil docket of these courts may include damage and contract claim suits up to $50,000 and requests for orders of protection, as well as traffic and parking infraction cases.

Courts of limited jurisdiction are the final stop in the judicial system in most instances. The number of cases filed in these lowest courts has remained relatively stable in recent years, consistently representing about seven of every eight legal cases filed in the state. More than 1.29 million limited jurisdiction cases were filed in 2001. Roughly one-quarter of Washington's citizens interact in some fashion with the court system each year. Non-parking judicial dispositions generated more than $126 million for state coffers in 2001. In terms of caseload, revenue, and the administration of justice, Washington's courts of limited jurisdiction obviously play a vital role in state government.

Superior courts, also called courts of general jurisdiction, hear far fewer cases than courts of limited jurisdiction. Cases are heard as mandatory original jurisdiction cases, such as juvenile justice and felony cases, or are heard on appeal from courts of limited jurisdiction. They represent cases that are too large to be heard at a lower level or important cases appealed from lower courts. In the case of appeals from municipal or lay courts of no record, appeals are frequently heard *de novo* ("over again")—i.e., treated as entirely new cases. Appeals from professional courts and district courts are heard and decided on the written or video record from the initial trial court. Superior courts are all courts of record. The 150 judges of the superior court system are all professional judges, elected by non-partisan ballot to four-year terms of office.

These courts of general jurisdiction are responsible for trying felonies for which the possible sentence exceeds one year in prison, and civil suits in excess of $50,000. In recent years, the number of cases filed in superior courts has remained relatively consistent. In 2001, Washington superior courts resolved some 274,000 of approximately 280,000 cases filed.[3] The largest percentage of these actions pertained to civil matters (38%), followed by domestic issues (15%) and criminal cases (13%). The remaining 34 percent was composed of probate, guardianship, mental illness, adoption, and juvenile cases.

Appellate Courts

While the superior courts and the courts of limited jurisdiction function primarily as trial courts, the *Court of Appeals* and Washington's *Supreme Court* function exclusively as appellate courts. The Court of Appeals serves as an intermediate appellate body, functioning much like the courts of appeal in the federal system, screening the Supreme Court from excessive caseloads, and serving as the final adjudicatory level in most cases. The Court of Appeals must review all properly filed appeals from lower courts. In practice, the court hears all appeals from superior courts that do not fall within the mandatory jurisdiction of the Supreme Court.

The Court of Appeals system is divided into three geographic jurisdictions and judges are drawn separately from those three areas. Each of the twenty-two total Court of Appeals judges is elected for a six-year term of office though nonpartisan election. Division I of the Court of Appeals is comprised of nine judges who are elected from northwestern Washington[4] and sit in Seattle. Division II is located in Tacoma and draws judges from western and southwestern

Washington.[5] Division III is located in Spokane; its judges are drawn from the counties of eastern Washington.[6]

The caseload of the three divisions varies somewhat, with Division I consistently hearing the most cases of the three, averaging 1,946 cases per year between 1997 and 2001. Division III heard the fewest cases during the same period, with 884 cases annually on average; and Division II fell in the middle, averaging 1,348 cases per year. In recent years, the caseload of the three divisions combined has remained remarkably stable. In 2001, 4,199 cases were heard. They were split relatively evenly between civil and criminal appeals, averaging 53% criminal and 47% civil across the three divisions.

The final piece of the structural puzzle for Washington courts is the state's court of last resort, the Supreme Court of Washington. The nine justices who sit on this highest court have a large and varied jurisdiction that is defined both by the state constitution and by statute. Justices are selected on a state-wide, non-partisan ballot and serve staggered six-year terms. The only requirement for service is admission to the Washington bar. The court has original jurisdiction over any petitions or charges against state officers and a mandatory jurisdiction over all capital case appeals in the state. In other instances, cases decided by a lower court in the state may be appealed to the Supreme Court if the total monetary value of the case exceeds $200, but these appeals are reviewed only at the discretion of the court itself. The court hears and decides all cases *en banc*, meaning all nine justices participate, although preliminary motions and petitions for review are heard by a five-member panel of the court.

The Supreme Court acts as the final arbiter of justice in the state. Its nearly 140 annual written opinions appear in *Washington Reports* and provide citable precedent for lower courts, state officials, and the Supreme Court itself. It is only the very exceptional case that can be appealed from this court to any outside court, such as the United States Supreme Court. Cases dealing entirely with state law are generally not subject to review by any other body. In its interpretation of state statutes, the state constitution or its administrative regulations, the Supreme Court acts in most instances as a true court of last resort. In addition to this profound legal responsibility, the Supreme Court has significant administrative responsibility over lower courts in the state. Lower courts may have limited autonomy on many issues of policy and procedure, but those policies must be within the guidelines established by the Supreme Court. The court serves this function by supervising the legal profession and is responsible for overseeing requirements for admission to the bar and defining and enforcing legal ethics. The justices on the Supreme Court approve the "Rules of Professional Conduct." They oversee application of those rules through the Washington State Bar Association and enforce penalties for violations, including disbarment, suspension, and censure.

Although the administrative responsibilities of the court are decidedly important, the primary duty of the Supreme Court is to resolve disputes. While the total number of cases decided by the Washington Supreme Court each year may appear small by comparison to other courts, the import of these cases and the lasting impact of the decisions rendered most certainly warrant the careful attention given to each case. The Court receives an average of nearly 1,500 petitions for review each year. This number is comprised of mandatory appeals, petitions for discretionary review, mandatory review of death penalty cases, attorney admission and discipline cases and requests from federal court for review. Some of the categories, such as review of capital cases, are usually a relatively small component of the overall court docket (e.g., only six were heard in 2001), but they can be important nonetheless.

As with other Washington courts, the Supreme Court's caseload also has remained relatively stable in recent years. Between 1997 and 2001, there was an average of 1,392 petitions filed annually, with a low in 1998 of 1,221 filings and a high of 1,557 in 2000.[7] The high court generally disposes of all filings each year, holding few cases over from one year to the next.

The number of opinions produced annually by the Supreme Court varies considerably. Types of cases brought before the court dictate the types of dispositions required, with the largest, most significant, and most interesting cases receiving full written opinions. The opinion-writing process is enormously time consuming and difficult. Supreme Court opinions are very important documents and become the citable precedent for future cases. They also figure as a means for the justices to explain their reasoning to the citizenry. Between 1997 and 2001, there was an average of about 131 opinions handed down by the court each year, with as many as 148 in 1998 and as few as 105 in 2000. Moreover, there were additional dissenting and concurring opinions also authored by one of more justices.

No judge in an elective system such as in Washington can act entirely autonomously or be totally insulated from the pressures of public opinion. Even at the Supreme Court level, the decisions rendered and opinions produced must be somewhat cognizant of public attitudes and preferences. In a system that relies on democratic input for its legitimacy, responsiveness to that input is required of all elected officials, including judges. If a judge deviates too far from the general public conception of the proper meaning of the law, he is inviting public displeasure, which in the next election might translate into nonreelection in favor of someone else perceived to be more in line with the electorate's views.

At the other extreme, however, any judge who seems too responsive to the expressed desires of particular groups might also be replaced at the next election. The judiciary is not immune to the efforts of interest groups to achieve particular policy goals, who may pursue their goals through the election of judges who are sympathetic to their causes. But if judgments appear to be too influenced by special interests and not guided by an authentic understanding of the law, arrived at independently, such a judge faces the prospect of not being reelected.

Paradoxically, perhaps, the very people who would want impartial judges elected to the bench would probably find the link between public opinion and judicial decisions tolerable, if not actually expected and encouraged. Public opinion thus can be seen as providing yet another factor to the framework within which judges act and decide cases. The institutional legitimacy of the courts as well as the personal careers of individual judges and justices is rooted in no small measure in their willingness and ability to balance the sometimes conflicting public demand for responsiveness and independence on the part of judges. However, the system for selecting and retaining judges in Washington—through non-partisan elections—creates problems in the relationship between democratic accountability and judicial independence even as it tries to solve others (Baum 1995; Dubois 1980).

Judicial Selection

The Washington State Constitution declares in Article I: "All political power is inherent in the people and governments derive their power from the consent of the governed." As with other government officials, judges in Washington are elected by the popular vote of the people, although in a slightly different way. A 1912 amendment to the constitution established a system of non-partisan elections for all judicial officers, replacing the previous system that required nomination by a political party for a candidate to appear on the ballot. The only general exception to the rule of elected judges occurs at the municipal-court or traffic-court level where judges may be appointed by county commissioners or mayors. Appointments may also be made by executive branch officials at the state, county, or municipal level in cases where a vacancy is created by the death, resignation, or recall of an elected judge. However, a judge appointed for one of those reasons must stand for reelection in the next general election.

Electing judges is thought to create a more direct link between the people and those interpreting and applying the law, thus increasing democratic accountability of state government. At the same time, however, the system attempts to work in the opposite direction by removing partisanship from the equation[8] and by thus assuming that judging and politics are distinct activities. In actuality, however, removing partisan or ideological labels from the ballot does not remove partisan calculations from the minds of the voters (Baum 1995). Voters often use proxy measures or "information shortcuts" such as endorsements or interest groups' support to stand in the place of partisan or ideological labels (Barber 1971; Dubois 1984; Welch and Bledsoe 1986). Voters may also try to infer partisanship through assumptions about ethnicity or sex. While these proxy measures can provide some information, the accuracy of that information can vary considerably. The assumption, for instance, that minority candidates are more liberal may be a convenient generalization, but it may be incorrect in particular cases. Nonrelated factors, such as name recognition or ballot placement, probably also play frequent and pivotal roles in voting patterns for judicial positions.[9] For example, in both the 1996 and 2000 election cycles, candidates whose names appeared first on the ballots won all but one contested election. Ironically, the single greatest effect of the system of nonpartisan elections may be caused by removing important information from the electorate about judicial candidates. This results in increased reliance on less precise, proxy measures of partisanship, increased voter roll-off, and decreased democratic accountability in the elected officials (Klein and Baum 2001; Schaffner et al 2001; Sheldon and Lovrich 1983).

The attempt to disconnect law and politics in the election process is probably best expressed by Washington's canons of judicial ethics. Canon 7 of Washington's Code of Judicial Conduct, for instance, prohibits candidates for judicial office from declaring a political party affiliation during the election. It also describes parameters for what candidates for judicial office may and may not disclose during a campaign. For example, brief biographies are permitted and simple statements about why a voter should choose a candidate are allowed. Prohibited is any mention of how the candidate might rule on any case presently before the Washington bench or that might occur in the future.

Canon 7 has come under significant scrutiny in recent years. The debate came to a head in 1997 when Justice Richard Sanders was censured by the Judicial Conduct Commission for giving a brief address at a pro-life rally in 1996 and for wearing a red rose at that rally (a widely recognized symbol of the pro-life movement). Sanders' critics claimed that the speech violated the "announce clause" of Canon 7, in that Sanders had in effect declared how he would vote on future reproductive rights cases.[10] In response, Justice Sanders argued that silencing him on this or any other issues would unconstitutionally violate his First Amendment rights to free expression. While Justice Sanders was eventually cleared of the ethics violation charges after a two-year battle, questions of the costs and benefits of Canon 7, and whether it provides any real protection for the judicial system or the public, are still being debated in Washington. In any case, this debate may have been made moot by a recent decision of the United States Supreme Court. In *Republican Party of Minnesota v. White* (2002), that court recently struck down as a violation of the First Amendment a similar "announce clause" in Minnesota's canon of judicial ethics. Whether Washington's restriction would fall in a similar federal challenge remains to be seen. What is clear, however, is that while Canon 7 attempts to remove partisanship and the overt influence of ideology from the judicial function in order to make the administration of justice appear independent of politics, it may actually oppose the purpose for holding democratic elections. Unless the electorate is able to make a decision between judicial candidates based on meaningful distinctions, it is unclear how the election of judges can be an expression of anything more than the "best guess" of the voters—a system that produces little if any real democratic accountability.

Other judicial selection factors also tend to dilute democratic control over the legal system in Washington. Much happens before an election that is just as important as the election itself (Sheldon and Lovrich 1991). There are actually three sets of actors responsible for selecting judges in the state. While the final decision rests with the people of the state, the selection, recruitment, and screening of judicial candidates takes place elsewhere, often behind closed doors. The Washington State Bar Association and the larger of its county-based counterparts often play a significant role in recruiting judges for all levels of the court system. These bodies identify potential candidates, screen, and evaluate them. For vacancies on the Supreme Court and the Court of Appeals, the Judicial Recommendation Committee of the State Bar Association investigates the background of potential judges, interviews the candidates, and recommends to the governor those judges whom the committee finds to be "well qualified" for appellate appointments. County and city bar groups often play a similar role for superior and other lower-court vacancies, providing names to the governor of the state or to county commissions or to mayors (in the case of municipal courts). While the governor is not obligated to follow the bar's recommendations, the professional group's input in the process carries considerable weight. That the governor's choice for appointed judges almost invariably coincides with the bar's recommendation is another indication of how judicial selection is responsive to important interest groups. Prior to elections, bar associations around the state interview and rate candidates in contested races, particularly those for Supreme Court and the Court of Appeals, publishing the results for the general public.

Gubernatorial appointments to fill vacancies on the bench can be a more informal and often an even more political process. Decisions in cases of appointment turn usually on consultation between the governor, his or her staff, members of the state bar association board of governors, and trusted political and judicial friends. A "well qualified" rating from the bar, some previous partisan activities in the state, endorsements from important interest groups,[11] and the ability to get reelected are usually necessary for appointment to an appellate bench. They can also be made as largely patronage appointments. This mirrors the way similar non-partisan election systems work across the country, where an average of two out of three justices reach the high bench of their state through appointment first and as many as 95 percent of these appointees are thereafter retained by the electorate (Ryan et al. 1980).[12] The chances governors receive to appoint judges to the high court varies. All of the current Supreme Court justices have been elected by the voters with only one, Justice Bridge, having first been a gubernatorial appointee. However, the importance of the vacancy appointment process should not be underestimated. These appointments are made with an eye to reelection possibilities and political constituencies.

At the primary and general election stages, judicial candidates selected and screened by others run on a non-partisan ballot and "the people" are expected to act as the final voice in selecting judges. However, it is not unusual for judicial candidates to run unopposed, with only a single candidate filing and appearing on the ballot. In the 2000 election, for instance, only nine of the 52 judicial positions were contested elections. If a candidate for a judicial position is running unopposed or receives more than half of the total votes cast in the primary, he or she is elected to the position and does not have to run in the general election. If three or more candidates are running and no one candidate receives more than half the votes, then the two receiving the most votes face each other in the general election.[13]

In general, however, even contested judicial elections suffer from significantly reduced voter participation or voter "roll-off," with fewer people voting in them than vote in the partisan races on the same ballot. The lack of political substance in judicial races, as required by Canon 7, undoubtedly decreases voter enthusiasm for judicial elections, as does the nonpartisan nature of the system and the lack of information available about the candidates (Klein and Baum 2001). The significant number of uncontested judicial elections probably serves also to depress turnout and participation, since statistically those elections that are contested have less roll-off than those that are not.[14] These general trends hold true for even the highest court in the state. Uncontested elections serve as a source of yet another problem in the system.[15]

Beyond the vast amounts of advertising that candidates supply, most voters in judicial elections depend for information on the voter's guide that is published by the secretary of state's office for each general election. The guide contains information on each candidate for judicial office as allowed under Canon 7, and is generally considered to be a source of reliable information about the candidates. As fewer elections are contested, however, the voter's guide becomes less valuable because it is not published until after the primary has selected the "winner." Thus, for the primary at least, voters lack a source of quality information on which to base their choice. In that absence, interest group politics, political advertising, and word of mouth tend to be the only guidance available. These voting cues and information shortcuts may lead voters to choose candidates on the basis of group ignorance rather than personal knowledge (Sheldon and Lovrich 1983a; 1999).

Whatever its causes, roll-off should be viewed as a problem for a system designed to produce some measure of democratic legitimacy and accountability, particularly at the highest level of the judiciary, where judges are more often asked to decide cases with important public policy implications. Even beyond arguments for democratic legitimacy, it seems that the people of Washington should care about the opportunity to select those individuals who will serve, largely without supervision, as the final arbiters of the law in the state. However, that is demonstrably not the case. In the 2000 election, for example, there were four Supreme Court positions on the ballot (one more than usual due to an appointed justice standing for retention after appointment). Two of the elections were contested and two were run uncontested; the differences are obvious. The two contested elections had roll-off rates of 25.9 percent and 27.9 percent, respectively.[16] The non-contested elections had roll-off rates of 39.5 percent and 40.8 percent, respectively—almost 60 percent greater. Even those percentages are misleading, because they represent only a percentage of total voters who cast ballots which, in the 2000 general election, was 75.4 percent of registered voters or only 57.6 percent of the voting eligible population. For the race with the lowest participation rate, the turnout was only 52.2 percent of those who voted for at least one other office—such as the president of the United States—and only 39.8 percent of Washington State citizens who were eligible to vote.[17]

Though this seems to suggest that judicial elections are not very competitive or highly contested, it is a false assumption. For the closest of the elections discussed above, the margin of victory for the winner was only five percentage points (52% to 47%) or about ninety thousand votes out of more than 2.5 million votes cast in that election statewide.[18] Lower court judges with smaller constituencies often encounter even closer results, with elections turning on a few thousand or even hundred votes. A contested superior court race in Benton County in that same election was decided by only 9,100 votes, and the closest contested election was decided in Pierce County by less than 5,000 votes. Because the margins can be so small, the pressures to campaign effectively are enormous. That pressure translates into the need to raise and spend large amounts of money on advertising and campaigning. The election mentioned above, decided by only 9,100 votes, cost the two candidates combined more than $160,000 to run.

The 2002 race for the Supreme Court was even more expensive. Close races between candidates has pushed the average total expenditures to more than $170,000, with one candidate spending in excess of $300,000 on his campaign.[19] Even local, lower court elections have become expensive propositions. In the 2002 campaign, an incumbent candidate for the Superior Court from King County spent almost $65,000. In Spokane County, a contested District Court seat in the 2002 election cost the two candidates $98,000 combined. That judicial candidates are able to raise such significant amounts of money from individuals and from interest groups suggests that the officials, once elected, are expected to be engaged in more than the abstract process of

administering justice. Rather, it conveys that they are engaged in a highly political undertaking.

Conclusion

In many ways Washington's courts represent a very stable system. The institutional structure of the system has changed little in recent years, the caseload has
not risen dramatically, and the output has been relatively consistent. In terms of
policy-making, the lower, trial courts, and even the Court of Appeals are relatively more constrained than the Supreme Court, due to the structure of their
jurisdiction and size. But even affecting the Supreme Court, the election of
judges creates an additional burden for the judiciary extending beyond hearing
and deciding disputes. Elected judges must try more explicitly to balance the
desire for judicial independence with the political need for accountability and
responsiveness. How those elements are balanced in the system depends on
several factors, including the involvement and attention of the electorate. The
nonpartisan system of judicial elections in Washington, by withholding relevant information from the electorate, probably accounts for a decrease in citizen participation; it certainly is responsible for a decrease of well-informed participation, evidenced by lower general turnout and in high roll-off rates. In
addition, judicial candidates are forced increasingly to jeopardize their independence, in appearance if not in fact, by a system that requires them to raise
large amounts of money from special interest groups and other potential bene-
factors of the courts in order to successfully compete for office.

The relationship between elections and judicial performance is certainly
not a simple one. Even judges themselves can seem of two minds about elections and elective systems. A recent survey of judges reported in *The Judges
Journal* suggests that judges are overwhelmingly concerned about the power of
money in judicial elections, the low levels of public involvement in elections,
and about the independence of the judicial system (Dierker 2002; Greenberg
and DiVall 2002). In the same issue of that journal, however, another article
decries the decision in *Minnesota v. White* as creating more problems than it
solves (Schotland 2002).

Many of these questions revolve around the real role of public opinion as
expressed at the ballot box and the strength of support for particular outcomes
in the court. It could be, as Stimson et al. (1995) suggest, that the Court is
removed from but not oblivious to the desires of the public. This would mean
that judges in the state of Washington consider themselves neither as pure delegates responding directly to the will of the people, nor as trustees interpreting
and applying the law independently. The court system and judges who work
inside it act within a larger framework of law and politics at the state level. This
framework or "political regime" (Clayton and May 1999) of the state is part

and parcel of the numerous variables affecting how judges perceive their role in particular cases and overall.

Undoubtedly, the most vitally affected judicial arena is the state Supreme Court. With the largest subject and geographic jurisdiction, the Supreme Court sits atop the judicial hierarchy. It is able to choose, in most instances, the cases that it will hear and is the most removed from the possibility of being reviewed and overturned. This court is the most free to act in innovative, responsive, and policy-creative ways, and to legislate from the bench. But its justices are, in the end, still elected officials. The candidates for the high court are subject to problems of voter roll-off, uncontested elections, inability to provide in-depth information for voters, and increased fundraising and monetary pressures in campaigning.

The remarkable, overall stability of the judicial branch of Washington government masks some important questions of law and politics in the state. Far from idle inquiry, these questions go to the heart of a system that aspires to be democratic in character and responsive in nature. The current arrangement calls into question the ability of the judicial system to live up to that ideal.

Endnotes

1. The court administrator is appointed by the Supreme Court and is responsible for execution of the administrative policies of the Washington judicial system. He or she compiles statistics, engages in studies of efficiency and management, provides information to the judicial system as directed, and prepares and submits the annual accounting of the judicial expenditures and appropriations.

2. The Commission on Judicial Conduct investigates allegations of misconduct on the part of judicial officers. The membership of the commission is composed of two lawyers, three judges, and six nonlawyer citizens. The commission cannot alter judicial decisions or actions, and objections to specific outcomes are not reviewed by the commission. It can, however, reprimand or censure a judge for official misconduct or recommend to the Supreme Court that a judge be removed or suspended for misconduct or incapacity.

3. Superior courts in the state have historically had a considerable backlog of cases on their dockets. They have been unable to deal with even the relatively low numbers of filings each year, holding many cases over until the next term. In recent years, that trend has begun to reverse itself, with the courts actually clearing more cases and beginning to decrease the decade-old backlog of cases.

4. Division I is divided into three districts. District one, King County, elects six judges. District two, Snohomish County, elects two judges. District three, composed of Island, San Juan, Skagit, and Whatcom counties together, elects one judge.

5. Division II is similarly divided into three districts. District one is Pierce County, from which three judges are elected. District two includes Clallam, Grays Harbor, Jefferson, Kitsap, Mason, and Thurston counties and is represented by two judges. District three, comprised of Clark, Cowlitz, Lewis, Pacific, Skamania, and Wahkiakum counties, elects two judges.

6. Division III is also divided into three districts. District one encompasses Ferry, Lincoln, Okanogan, Pend Oreille, Spokane, and Stevens counties, from which two judges are elected. District two includes Adams, Asotin, Benton, Columbia, Franklin, Garfield, Grant, Walla Walla, and Whitman counties, from which one judge is elected. District three is Chelan, Douglas, Kittitas, Klickitat, and Yakima counties, from which two judges are elected.

7. The largest factor in that year's high filing rate is the number of personal protection petitions. Between 1997 and 1999, the total number of these filings rose more than 340 percent, while most other types of filings remained constant or even fell slightly.

8. As with many other states, other identifying information is also stripped away from the ballot. Incumbency and occupation are also not listed. In the particular case of Washington, voters have the resource of the Voter's Pamphlet, produced by the secretary of state's office, that is available prior to the general election and which contains the best available information to assist in making reasonably informed choices. However, this is of little help in the primary election, when many judicial races are actually decided.

9. One example of problems caused by scanty information is the defeat in 1990 of the then sitting Washington State Supreme Court Chief Justice, Keith Callow. Despite the absence of any negative information about his job performance, Callow was defeated by Charles Johnson, a lawyer who ran an aggressive campaign and who also happened to shares the same name as a Seattle trial judge of some reputation. While there is little empirical evidence to support it, the claim is frequently made that pseudo-name recognition played a decisive factor in the election. (See also London, Robb. 1990. "For Want of Recognition, a Chief Justice Is Ousted," *New York Times* September 28: Sec. B).

10. For a more complete account, see Tyrone Beason's article in the Seattle *Times,* "Sanders Denies Ethics Violation" (December 27, 1996: Local News) and David Postman's article, "Panel Clears Justice Sanders," also in the Seattle *Times* (April 29, 1998: Local News).

11. In a nominally non-partisan electoral system, interest group endorsements can often serve as proxies for partisan labels. Important interest groups, such as police officers associations or education interest groups, may conjure in the minds of voters the expectation of partisan affiliation on the part of the candidate, even if none is expressed.

12. For a more complete account of the Washington high courts, see Charles H. Sheldon's definitive history of the court, *A Century of Judging: A Political History of the Washington Supreme Court* (1998. Seattle: University of Washington Press).

13. District court positions are an exception. By state law (RCW 29.21.015), two-candidate races for district court positions are not placed on the primary ballot but must appear on the general election ballot. If there are three or more candidates for the position, the process of primary election and advancement to the general election is the same as other positions.

14. Schaffner et al. (2001) also argue that the non-partisan ballot has a general depressive effect on turnout. This translates into judicial elections as well.

15. In Spokane County, for example, the 2002 general election saw thirteen judicial positions on the ballot, but only four were contested. Those four included only two of the three Supreme Court positions and two district court positions. Statewide in the 2002 general election only 27 judicial positions were contested in the November election.

16. National roll-off rates average between 25–35 percent for judicial elections across the entire range of partisan and non-partisan state elections. Retention elections, common

in the Missouri Plan system of judicial selection, often see much higher roll-off rates—often in excess of 75 percent (Dubois 1980).

17. It is worth noting that roll-off rates for the 2000 election were lower than average roll-off rates for the state. Presidential election years produce generally higher roll-off that correlates roughly to the higher overall turnout rates in those elections. In the 1996 election, roll-off in the contested Supreme Court position was 32 percent, while the 1998 contested Supreme Court position experienced an average of 22 percent roll-off. This judicial roll-off occurred while the general rate of participation declined from 75 percent in the 1996 election to 62 percent of registered voters participating in 1998.

18. That margin of victory is similar to others in recent years. In 1996, ten of the forty-four judicial elections in the state were contested. The winner in those elections received an average of 54 percent of the vote, to the loser's average of 46 percent. A similar result can be seen in the nine contested elections (of fifty-two total judicial elections) in 2000, where the average margin for the victor was only 57 percent.

19. These expenditure figures are taken from Public Disclosure Commission C-4 filings by the candidates. They do not include independent expenditure made by third parties.

References

Barber, Kathleen. 1971. "Ohio Judicial Elections—Non-partisan Premise with Partisan Results." *Ohio State Law Journal* 32: 762-89.

Baum, Lawrence. 1995. "Electing Judges." In *Contemplating Courts,* ed. Lee Epstein. Washington, D.C.: Congressional Quarterly Press.

Clayton, Cornell, and David May. 1999. "A Political Regimes Approach to Legal Decision Making." *Polity* 32: 233-52.

Dierker, Robert. 2002. "The Missouri Nonpartisan Court Plan—Still a Good Model." *The Judges Journal: A Quarterly of the Judicial Division* 41: 11-15.

Dubois, Phillip. 1980. *From Ballot to Bench: Judicial Elections and the Quest for Accountability.* Austin: University of Austin Press.

Dubois, Phillip. 1984. "Voting Cues in Nonpartisan Trial Court Elections: A Multivariate Assessment." *Law & Society Review* 18: 395-436.

Greenberg, Stan, and Linda DiVall. 2002. "Courts Under Pressure—A Wake-up Call from State Judges." *The Judges Journal: A Quarterly of the Judicial Division* 41: 11-15.

Klein, David, and Lawrence Baum. 2001. "Ballot Information and Voting Decisions in Judicial Elections." *Political Research Quarterly* 54: 709-28

Lovrich, Nicholas, and Charles Sheldon. 1985. "Assessing Judicial Elections: Effects upon the Electorate of High and Low Articulation Systems." *Western Political Quarterly* 38: 276.

Ryan, John, Allan Ashman, Bruce Sales, and Sandra Shane-Dubow. 1980. *American Trial Judges.* New York: Free Press.

Schaffner, Brian, Gerald Wright, and Matthew Streb. 2001. "Teams without Uniforms: The Nonpartisan Ballot in State and Local Elections." *Political Research Quarterly* 54: 7-30.

Schotland, Roy. 2002. "*Republican Party of Minnesota v. White:* Should Judges be More Like Politicians?" *The Judges Journal: A Quarterly of the Judicial Division* 41: 11-15.

Sheldon, Charles, and Frank Weaver. 1980. *Politicians, Judges and the People: A Study in Citizen Participation.* Westport, Conn.: Greenwood Press.

Sheldon, Charles, and Nicholas Lovrich. 1983. "Voters in Contested, Nonpartisan Judicial Elections: Responsible Electorate or Problematic Public?" *Western Political Quarterly* 36: 241.

Sheldon, Charles, and Nicholas Lovrich. 1983a. "Knowledge and Judicial Voting: The Oregon and Washington Experience." *Judicature* 67: 234-45

Sheldon, Charles, and Nicholas Lovrich. 1991. "State Judicial Selection." In *American Courts: A Critical Assessment,* eds. John Gates and Charles Johnson. Washington, D.C.: Congressional Quarterly Press.

Sheldon, Charles, and Nicholas Lovrich. 1999. "Voter Knowledge, Behavior and Attitudes in Primary and General Elections." *Judicature* 82: 216-23.

Stimson, James, Michael MacKuen, and Robert Erickson. 1995. "Dynamic Representation." *American Political Science Review* 89: 543.

Welch, Susan, and Timothy Bledsoe. 1986. "The Partisan Consequences of Nonpartisan Elections and the Changing Nature of Urban Politics." *American Journal of Political Science* 30: 128-39.

Chapter Seven

The Executive Branch in Washington State Government

Steven D. Stehr and Steven J. Ellwanger

ADMINISTRATIVE ARRANGEMENTS in state governments are a reflection of the cumulative political, social, and economic forces—national, regional, and local—that shape the scope and functions of contemporary American bureaucracy. Painting with broad strokes, the development of the executive branch in Washington can be viewed as a product of two, at times contradictory, forces. The first is a long-standing ambivalence on the part of the citizens of the state regarding the proper scope of governmental authority and the firm belief that the authority state government does possess should be highly constrained. These sentiments are reflected in institutional arrangements such as the use of the long ballot to elect statewide executive-branch officials, a reliance on a multitude of boards and commissions to oversee the activities of many state agencies, the frequent use of the initiative process to make statewide policy, and steadfast resistance to establishing a state income tax. At the same time, Washington's social and economic development has been closely tied to active (and typically welcomed) intervention in state affairs by both federal and state agencies. Washington as we know it today would look much different were it not for the influx of federal dollars made possible by the growth of the national defense industry, the construction of the Hanford nuclear facility, the network of dams on the Columbia and Snake rivers which provide abundant hydroelectric power, and the Columbia Basin Irrigation and Reclamation Project that made much of Eastern Washington both habitable and economically viable. In addition, Washington citizens have come to expect that state and local governments will provide necessary goods and services in areas such as transportation, education, health care, fire and police protection, parks, environmental protection, and engage in many other activities that enhance the quality of life in the state. As we shall see, Washington state government ranks above national averages in the provision of many publicly provided goods and services.

Thus, the story of the administrative state in Washington is based on a mixture of ambivalence toward government coupled with a heavy reliance on the services it provides. In their centennial history of the state, Robert Ficken and Charles LeWarne point out what, for some, is an uncomfortable truth about the relationship between Washingtonians and the public sector: "Government [has] always been a vital presence in the Pacific Northwest. Settlers and their entrepreneurial progeny might think of themselves as self-reliant and independent from public assistance, but the reality was otherwise" (Ficken and LeWarne 1988, 106).

This chapter proceeds as follows. First, we briefly discuss the historical roots of the modern administrative state in Washington. This review highlights the intersection of national and local trends, and reveals some perennial thematic currents that have shaped the institutional structures of state government. Second, we examine the contemporary structure and activities of the executive branch in Washington, concentrating on personnel and budgets. Third, we look at the administration in Washington from a comparative perspective, focusing on questions such as: How does Washington compare to other states in the scope and content of governmental activities? What trends in the provision of government services are evident over the past two decades? To what extent have state government priorities changed, and what impact have these changes had on the executive branch? Finally, we briefly discuss the near term challenges facing state administrative agencies.

The Development of the Administrative State in Washington

Like many Western states, the structure of government in Washington was highly influenced by national reform movements that took place near the turn of the twentieth century. Populism and Progressivism were reform movements that began in response to the corruption and inefficiencies flowing from power-heavy legislatures and political machines that characterized government administration in the nineteenth century, and to the emerging social problems accompanying a shift from a rural agrarian to an urban industrial economy (Knott and Miller 1987). The essence of the Populist movement, which was largely a rural western, midwestern, and southern phenomenon, was a deep-seated concern about America's economic, social, and political development that sought to wrestle political and economic power from the "urban-oriented oligarchy" (e.g., banks, trusts, monopolies, railroads) and return it to the common people. Progressivism, on the other hand, was urban, middle class, and national in character (Francis and Thomas 1991, 39). The Progressive movement sought to dismantle an emerging plutocracy while addressing the needs of an increasing number of poor people. As a result, Progressive reforms favored efforts directed at controlling monopolies and trusts and restoring economic competition; aiding small businessmen and farmers; protecting labor and enhancing its rewards; conserving the nation's resources and protecting the environment; and protecting consumers through regulation (Francis and Thomas 1991, 39). Lastly, Progressive political ideology favored replacing the "politics of administration" with "administrative expertise" by employing "merit" rather than "patronage" in the design and operation of personnel systems.

Territories admitted to statehood during the late 1880s and early 1900s often ratified constitutions imbued with the ideals and values of the Progressive and Populist movements. In 1889, the people of Washington voted to accept the constitution by nearly a 4:1 ratio (Avery 1973). As adopted, the constitution contained administrative arrangements that attempted to institutionalize the Progressive and Populist ideals of the period. Later, in 1912, the constitution was amended, introducing instruments of direct democracy—the initiative, referendum, and recall—to further increase popular control of government.

In response to legislatures which often abused their substantial powers, along with a deep-seated distrust of centralized authority, institutional arrangements were adopted by the framers of Washington's constitution that fragmented government authority and moved important policy decision making areas under the purview of a variety of independent expert boards and/or commissions (Cox III 1991). In fact, distrust of the concentration of authority ran so high that the framers of Washington State's constitution subjected eight separate executive officers to independent elections at the ballot box—the superintendent of public instruction, the commissioner of public lands, the state auditor, the attorney general, the secretary of state, the state treasurer, the lieutenant governor, and the governor. Later, in 1907, a ninth elected executive officer position, that of the state insurance commissioner, was created by legislative statute.

The fragmentation of government authority has also been achieved through institutional arrangements within the administrative state that ultimately shape the power bases and agendas of Washington's bureaucracies. Similar to the federal government, most executive branch functions are carried out by administrative departments, agencies, boards, and commissions, all of which limit the amount of formal power the governor is able to exercise over the bureaucracy. This limits the governor's authority for two reasons. First, many nonelected officials are under the formal authority and control of elected executive officials other than the governor. Secondly, many bureaucratic entities are under the control of boards, commissions, and councils that act independently of the governor and over which the governor possesses only appointive powers. As a case in point, in fiscal year 2001 there were roughly 100,000 full-time employees working for the state of Washington; approximately 68 percent of those employees worked in agencies that did not report directly to the governor (OFM 2002).

An illustrative example of the fragmentation of authority in the state executive branch is the set of peculiar administrative arrangements governing the Department of Natural Resources (DNR). The DNR was legislatively authorized in 1957 to bring together seven boards and agencies, and the agency is managed by the independently elected commissioner of public lands. Today, not only does the commissioner manage the Department of Natural Resources, he/she serves on the six-member Board of Natural Resources consisting of the governor, superintendent of public instruction, a county commissioner from a county containing Forest Board trust land, the dean of the University of Washington College of Forest Resources, and the dean of Washington State University's College of Agricultural, Human and Natural Resources Sciences. The members of the eight remaining boards, councils, and committees within the Department of Natural Resources are similarly selected (some are appointed by the governor, while others serve as designees for agency heads or are ordinary citizens appointed by the commissioner). As a result of these provisions for governing this agency, the influence exercised by the governor within DNR is greatly circumscribed because of the authority of these boards, committees, and councils that often express and reflect divergent values, incentives, and power bases. The departments of Public Education and Transportation, two of the most important in state government, are beyond the governor's direct control.

The shape and form of the modern administrative branch did not develop solely due to factors peculiar to the state. The federal government became an important factor in the delivery of public goods and services in Washington during World War I as numerous military installations were erected and the modern military-industrial complex (which greatly benefited industries in the state) was born. This presence would grow during the era of Franklin D. Roosevelt and the New Deal. Between 1933 and 1939, Washington ranked first among all states in per capita federal spending (Reading 1973). The construction of the Grand Coulee and other dams, the Columbia Basin Irrigation Project, the creation of the Bonneville Power Authority, the establishment of national parks, and hundreds of other projects cemented the close relationship between state and federal administration. The state was both a large contributor to and beneficiary of World War II, the Korean conflict, and the Cold War.

For example, the availability of cheap hydroelectric power (made possible by the network of federally funded dams) allowed for the development of power-sapping aluminum production plants that were needed to provide materials for the production of Boeing airplanes, and naval and Merchant Marine ships in Bremerton. The Manhattan Project was responsible for the creation of a nuclear weapon production facility in Richland (known as the "Atomic City"), and Cold War fears of a confrontation with the Soviet Union made the Hanford works important well into the 1980s. As in other states, the Great Society

Programs of the Johnson administration greatly increased the responsibilities of state government in Washington, as did the shift toward decentralizing the responsibility for managing programs through various "new federalism" initiatives (Denhardt 1993). The champions of decentralization expected increased state and local control over the design and implementation of federally funded programs, and an increase in the institutional capacity of states to assume these responsibilities. Thus, state governments became increasingly responsible for funding government initiatives and for increasing their administrative capacities (Barrilleaux 1999).

As the figures displayed in Table 1 show, for most of the last forty years Washington has depended upon the federal government for between 20–25 percent of its total revenues. This is a significant factor in Washington government as it demonstrates the extent to which the delivery of public services in the Evergreen

Table 1

Total State Revenues and Percentage of Revenue from Federal Sources, by Fiscal Biennium, 1963-65 to 1999-2001

Fiscal Biennium	Total Revenue*	Percent from Federal Sources
1963-65	$1,818	21.0%
1965-67	2,305	21.5
1967-69	2,998	20.2
1969-71	3,663	22.0
1971-73	4,392	25.6
1973-75	5,137	24.7
1975-77	6,730	24.4
1977-79	8,321	23.1
1979-81	10,319	25.7
1981-83	12,805	20.6
1983-85	18,710	16.2
1985-87	17,865	19.7
1987-89	21,763	19.2
1989-91	25,200	21.1
1991-93	28,758	23.6
1993-95	35,887	22.0
1995-97	38,705	21.3
1997-99	43,598	20.5
1999-2001	47,312	22.5

Source: Author's calculations from Office of Financial Management 1995 and 2001 Data Book.
*In millions of dollars

State has been linked to national economic and political trends. This factor of state politics also speaks to the considerable influence of the state's congressional delegation during this time period, in particular senators Warren Magnuson and Henry "Scoop" Jackson and Speaker of the House Tom Foley.

During the late 1970s and early 1980s the political legacy of the Progressives and the Populists resurfaced and converged to incite a taxpayer revolt that led to several attempts to limit government revenues and expenditures (Schwantes 1996, 475). The "taxpayer revolt," in conjunction with the social and political forces that led to a devolution of responsibility for program implementation to the state government, set the basic foundation upon which Washington's administrative state now operates. Indeed, the current environment is characterized by the now familiar situation of citizen demands for increased government services while circumscribing the ability of state and local government to generate revenues to fund such services. To address these challenges, the state searched for alternative sources of revenue (for example, the State Lottery was established in 1982) while administrative agencies attempted to satisfy the demands of an increasingly larger and more diverse population. The economic boom of the mid-to-late 1990s (and the tax revenues that resulted) enabled state agencies to provide necessary services despite the growth in key demographic groups, such as the K-12, college-age, and elderly populations; dramatic increases in the size of the prison population; and other factors that drive government spending. However, beginning in 2000 an economic slowdown forced policy makers to make difficult choices regarding the scope and level of government services in Washington.

The Contemporary Executive Branch

State administrators are responsible for carrying out a wide range of public functions. They are responsible for maintaining a network of over 8,000 miles of highways and roads, and a ferry system (the largest of any state) that carries about eighteen million passengers annually. They monitor and partially finance the education of over one million elementary and high school students and are directly responsible for the education of over a quarter-million students in public colleges and universities. State agencies also oversee the care and rehabilitation of more than 16,000 prison inmates and provide state-subsidized childcare to over 76,000 children under the age of 12. The state is responsible for managing the state's natural resources, parks, fish and wildlife, public lands, clean air and water programs, and the use of its over 2,300 miles of shorelines. The state also regulates a wide variety of economic enterprises. Public administrators set rates for telephone and electric service, enforce health and safety standards in business, and license many occupations and professions.

Depending on how they are counted, there are approximately 250 statutory agencies charged with interpreting and implementing policies and programs in

Washington (see organization chart, next two pages). Twenty-one of these are cabinet agencies headed by an executive who serves at the pleasure of the governor. These include such major units as the departments of Ecology, Agriculture, Social and Health Services, Labor and Industries, Employment Security, and Corrections. Another dozen or so agencies serve under separately elected statewide office holders, such as the superintendent of public instruction. Approximately 200 boards and commissions are charged with responsibilities in a wide variety of more specialized areas. At least three dozen boards license individual professions and occupations, monitor their conduct, and hear complaints filed by citizens. There are commissions to regulate boxing, gambling (with a separate one for horse racing), and to oversee the state's sale and distribution of liquor and lottery tickets. The governor appoints all or some of the members of three-fourths of the commissions to overlapping terms. However, after the appointments have been made, gubernatorial control over these commissioners is typically quite limited, as program clients and interest groups take an active interest in their decision making.

Personnel and budgets are two indices of the size and scope of state administration. More than 100,000 men and women are currently employed by the state (see Table 2). This represents a doubling of the workforce since the mid-1970s, and an increase of 16 percent over the last decade. When the number of state employees is adjusted to reflect changes in state population over time, this growth appears more moderate. In 2002, there were 16.9 executive branch employees for every 1,000 persons in the state population (see Table 2), a ratio that has changed relatively little since the late 1980s. For comparison purposes, the average state employed approximately 15 people per 1,000 population in the mid-1990s (Barrilleaux 1999).

Over three-fourths of all state employees work in the fields of human services (broadly defined) or higher education. Approximately 42 percent of state employees currently work for universities, colleges, or community colleges, and another 18 percent work in the Department of Social and Health Services. An additional 15 percent work in various "human services" agencies such as the Department of Labor and Industries, the Department of Corrections, and the Department of Employment Security (see Table 3). Nearly all of the remaining employees work in the areas of transportation (8.2%), natural resources (6.1%), and governmental operations (7.4%). The largest percentage increase over the last decade or so has been in the area of human services (from 13.1% of total state employees in 1989-91 to 15.1% of the total in 2001-03). Much of this increase in personnel took place in the Department of Corrections, which saw a 40 percent increase in the number of employees (from 4,549 to 7,547) between 1991 and 2001.

Taking a longer-term view, there has been remarkably little change in the distribution of employees by functional area in the state since the mid-1970s

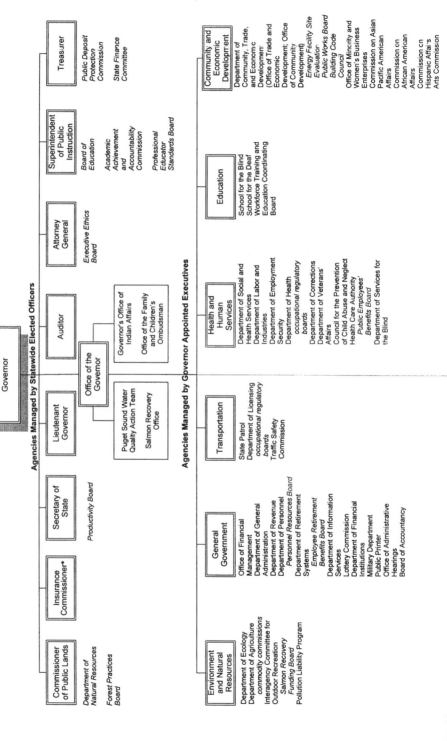

2001-2002 Washington State Executive Branch Organization Chart†

Agencies Under Authority of a Board

Fish and Wildlife Commission
Department of Fish and Wildlife
Parks and Recreation Commission
Environmental Hearings Office
Pollution Control Hearings Board
Shorelines Hearings Board
Forest Practices Appeals Board
Hydraulic Appeals Board
Conservation Commission
Columbia River Gorge Commission
Growth Management Hearings Board
Eastern Washington
Central Puget Sound
Western Washington
Board of Natural Resources

Personnel Appeals Board
Liquor Control Board
Public Employment Relations Commission
Board of Tax Appeals
Public Disclosure Commission
Board for Volunteer Firefighters and Reserve Officers
Gambling Commission
Horse Racing Commission
Utilities and Transportation Commission
Investment Board
Statute Law Committee
Code Reviser
Municipal Research Council
Economic and Revenue Forecast Council
Caseload Forecast Council
Pension Funding Council
Forensic Investigations Council
Citizens' Commission on Salaries for Elected Officials
State Capitol Committee

Transportation Commission
Department of Transportation
Board of Pilotage Commissioners
Marine Employees' Commission
Transportation Improvement Board
Freight Mobility Strategic Investment Board
County Road Administration Board

Human Rights Commission
Indeterminate Sentence Review Board
Board of Industrial Insurance Appeals
Criminal Justice Training Commission
Sentencing Guidelines Commission
Health Care Facilities Authority
Board of Health

Higher Education Coordinating Board
Governing Boards of Four Year Institutions of Higher Education
University of Washington
Washington State University
Central Washington University
Eastern Washington University
Western Washington University
The Evergreen State College
Board for Community and Technical Colleges
Boards of Trustees
Community Colleges
Technical Colleges
Spokane Intercollegiate Research and Technology Institute
Library Commission
State Library
Higher Education Facilities Authority
Washington State Historical Society
Eastern Washington State Historical Society

Convention and Trade Center
Housing Finance Commission
Economic Development Finance Committee

† 2001-2002 Executive Branch organization information provided by Washington State Office of Financial Management.
* Statutory position created by the first state legislature 1889-90.

Table 2

Full-Time Equivalent Executive Branch State Employees
Per 1,000 Population, 1984 to 2002

State Fiscal Year	FTE Executive Branch Employees	Population	FTE Executive Branch Employees Per 1,000 Pop.
1984	64,393.7	4,354,067	14.8
1985	68,837.0	4,415,785	15.6
1986	69,086.3	4,462,212	15.5
1987	70,910.7	4,527,098	15.7
1988	72,819.9	4,616,886	15.8
1989	75,717.6	4,728,077	16.0
1990	78,968.3	4,866,669	16.2
1991	83,103.4	5,021,335	16.5
1992	86,291.3	5,141,177	16.8
1993	88,793.1	5,265,688	16.9
1994	88,344.6	5,364,338	16.5
1995	90,591.9	5,470,104	16.6
1996	90,585.8	5,567,764	16.3
1997	92,375.9	5,663,763	16.3
1998	93,746.4	5,750,033	16.3
1999	96,564.1	5,830,835	16.6
2000	98,560.8	5,894,121	16.7
2001	100,618.8	5,974,900	16.8
2002	102,402.8	6,041,700	16.9

Sources: Authors' calculations based on data drawn from Office of Financial Management. (2001). *2001 Data Book.* Olympia, Washington: Office of Financial Management.

Office of Financial Management. (2002). *Population and components of population change for the state:* 1920 to 2002 [Internet]. Office of Financial Management. Retrieved August 12, 2002, from the World Wide Web: http://www.ofm.wa.gov/2002Pop/cmp_chg.pdf.

Office of Financial Management. (2002b). *State of Washington office of financial management special agency grouping trend report for FTEs: operating and capital (includes higher education funds).* Olympia, Washington: Office of Financial Management.

(transportation is a notable exception). The distribution of employees by category in 1975 was as follows: education—42 percent; human resources—30 percent; transportation—14 percent; government operations—8 percent; and natural resources—6 percent (Mullen and Swanson 1985). The largest individual units of state government in 2001 included the University of Washington (18,892), the Department of Social and Health Services (18,199), the Community and Technical College System (14,272), the Department of Corrections

(7,547), the Department of Transportation (6,707), and Washington State University (5,453).

The expansion of the activities of state government is graphically illustrated by the increase over time in state expenditures. Over the last four decades, total public expenditures of the state executive branch increased by more than twenty-five times (see Table 4). State budget expenditures for the 1999–2001 biennium were approximately $44.5 billion, more than double the budget of fifteen years earlier. One commonly used method to examine state budget spending over time is to express expenditures as a percent of total personal income. As the last column in Table 4 shows, state spending actually declined over the past six years using this conventional measure of size of government. This is largely the result of rapidly increasing personal income in the mid-to-late 1990s (which went up 33 percent) relative to increases in state spending (which went up 26 percent).

Table 3

Percentage of State Employees by Function, Selected Fiscal Years 1989-2003

	1989-91	1995-97	2001-2003
Governmental Operations*	7.8%	7.6%	7.4%
Human Services**	13.1	14.6	15.1
Dept of Social & Health Services	19.6	18.7	18.4
Natural Resources***	6.9	6.4	6.1
Transportation****	8.6	8.3	8.2
Higher Education	41.3	42.2	42.5
Other	2.7	2.2	2.3
Total	100.0%	100.0%	100.0%

*Includes Dept. of Revenue, Dept. of Personnel, Attorney General, State Auditor, Office of the Governor, Liquor Control Board.

**Includes Dept. of Labor and Industries, Dept. of Corrections, Dept. of Employment Security.

***Includes the Dept. of Natural Resources, Dept. of Ecology, Dept. of Fish and Wildlife, Agriculture.

****Includes Dept. of Transportation, Dept. of Licensing, State Patrol.

Source: OFM 2002

Table 4

Budgeted Expenditures as a Percent of Total Personal Income
($ in Millions)

Biennium	Total Personal Income	Total Expenditures	Expenditures as a Percent of Total Personal Income
1963-65	16,279.00	1,795.6	11.0
1965-67	19,786.00	2,146.9	10.9
1967-69	24,296.00	2,830.5	11.7
1969-71	28,536.00	3,840.8	13.5
1971-73	32,510.00	4,305.3	13.2
1973-75	41,315.00	4,986.4	12.1
1975-77	51,941.00	6,432.6	12.4
1977-79	67,889.00	8,027.8	11.8
1979-81	89,255.00	10,857.8	12.2
1981-83	104,537.00	12,388.1	11.9
1983-85	121,595.00	15,462.5	12.7
1985-87	138,062.00	17,928.0	13.0
1987-89	161,190.00	19,788.7	12.3
1989-91	195,039.00	24,690.8	12.7
1991-93	223,894.00	29,432.2	13.2
1993-95	246,916.00	32,853.5	13.3
1995-97	278,883.00	36,009.7	12.9
1997-99	323,911.00	39,394.2	12.2
1999-01	371,497.00	44,547.8	12.0

Sources: Authors' calculations based on data drawn from Office of Financial Management. (1995). *1995 Data Book*. Olympia, Washington: Office of Financial Management.

Office of Financial Management. (2001). *2001 Data Book*. Olympia, Washington: Office of Financial Management.

The majority of state administrative spending is in the areas of education and social services (see Table 5). Nearly 42 percent of the 1999–2001 budget was devoted to education (this figure includes transfers to elementary and secondary schools and higher education) and another 31 percent was expended through the Department of Social and Health Services (DSHS). A decade earlier, education accounted for approximately 46 percent of state spending, while DSHS accounted for 27 percent. Over the last decade, the DSHS budget increased an average of nearly 17 percent in each biennium. This budgetary growth has been

Table 5

Percent of State Operating Budget by Function,
Selected Fiscal Years 1989-2001

	1989-91	1995-97	1999-2001
Governmental Operations*	6.6%	6.6%	6.5%
Human Services**	6.4	7.5	8.0
Dept of Social & Health Services	26.9	30.4	31.3
Natural Resources***	3.7	2.6	2.5
Transportation****	4.7	4.4	4.0
Total Education	46.3	43.5	41.9
Other	5.4	2.8	5.8
Total	100.0%	100.0%	100.0%

*Includes Dept. of Revenue, Dept. of Personnel, Attorney General, State Auditor, Office of the Governor, Liquor Control Board.

**Includes Dept. of Labor and Industries, Dept. of Corrections, Dept. of Employment Security.

***Includes the Dept. of Natural Resources, Dept. of Ecology, Dept. of Fish and Wildlife, Agriculture.

****Includes Dept. of Transportation, Dept. of Licensing, State Patrol.

Source: OFM 2001.

fueled in recent years by increased spending on medical assistance payments, developmental disabilities programs, and long-term care services. Spending on other human services also claimed a larger share of state spending when comparing the 1999–2001 and the 1989–91 budget years. This reflects increased spending by the Washington State Health Care Authority and the Department of Corrections. Like education, agencies responsible for natural resources and transportation claimed smaller shares of the state budget in 2001 than they did in 1991. It is apparent that a combination of increasing demands for social and health services, a growing prison population, and major federal reforms that placed greater responsibility on state governments for implementing social welfare and health programs led to this dramatic shift in state spending patterns over the last decade.

One area where this shift in state spending priorities is apparent is in the area of elementary and secondary education. Compared to other states, spending on elementary and secondary education was well above the national average into the early '90s, when measured by the index of expenditures per $1000 of personal income. For example, in fiscal year 1991 the state spent $52 on local education for every $1,000 of personal income. This ranked Washington ninth among all states. Beginning in fiscal year 1993, however, state spending on K-12 education as a share of personal income began to decline. In 1995, Washington ranked eighteenth among all states in education spending adjusted for personal income ($50.46 per $1000). State spending on local education continued to decrease even as the national average continued to increase. In fiscal year 1999, the average state was expending $46.03 per $1000 of personal income on K-12 education compared to just $45.05 in Washington (by then the state had dropped to thirty-second among all states). For comparison purposes, the state expended $50.32 per $1000 of personal income on this function in 1976 (Washington Research Council 2001).

The story is similar with respect to state spending for higher education. Until the mid-1990s, Washington spent more on higher education per capita and as a share of personal income than did the average state. In fiscal year 1995 Washington ranked twenty-second among the states, expending $21.14 per $1000 of personal income. By fiscal year 2001, however, state spending on higher education declined to $19.23 per $1000 of personal income (ranking twenty-sixth that year among all states) (Washington Research Council 2001).

The federal role in the changing distribution of state delivery of goods and services should not be overlooked in this discussion of the scale of government in Washington. As Barrilleaux points out, developments in state administrative arrangements are often closely linked to changes in federal policy initiatives. For example, during the 1970s—and later in the mid-1990s—the federal government provided incentives to build state social service capacity and, during the 1980s and 1990s, to build and staff correctional facilities (Barrilleaux 1999). In both cases, the states—including Washington—responded as expected.

Given the foregoing discussion, a listing of the units of state government that had the largest budgets in fiscal year 1999–2001 should come as no surprise:

- DSHS—$12.155 billion (including $4.6 billion for medical assistance payments, $2.2 billion for economic services, $1.9 billion for long-term care, and $1.0 billion for developmental disabilities programs)
- University of Washington—$2.711 billion
- Community/Technical College System—$1.505 billion
- Department of Transportation—$1.039 billion
- Department of Corrections—$976.4 million

These units accounted for just over 40 percent of state spending during the last budget cycle.

Washington's Executive Branch in Comparative Perspective

Despite their ambivalence toward government, citizens in Washington are provided with relatively high levels of public services when compared to national averages. Indeed, Washington is a leader among the states in providing a variety of goods and services. As the figures displayed in Table 6 show, in fiscal year 2001 the state expended $259.93 per $1000 of personal income for all state government functions (this ranked ninth among all states); the national average was $223.42. During the same year, Washington ranked fifth in total state expenditures per capita ($6,544 per person compared to the national average of $5,508) (Washington Research Council 2001).

In 2001 Washington ranked in the top ten among the states in expenditures per $1000 of personal income in the following functional categories: water transportation (ranked 1), seaports (2), fire protection (3), health (3), libraries (5), social insurance administration (5), and natural resources (8). It ranked in the top twenty among the states in cash assistance payments (ranked 12), parks

Table 6

State Expenditures on Selected Functions Per $1000 of Personal Income and Rank of Washington Compared to All States Average

	Per $1,000 of Personal Income	Washington Rank	All States
Total State Spending	$259.23	9	$223.42
Water Transportation	2.76	1	0.43
Seaports	2.82	2	0.40
Health	10.27	3	6.41
Fire Protection	3.84	3	2.93
Libraries	1.31	5	0.96
Social Insurance Admin.	1.16	5	0.61
Natural Resources	4.65	8	2.52
Cash Assistance Payments	4.10	12	3.21
Parks and Recreation	4.41	13	3.23
Corrections	6.09	17	6.11
Housing and Community Develop.	3.47	18	3.56
Highways	14.35	25	12.59
Higher Education	19.23	26	16.29
Police Protection	5.98	36	7.28

Source: Washington Research Council, *How Washington Compares,* 2002.

and recreation (13), corrections (17), and housing and community development (18). Among the major expenditure categories Washington ranked in the bottom half of the states when measured by state expenditures per $1000 of personal income only in K-12 and higher education spending (Washington was ranked twenty-sixth in each) (Washington Research Council 2001).

The higher-than-average expenditures are partly explained by social and demographic changes (for example, increases in school-age children), and by political decisions (for example, implementation of mandatory sentencing laws), which have forced state agencies to provide higher levels of goods and services. Some of the key factors driving the increased levels of service provision in Washington over the past decade include:

- Larger enrollments in K-12 education. Enrollments in public schools increased by 17 percent between 1990 and 2001. In inflation-adjusted dollars (year 2000), per capita spending in this area increased from $1,096 to $1,298.

- Larger enrollments in institutions of higher education. Between 1990 and 2001, enrollments in Washington's colleges and universities increased by 23 percent. Per capita spending (adjusted to year 2000 dollars) increased from $437 to $564 during this period.

- Increasing numbers of people receiving state social services. For example, the number of children receiving subsidized childcare increased by 78 percent between 1990 and 2001. Total per capita public welfare expenditures in inflation-adjusted dollars increased from $533 to $863 over the last decade.

- Increasing numbers of prison inmates. The number of people incarcerated in Washington has increased by 54 percent since 1990. Correctional expenditures per capita increased from $105 to $176 between 1990 and 2001 (OFM, Washington Trends, 2003).

These trends are forecasted to continue through the decade. According to the Office of Financial Management, those populations that receive a high proportion of state government services are projected to grow particularly rapidly over the next five years. For example, it is forecast that those seeking state assisted long-term care will increase by over 16 percent, and that the demand for higher education will increase by over 8 percent over this time period (OFM 2003).

Conclusion

Washington State government agencies face enormous challenges in the near term. As was the case in the early 1980s, a slowdown in economic growth in the early 2000s has prompted new rounds of budget cuts in state government. In addition, citizen-supported initiatives that passed in the 1990s make it difficult for state officials to raise taxes or find new sources of revenue. This occurs at a time when demands for essential government services such as education, transportation, social services, and public safety continue to grow. Indeed, in the post-September 11 environment, state and local governments are expected to take on increasing responsibilities in the area of homeland security. The federal government, facing its own challenges, may be unable to provide the same budgetary stimulus for state programs as it has in the past. Whether these new challenges will prompt a reexamination of the size, scope, and content of state government programs remains to be seen.

References

Avery, Mary Williamson. 1973. *Government of Washington State*, 6th ed. Seattle: University of Washington Press.

Barrilleaux, Charles. 1999. Statehouse Bureaucracy. In *American State and Local Politics: Directions for the 21st Century*, ed. P. Brace. New York: Chatham House Publishers of Seven Bridges, LLC.

Cox III, Raymond W. 1991. Gubernatorial Politics. In *Politics and Public Policy in the Contemporary American West*, ed. C. S. Thomas. Albuquerque: University of New Mexico Press.

Denhardt, Robert B. 1993. *Theories of Public Organization*, 2d ed. Belmont, Cal.: Wadsworth Publishing Company. Seattle: University of Washington Press.

Ficken, Robert E., and Charles P. LeWarne. 1988. *Washington: A Centennial History.* Seattle: University of Washington Press.

Francis, John G., and Clive S. Thomas. 1991. Influences on Western Political Culture. In *Politics and Public Policy in the Contemporary American West*, ed. C. S. Thomas. Albuquerque: University of New Mexico Press.

Knott, Jack H., and Gary J. Miller. 1987. *Reforming Bureaucracy: The Politics of Institutional Choice*. New York: Prentice Hall.

Mullen, William, and Thor Swanson. 1985. "The Executives and Administration." In *Political Life in Washington: Governing the Evergreen State*, ed. T. Swanson, et al. Pullman: Washington State University Press.

OFM, 2002. Washington State Office of Financial Management, "Special Agency Grouping Trend Report for FTEs." From OFM website, September 2002.

OFM, 2003. Washington State Office of Financial Management, "Washington Trends." Available at www.ofm.wa.gov/trends. From OFM website, March 3, 2002.

Reading, Don C. 1973. "New Deal Activity and the State, 1933-1939." *Journal of Economic History.* 33:794-795.

Schwantes, Carlos A. 1996. *The Pacific Northwest: An Interpretive History.* Lincoln: University of Nebraska Press.

Washington Research Council. 2002. *How Washington Compares 2002.* Seattle: Washington Research Council.

Washington Research Council. 2001. *How Washington Compares 2001.* Seattle: Washington Research Council.

Chapter Eight

The Office of the Governor

David Nice and Erin Otte

A S THE HIGHEST-RANKING and most visible government officials in state politics, governors are in a position to make substantial contributions to policies that will improve the lives of the citizens of their states. However, the governor's mansion is often the springboard to higher office: many members of Congress and presidential candidates—as well as presidents—have previously been governors. Because of the opportunities for fostering policy change, as well as furthering personal goals, state governors must maintain a fine balance between present and future aims.

This chapter will explore the numerous contradictory aspects of the Washington governor's office. It will first present a brief historical explanation of the evolution of the governor, both on a national as well as a state-specific timeline. It will then discuss the roles a governor must fill and the challenges that may help or hinder governors in exercising those responsibilities. The third section will briefly examine careers of governors—where they come from, what experience they bring to the job, and where they head after leaving the governor's mansion. Finally, this chapter will examine the eight other statewide-elected officials in Washington and briefly discuss their job descriptions and interactions with the governor.

Evolution of the Office of Governor

Washington has had its own governmental structures since its separation from Oregon Territory in 1853. The first territorial governor, Isaac I. Stevens, is most widely known for his settlement of Native American land claims and moves to improve transportation, both of which he perceived as critical to the economic development of the new territory. Territorial governors following Stevens were also political appointees and most served short terms, which inevitably influenced the kind of leadership, as well as the policies, they were able to pursue. Because territorial governors were presidential appointees, they were often viewed as political puppets of the then-current White House administration, an image which ultimately undermined their credibility and legitimacy in the territory's political scene.

After Washington was admitted to the Union in 1889, the situation changed for the governorship. No longer appointed by the president, governors were obligated to forge their own political careers, which in turn influenced the approaches those individuals took to leadership. The Progressive reform movements of the late nineteenth and early twentieth centuries contributed to increasing demands for accountability in state government, while strengthening the previously weak executive branch. In response to this trend, Washington's governors asserted greater leadership and assumed a dominant role in the politics and government of the state. The Washington governor's strength is evidenced by the power to call extra sessions, the ability to propose and veto legislation, and the opportunity for (and sometimes burden of) setting the state's agenda through creating the budget.

The new state's concern and reaction to the national move for accountability in government is evident in the state constitution, which resembles many other state constitutions, as well as the Constitution of the United States of America. Checks and balances were established in an attempt to minimize the opportunity for corruption, with executive, legislative, and judicial branches assigned some overlapping responsibilities. At the same time, prevailing skepticism about politicians was reflected in the low salaries paid to the citizen-legislators, who would spend most of their time in their regular employ, rather than as legislators.

The period of cooperative federalism following the end of World War II, too, displayed a relationship between federal and state government in which state governments were not altogether trusted, due to a legacy of corruption and misappropriation of federal funds. Governors were inevitably affected when federal programs circumvented the state governments and funneled monies directly to local governments instead. In response, state legislatures and governors started to institute policies to prove their responsibility and to reduce the amount of pork in state politics. The 1950s saw the creation of formulas to determine the allocation of resources instead of basing allocations on promises made by legislators to vote for gubernatorial proposals, and the capital budget began going through prioritization processes prior to its submission to the legislature.

Divided government was the norm from the 1950s through the 1970s, and intermittently since then—a situation creating difficulties for Washington governors interested in policy change. From the 1950s through the 1970s, the governor's office was occupied by Republicans for twenty years, while the Democrats were in control for twelve years. In that period, ten legislative sessions featured different parties controlling the governor's mansion and the state legislature. Legislative accomplishments required careful negotiation between governors and legislature, and governors sometimes used the line-item veto to delete individual words in legislation, changing the entire meaning of a bill's provisions. The latter practice eventually led to a constitutional amendment that permitted individual deletion of spending items, but limited the governor's ability to make substantive legislative changes by veto action.

Today the governor's office still encounters some of the widespread public skepticism common in American politics, but as the office has become increasingly professional, it has generally been afforded greater respect, authority, and compensation. In 2003, Washington's governor received $142,286 annually, which was currently one of the highest salaries in all of the fifty states. (In comparison, Oregon's governor received $93,600, while Idaho's governor earned $98,500. The highest paid governor was New York's, with an annual salary of $179,000. The lowest gubernatorial salary of 2003 went to the governor of Nebraska, at $65,000.) In addition, the job of governor includes other perks, such as state-provided housing, and auto and air transportation.[1] The governor is also afforded protection by the Washington State Patrol, both on the capitol campus in Olympia and around the state.

Governors are regularly viewed as advocates for their states' interests, both nationally and internationally, and often use their office and its affiliated power and prestige to promote those interests. The formation of the National Governors' Association gives further evidence of an increase in governors' power nationwide. Governors come together on a regular basis to discuss not only how best to lead their states, but also to mobilize their power to further states' interests in the federal system. Most states maintain representatives permanently in the nation's capital to keep an eye out for legislation that may affect them corporately or individually. Governors and their advocates regularly lobby and seek to influence Congress and the president now more than ever before.

The Roles of the Governor

The duties of the state's governor are complex, due particularly to the numerous roles a governor must play. A governor must try to lead the public, his party, and the legislature, while looking out for his own political interests. It is not unusual for these roles to conflict and create a difficult balancing act for a governor to maintain.

Politician and Party Leader

First and foremost, governors are politicians. They cannot pursue any of the other jobs delegated to their office without first gaining, then maintaining, their access to the office. While they may not overtly consider their political career in all actions, governors often have career interests in the back of their mind. If they hope to survive in office and accomplish their goals, they must gain support and cooperation, while coping with opposition and criticism. Washington is one of twelve states nationwide that has no limit on the number of terms a governor can serve, which may affect a governor's actions in office.

The politician role becomes particularly prevalent when a governor exercises his or her responsibility as a party leader. A state's governor is often the highest-ranking member of his or her state political party. Governors are often required to not only lead their party in the state's legislature, but to also lead the party within the state. Washington's governor, Democrat Gary Locke, was quite active in his party's politics, not only in making appearances for Democratic candidates throughout the state, but also in attending party functions and fundraisers. The governor's presence at fundraising events is especially critical for lesser-known candidates; without the governor in attendance, there may be considerable difficulty attracting people to these events.

Washington's governor, however, faces significant challenges as a politician and party leader. In particular, the geopolitical conditions of Washington make it difficult for a partisan governor to connect with the entire state. The Cascade Range divides the state not only geographically, but also politically. The western side of the Cascades, home to most of the larger metropolitan areas, has an economy primarily driven by industry and business, while the eastern half is an agriculturally-dominated economy. These economic differences between the two parts of the state also perpetuate distinct differences in politics. The western half of Washington, particularly in the greater Puget Sound area, tends to vote primarily Democratic, while the eastern half leans more toward the Republican Party.

In formulating a campaign strategy, a governor must adapt to this, as well as the distinct urban-rural divide that also influences the division of political power in Washington. The major population centers—Seattle, Tacoma, Vancouver, Everett, and Spokane—tend to be liberal (i.e., Democrat) strongholds, while the remainder of the state, encompassing the rural areas and the smaller towns and cities, tends to hold more conservative ideals.

A governor's role as party leader only extends as far as other members of the party will allow. While the governor is involved with the political party he or she represents, the governor's power as the leader of his party has declined significantly in recent years in Washington, primarily due to the weakness of political parties in the state. Because of the distinct differences between the east and west and urban and rural areas, political parties have had to adopt different strategies in different parts of the state to facilitate electoral and legislative success. This has led to a lack of unified policies for the parties at the state level, which can make it difficult for a governor to find common ground within his party. Not only are Washington's political parties regionally oriented, they also tend to be independent, further limiting the governor's power and ability to lead the party as a whole. The need to appeal to the large number of political independents in the state, as well as concerns that too much party involvement may tarnish a governor's public image, also work against vigorous party leadership at times.

Chief Legislator

The Washington State governor also functions as the chief legislator in the state. The governor exercises many duties associated with introducing, approving, and lobbying for legislation. The governor's office, too, is required to introduce all budgeting legislation. Governors, in fact, often exercise the most influence on their particular issues through the budget, therefore it has become one of the governor's chief tools for policy leadership.

The Washington governor can also exercise influence as chief legislator by calling special sessions. The constitution gives the governor authority to reassemble the legislature after their regularly scheduled annual session has ended. While special sessions are usually called to address issues not covered during the regular session, or to reconsider a veto, in recent years Governor Locke has used the special sessions to deal with some of his priority issues, particularly transportation. During the summer of 2001 alone, the governor called three special sessions to address transportation issues not resolved during the regular session.

However, the governor's position as legislative leader is not absolute. There are several institutional characteristics and political factors limiting a governor's ability to lead the legislature. In recent years, at least one house of the legislature often has been controlled by the opposition party (see Table 1). In the 2001 legislative session, the House was evenly split, with each party holding 49 seats, and the Senate was divided almost evenly with the Democrats holding the majority by only one seat. The 2002 legislature also was closely divided, with the Democrats controlling the House, 50 seats to the Republican's 48, while the Senate retained the same partisan composition as the 2001 session. The 2003–04 legislature also was divided, with the Democrats in control of the House and the Republicans holding a one-vote majority in the Senate. Divided government is not unique to Washington. Prior to the fall 2002 elections, fifteen states had divided legislatures, and after the election, twelve states still witnessed different parties controlling the two houses of their legislative branch.

Table 1

United or Divided Party Control of the Governor and Legislature

Governor	Year	United or Divided Party Control
Langlie (R)	1949	Divided
	1951	Divided
	1953	United
	1955	Divided
Rosellini (D)	1957	United
	1959	United
	1960	United
	1963	United
Evans (R)	1965	Divided
	1967	Divided
	1969	Divided
	1971	Divided
	1973	Divided
	1975	Divided
Ray (D)	1977	United
	1979	Divided
Spellman (R)	1981	United
	1983	Divided
Gardner (D)	1985	United
	1987	Divided
	1989	United
	1991	Divided
Lowry (D)	1993	Divided
	1995	Divided
Locke (D)	1997	Divided
	1999	Divided*
	2001	United**
	2003	Divided

Sources: *Book of the States* (Lexington, KY: Council of State Governments, various volumes).

*In 1999, the governor's party had a majority in one house; the other house was evenly divided between the two parties.

**In 2001, the House remained tied until a special election in November gave Democrats unified control.

Even when one party controls the governor's mansion and both houses of the legislature, party majorities are sometimes too small to give the governor dependable support. When party control of the state House of Representatives was evenly split between the two parties, the dual leadership structures created to cope with the tie led to nearly insurmountable obstacles to leadership, both within the house and from the governor. While the close division of both houses of the legislature reflects the close political divisions of the state, and indeed, the nation as a whole, the nearly evenly divided government and the increasing polarization of the two parties make it extremely difficult for the governor to exercise effective leadership.

Though the governor exercises leadership through budget submissions, this too is constrained. In Washington State, due to the initiative and referenda processes and other requirements set forth in the constitution and statutes, perhaps upward of 80 percent of the state's budget already is allocated. In recent years, voters have passed several initiatives mandating spending on K–12 education, health care, and road maintenance, while simultaneously passing initiatives cutting property and excise taxes that have decreased tax revenues substantially. This leaves less money for the governor to utilize politically to placate constituents or legislators. Ultimately, due to a high level of already allocated funds, the governor has fewer opportunities to effect policy through spending decisions, and must often capitulate to demands from legislators in order to ensure passage of the budget (see Chapter 10; "Budgeting and Public Finance in Washington").

Budgetary problems are further complicated by the economic constraints faced by state government. Washington has two major sources of revenue from individual citizens: property taxes and sales taxes. The reliance on these two taxes becomes particularly problematic when the state faces an economic recession, as Washington has during the early 2000s. As the recession worsened, sales tax revenues continued a dramatic drop-off. In October 2002 the Office of Financial Management predicted that the deficit for the 2003–05 biennium, just to maintain 2002 services levels, would be approximately $2.5 billion. Initiatives that require voter approval for tax increases or limit the percentage by which taxes may be increased limit the ability of the legislature or governor to make up the shortfall in tax revenue. Thus, the governor may look to other avenues to address temporary economic difficulties.

Washington also gathers revenue from taxes levied on businesses. However, the number of large companies from which a majority of state tax revenue relies—such as Microsoft and Boeing—are few. Since companies are susceptible to the volatility of the economy, their tax contributions decrease during recessions. Boeing, in the wake of the September 11, 2001, terrorist attacks and the resulting financial difficulties for the airline industry, has seen orders for airplanes decline dramatically, and has not won enough lucrative federal contracts to make up the difference in revenue.

Further complicating the budgetary maze are constitutional limits put on the amount of debt the state can incur. These limitations may reduce the risk of future financial difficulties, but in times of recession, those limits can almost be debilitating. The reliance on two taxes——one of which is subject to economic volatility (sales taxes), the other of which is not quickly adjustable (property taxes)—and the constitutional limits placed on spending have the combined effect of making the budgetary leadership role quite challenging for the governor.

The governor faces other challenges regarding the legislature. Washington's governor, like others, has the power to veto legislation to which he objects. He also has line-item veto power, but is constrained by the state's constitution to vetoing not less than entire paragraphs of legislative language, except in the cases of spending bills, when the governor may delete individual appropriations items. The governor's veto power may be used for more than blocking legislation; it can be used in negotiating with the legislature in order to further the governor's policy goals. However, casting large numbers of vetoes risks angering legislators and political opponents; consequently, governors tend to use their veto power cautiously.

Finally, the governor's leadership can be constrained by the judicial branch of state government. Decisions by Washington State's Supreme Court have had impacts on budget allocations and other policy decisions that must be adhered to by the governor. For example, in several rulings the Supreme Court has indicated the priority status of education, relative to other policy areas. Support for primary and secondary education in the state of Washington is already constitutionally mandated, and Article IX requires the state to fund schools to appropriate levels by allocating funds out of general revenue sources. However, as the Supreme Court has reinforced the constitutional provision for education, it has in essence given K–12 education priority status in the state budget.

Administrator and Chief Executive

Another large area of responsibility for Washington's governor is the oversight of numerous state agencies. Governors influence the bureaucracy by requiring reporting from state agencies and by ensuring that laws are properly executed. While a governor usually minimizes involvement in the day-to-day operations of each state agency, the governor still holds ultimate oversight responsibility, and usually works very closely with state agencies on policies important to the gubernatorial office. As provided for in Washington Administrative Code (WAC), the governor also is provided with professional staff assistants to help in fulfilling these duties. These personnel totaled thirty-six in 2002, which is close to the national average. The governor also has a personally appointed, twenty-eight-member cabinet with whom he meets on a weekly basis during legislative sessions, and a bi-weekly basis when the legislature is not in session. WAC also requires that commissions, task forces, or similar entities must report to the chief executive, which thereby, by default, falls under the governor's purview.

The job as administrator is particularly challenging for the governor. As with bureaucracies at any level of government, the amount of time and energy required to effectively oversee state agencies is extensive and generally requires special attention to detail. Washington, as already mentioned, relies quite heavily on task forces and citizen boards, which also report to the governor in implementing policies passed by the legislature. The sheer volume of entities involved, not to mention the increasing numbers of policies they deal with, contribute to the gubernatorial quagmire. Due to other overall governmental responsibilities, governors have little time to sufficiently administrate all agencies, task forces, and boards.

In addition, it is up to the governor to fill numerous appointed positions on boards and task forces. Finding or hiring appointees is an extremely time-consuming process, often requiring a coordinated effort with others. The governor's acquaintance with individuals throughout the state and the ability to draw on networks may ease the job of filling appointed positions, but the chief administrator always must consider potential political consequences resulting from these selections.

In another aspect of administrative duties, the governor fulfills an additional role as chief executive. The state of Washington provides for an executive branch headed by the governor, but also features eight other independently elected state executives—a larger number than in most other states. Although the governor has no direct involvement in their selection, to be effective a governor must ultimately work with them. Most of the statewide elected officials are partisan, which means party politics are inevitable in the management of the executive branch. The chief executive often faces divided political loyalties that must be overcome; deciding which battles to fight and which ones to forego can have long-lasting consequences.

Another executive power has gained in significance since September 11, 2001. The governor has the authority to issue executive orders in order for the state to cope with civil defense problems, disasters, and other public emergencies. Governors in several other states have broader authority in this regard than Washington's governor, however.

Ceremonial Leader and Figurehead

Finally, the governor has an important role as the ceremonial leader and figurehead for the state. This has many aspects. The governor may represent the state either on a national or international level. Washington governors regularly attend the National Governors' Association Conference, and frequently travel to the nation's capital to lobby for policies relevant to the state, or to meet with Washington's congressional delegation. The governor also is often involved with international trade delegations and promoting Washington's overseas trade interests. In recent years, Governor Locke has traveled to Korea, Japan, China, and Mexico to advocate markets for Washington goods, including agricultural and technological products.

Within the state, the governor performs responsibilities as a ceremonial leader and chief of state. As a ceremonial leader, the governor may speak at public commemorations, welcome dignitaries, or attend events of importance to a large segment of the population. The governor makes regular appearances at events on holidays such as Veteran's Day or Memorial Day. The governor's job as ceremonial leader and figurehead is probably the least controversial of the position's duties.

Where do Governors Come From?

The governor's office has become increasingly professional because of the many demands attending it. Individuals seeking election to state government have responded to this change and gubernatorial candidates are increasingly well skilled and experienced in government. This is a considerable contrast to Washington's territorial governors who, as political friends of presidents, were appointed on the basis of politics rather than because of skill or governing experience.

Contemporary governors tend to be younger than their historical predecessors, and better educated. According to information recently compiled by the National Governors' Association, the most common degrees for governors holding office are in business, history, and political science; twenty-three governors hold law degrees; and two are doctors.

Generally speaking, most governors now have some degree of previous political experience. Most have served in a legislative capacity, either at the state or national level, as well as in different levels of state or local government. Washington Governor Gary Locke served five terms in the state's House of Representatives prior to his election as governor. Idaho's governor, Dirk Kempthorne, was a U.S. Senator, and Oregon's governor, Ted Kulongoski, also was a member of the state legislature. This trend is not unique to the Pacific Northwest; in 2003, thirty-five state governors had legislative experience at the national or state level (National Governors' Association fast facts website), and seven governors formerly were mayors. Only eight governors had never held political office prior to their election as governor.

State governorship is also straying from being dominated exclusively by white males. Women and ethnic minorities have been elected to the governor's office. For example, Washington's Governor Locke, son of immigrant parents, was the first Chinese-American elected to the governorship. At the time of this writing, there are two governors from minority ethnic groups in the United States.

Women are also assuming a rightful place in state leadership. Prior to the 2002 election, there were five female governors in the United States. Although several women had been elected governor on the death of their governor husbands or as stand-ins for their husbands who were not eligible to run for another term, Dixy Lee Ray of Washington State was one of the first female governors elected in her own right. Carroll (1994) and O'Regan (2000) have shown that the presence of women in government has an impact on the kinds of policies addressed. If government is supposed to reflect the citizens it represents, and if ideally the population of government should mirror the population in terms of gender, ethnicity, and religious composition, the presence of representatives from all groups in society is necessary. Therefore, it is to the great pleasure of those concerned with equal representation that more ethnic minorities and women are being elected to gubernatorial positions. The talent pool from which governors are chosen has expanded.

However, the increasing cost of running for office may hinder access to the position. In Washington's 2000 governor's race alone, spending by the two major party candidates totaled almost $6.5 million, with Governor Locke spending just over half of that amount. Most of this was spent on television access. As the importance of television and other media exposure in campaigning continues, the costs will rise, limiting those who can run successful campaigns. Gubernatorial candidates accrue more expenses than, say, legislative candidates, because of the necessity of reaching the electorate in all parts of the state.

The governor's office often is a springboard for individuals aspiring to higher public office. There were thirteen former governors in the 107th Congress, and seventeen governors have become presidents, including former President Bill Clinton, who was governor of Arkansas, and President George W. Bush, who served as governor of Texas. Many governors have entered various positions at the federal level, either after finishing their terms, or sometimes in the middle of a term. Former governor of Massachusetts, William F. Weld, left the governor's mansion to pursue an unsuccessful ambassadorial appointment, and his successor, Paul Cellucci, left the governor's office to become the ambassador to Canada in 2001. Still other governors have become a part of the federal executive branch, including the first Homeland Security Secretary, Tom Ridge, the former governor of Pennsylvania. Christine Todd Whitman, the ex-governor of New Jersey, became administrator of the Environmental Protection Agency.

Thus, governors throughout history often have followed their tenure in the governor's mansion by assuming elected and appointed positions at other levels of government. As governors enter office at a younger age, however, the opportunity for an extended political career increases. Personal considerations for a future in politics may inevitably influence a governor's actions, but those considerations do not require that a current governor ignore the issues and policies relevant to his or her constituency. Regardless of what the future may hold for them personally, most governors are concerned with the well being of their states, and work for the greater benefit of their citizens.

Other Statewide-elected Officials

Article III of the Washington State Constitution designates seven other state-wide elected officials besides the governor as part of the executive branch of state government. Their responsibilities range from oversight of the legislature, to protection of the legal interests of the state, to management of the vast state-owned public lands in Washington. In addition to these seven constitutionally mandated officers there also is an insurance commissioner, who is elected by a statewide constituency. These elected officials each serve four-year terms and, like the governor, walk the fine line between public responsibility and self-interest.

Lieutenant governor. As the title would suggest, the lieutenant governor is the governor's second-in-command. In the event that a governor is incapacitated or out of the state, the lieutenant governor may act on the governor's behalf. The lieutenant governor's primary responsibility is to oversee the Senate in the capacity as that body's president. The lieutenant governor also is an appointed member and chair of the Senate Rules Committee. Finally, the lieutenant governor may, on occasion, nominate individuals to various statewide commissions or task forces. Lieutenant Governor Brad Owen has been particularly active in addressing children's issues, especially regarding health and safety needs. He also has been involved in promoting Washington's international trade.

Secretary of state. The secretary of state has a wide variety of responsibilities. The state constitution requires that the secretary of state keep the record of the legislature and executive department, and also delegates possession and regulation of the state seal to this office. Over time, the office been given responsibility for supervising elections and verifying signatures on the filing of initiatives. Secretary of State Sam Reed was particularly active in voter mobilization, as well as in updating Washington's voting technology and accuracy following Florida's voting problems in the 2000 presidential election. Reed also was instrumental in bringing the state archives, another of the secretary's responsibilities, into the digital age and has documented the oral histories of previous members of state government. In addiiton, the office of the secretary of state has been active in rewarding governmental innovation and efficiency through the Employee Involvement and Recognition Board.

Attorney general. The attorney general is the primary legal counselor for the state. The attorney general's duties include representing state interests in any supreme or appeals court proceedings, and, when requested by other state officials or the legislature, issuing opinions on constitutional or legal questions pertaining to the duties of those officials. The attorney general is responsible for oversight of deputy attorneys and has the authority to initiate or intervene in local prosecutions, either at his or her own discretion or by request of the governor. The attorney general also may instigate civil or criminal proceedings on a limited basis, and also serves the public through administering consumer protection programs and handling consumer complaints. The attorney general's office also may review legislation prior to passage or before signing.

Attorney General Christine Gregoire received national recognition during the state's lawsuit against the tobacco industry in 1999. She was one of the chief architects of the settlement that allocated $206 billion to Washington and 45 other states, to be dispersed over a 25-year time span, and she also disputed the federal government's attempt to use settlement money to pay Medicare and Medicaid costs associated with treating patients suffering from tobacco-related illnesses.

State treasurer. The state treasurer has the primary responsibility for managing state finances and serves as the state's representative in any financial contracts into which the state may enter. The treasurer's office also manages all state financial accounts and provides annual updates of those accounts to the legislature and governor.

State auditor. The state auditor has the responsibility of overseeing all the public accounts of approximately 2,400 governmental units throughout the state. The auditor must account for all these public resources to prevent their misappropriation or misuse, while simultaneously ensuring that units throughout Washington adhere to laws and regulations relating to state finances. The auditor's office sets forth standards for uniform budgeting, accounting, and reporting, and provides training and technical assistance to implement those standards. It is also the auditor's responsibility to provide mandatory reports to the governor and legislature of any financial accounting problems that may have arisen in state units.

Superintendent of public instruction. The superintendent of public instruction is Washington's chief educator. This individual has oversight of all concerns pertaining to public education from kindergarten through the 12th grade, and acts as the liaison between public schools and the governor and legislature, particularly in matters concerning management and policy. The office prepares and publishes the state's common school code, administers basic education programs, and issues and keeps the record of all teaching certificates in the state. The superintendent also is responsible for implementing educational reform. Superintendent of Public Instruction Terry Bergeson has been particularly active in the debate over the use and reform of the state's standardized tests, and has been a strong advocate for increased pay for teachers and for smaller class sizes.

Commissioner of public lands. The last of the constitutionally mandated offices, the commissioner of public lands manages the more than five million acres of state-owned public land and real estate in Washington, including forests, farms, commercial properties, and underwater areas. The office is charged with the duty of managing lands in a way that generates profits to benefit public schools and universities by selling products such as timber or wheat, while simultaneously ensuring that the properties will be useful and profitable in the future. The commissioner of public lands also is responsible for managing natural resources such as fish, wildlife, and waterways. During the annual summer fire season, the commissioner of public lands oversees fire prevention and protection measures. Commissioner Doug Sutherland was elected in November 2000.

Insurance commissioner. The insurance commissioner is the only non-constitutionally mandated officeholder selected by a statewide election. The office was established in 1907 to enforce the state's insurance code through implementing and enforcing rules and regulations. The insurance commissioner is responsible for investigating and, if necessary, bringing charges or fines against any insurance company engaged in fraudulent behavior. The commissioner has authority to revoke licenses or fine insurance agents, brokers, solicitors, or adjusters found to be engaging in unethical behavior. Additionally, the insurance commissioner is responsible for enforcing the rights of Washington citizens as promised to them by insurance companies or providers, and ensuring that requirements for insurance policies set forth in Washington State law are adhered to by providers. The current insurance commissioner is Mike Kreidler.

Conclusion

The governor's office has evolved since Washington's statehood from a position with little power or public trust, to an institution that has not only state, but national, influence as well. As state governors have come to work together, they have been able to exert tremendous influence at the federal level.

However, the governor is only one person in a state system designed to prevent the accrual of absolute power in any one individual or institution. The governor, as the chief executive, has the great responsibility of leading the state in both policy and administration. A governor faces numerous obstacles and challenges, but these are not insurmountable. A governor who can negotiate the political and partisan terrain is a governor who can have lasting impact.

Endnote

1. From *The Book of the States, 2002* edition, Table 4.3, The Governors: Compensation. For discussions and comparisons of gubernatorial authority across the nation, see *The Book of the States, 2002* (Lexington, KY: Council of State Governments, 2002), chapter 4, and the sources cited there. For an earlier discussion of Washington's governor, see George Scott, "The Office of Governor and Elected Statewide Officials," in David Nice, John Pierce, and Charles Sheldon, *Government and Politics in the Evergreen State* (Pullman: Washington State University Press, 1992), pp. 17-32.

References

Bowman, Ann O'M., and Richard C. Kearney. *State and Local Government*, 4th ed. Boston, Mass.: Houghton Mifflin Company.

Carroll, Susan J. 1994. *Women as Candidates in American Politics*. Bloomington: Indiana University Press.

Council of State Governments. 2002. *The Book of the States, 2002*. Vol. 34. Lexington, Ky.: Council of State Governments.

Harrigan, John J., and David C. Nice. 2001. *Politics and Policy in States and Communities*, 7th ed. New York: Longman.

National Governor's Association Fast Facts. 2002. www.nga.org/governors. (October).

Office of the Code Reviser. 1995. *Washington State Constitution*. Olympia, Wash.: Office of the Code Reviser.

O'Regan, Valerie R. 2000. *Gender Matters: Female Policymakers' Influence in Industrialized Nations*. Westport, Conn.: Praeger.

Scott, George. 1992. "The Office of Governor and Elected Statewide Officials." In *Government and Politics in the Evergreen State,* eds. David Nice, John Pierce, and Charles Sheldon. Pullman: Washington State University Press. Pp. 17-32.

Statute Law Committee. 2001. *Washington State Administrative Code*. Olympia, Wash.: Statute Law Committee.

Washington State Office of Financial Management. 2002. www.ofm.wa.gov. (October).

Washington State Secretary of State Elections and Voting. 2002. www.secstate.wa.gov/elections. (October).

| Chapter Nine |

The Legislature

Todd Donovan

"The legislative authority of the state of Washington shall be vested in the legislature…but the people reserve to themselves the power to propose bills, laws, and to enact or reject the same at the polls, independent of the legislature, and also reserve power, at their own option, to approve or reject at the polls any act, item, section, or part of any bill, act, or law passed by the legislature." - Article II, Section 1 of the Washington State Constitution.

AMERICANS ARE RELATIVELY AMBIVALENT about representative government. Although most claim great regard for the institutions and traditions of the U.S. Congress (Hibbing and Theiss-Morse 1995), few trust in the people who serve in Congress. In the state of Washington, this tension between the public and representative democracy is exacerbated by the initiative process. There are probably only six other states in America where the legislature is more exposed to laws that "the people" enact or reject at the polls "independent of the legislature" (Bowler and Donovan 2003). The Washington legislature thus operates in a unique environment where initiative proponents often succeed in undoing—for better or for worse—the work that elected representatives accomplish in Olympia.

This chapter describes this unique legislative context as it existed at the beginning of twenty-first century. We also examine the partisan environment during this period, and find that despite Washington's wide-open style of direct democracy, political parties have become even more dominant in organizing how the legislature conducts its business. We begin with a look at how citizens are represented in the legislature.

The Nature of Representation: Districts

The Washington state legislature is composed of two houses: the 98-member House of Representatives and the 49-member State Senate. There are 49 state legislative districts in Washington, with two members of the House and one state senator elected from each district. The entire membership of the House is elected every two years to a two-year term, while one-half of the State Senate is elected every two years. State senators serve four-year terms. At the time of the 2000 reapportionment, each legislative district had about 120,000 people. Each district is expected to have roughly the same population, and districts are drawn to coincide with city and county lines, and "communities of interest." On average, about 44,500 voters cast ballots in each legislative district. Population growth and change means that the composition of districts changes every decade.

Laws require that the boundaries of legislative districts be redrawn after each decennial census. In many states, the legislature and governor have complete discretion over the way legislative districts are crafted. This means that the party in control of government can use data from the census and previous elections to maximize the number of seats that are "safe" for its party. Even in states with divided government, legislators of both parties may agree to create "safe districts" that protect incumbents.

After the Republican-controlled legislature passed plans for U.S. Congress and state legislature redistricting in 1981, Governor John Spellman (R) vetoed the congressional portion of the plan. The partisan conflict over legislative districting led to voter approval of a 1983 constitutional amendment limiting the legislature's direct influence over the determination of districts. Under the present system, a five-member bipartisan commission draws district boundaries. The legislature may only make minor amendments to the commission's plan, and only with a two-thirds majority. The governor cannot veto the plan.[1]

Commissioners cannot have held elected office within two years of serving; however, they are closely tied to the two major political parties. Each party's legislative caucus organization appoints one citizen member to the commission. The commissioners then appoint a fifth non-voting member to serve as chair. Three of four voting members must agree to a plan, which is then sent to the legislature. In 1991 and 2001, legislative districts were drawn by the commission. In 2001, partisan conflict among commissioners caused them to fail to meet the statutory deadline for completing their congressional plan. It was completed soon after the deadline, and court intervention was not required.

What does it matter if redistricting is done by commission? It may be that lacking direct, constant pressure from legislators concerned about protecting their seats that the commission may create a few more districts where neither party holds the loyalties of an overwhelming majority of voters. This means that some legislative elections could be more competitive, and that a statewide swing of relatively few votes from one party to the other could produce a large change in the partisan control of the legislature. Some observers suggest that partisan maneuvering endemic to districting may simply become less visible when done by commission rather than the legislature. Recent elections, however, suggest that Washington's districts are more competitive than those in most states. In 2000, three of the nation's most competitive U.S. House races were in Washington. The dramatic shift in control of the state's congressional delegation and the state legislature in 1994 (see Figure 1) resulted from a relatively small shift in popular votes toward the Republicans—another illustration of the competitiveness of some Washington legislative districts.

Figure 1

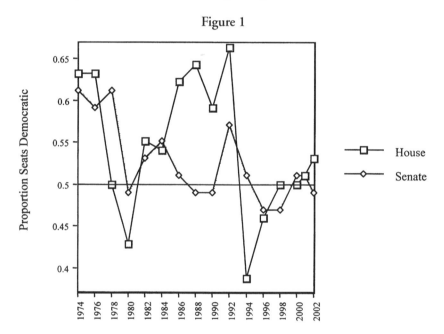

Representation of Voters in the Legislature

At the end of the twentieth century, party control of the legislature was so closely balanced that the House was deadlocked in a 49–49 tie for three consecutive sessions (1999, 2000, and 2001). At the same time, the majority party had just a single seat advantage in the Senate. The House had been deadlocked before, as recently as 1979, but the close partisan balance in both houses evident by 2000 had not been seen since the 1950s.

The tightly balanced partisan composition of the legislature circa 1996 to 2004—and outright ties—represented the roughly balanced support that

Democrats and Republicans received from the state's voters. The 49–49 ties in the House, however, masked the fact that Democratic candidates received significantly more votes than Republicans in most state races. In the 2000 and 1996 presidential elections, for example, 50% of the state voted Democrat, with Republicans capturing 45% and 37% in respective years. Both of Washington's U.S. senators and the governor were Democrats, although Republican Senator Slade Gorton narrowly lost in 2000.

The state's system of drawing legislative districts does not always translate votes for one party's candidates into seats with much accuracy. In 2000, for example, Democrats won over 50 percent of votes cast for all candidates for the House of Representatives, and Republican candidates received just 46 percent. Yet each party ended up with 49 seats. This disparity in translating votes to seats reflected a lack of candidates of both parties in many districts. In 2002, the situation was reversed. Over 50 percent of all votes cast for state House of Representative candidates went to Republicans, but the Democrats won a clear majority of seats.

The Washington State legislature receives high marks nationally for representation of women. Starting in 1992, Washington began to lead all states in the proportion of women in the legislature. By 2000, women held 40 percent of all seats—up from 18 percent in 1983 when the state ranked eleventh nationally.[2] The recent success of women candidates is attributed to Washington's political culture, and to the aggressive recruitment of women candidates by both parties in the 1990s. Some political scientists also suggest that states with lower campaign costs tend to elect more women; however, as noted below, legislative campaign costs have been increasing while women have been winning more seats.

Legislators and the Washington Public

Most Washington voters were reasonably satisfied with their legislature in 2000, yet they are often unwilling to delegate much responsibility to them. As Table 1 illustrates, few Washington voters rated their state legislature as doing a "poor" job. Although few rated the legislature as doing "very good," these opinions suggest voters are relatively satisfied with the legislature's performance. Nearly one-half thought the legislature did a "fair" job, and over one-third said it did a "good" job.

In 1999 voters passed Initiative 695, which repealed the Motor Vehicle Excise Tax (MVET) and required that any new tax passed by the legislature must be approved by voters. This was one of many recent cases where voters approved an initiative designed to constrain how the legislature functions. Throughout the 1990s and into the twenty-first century, Washington voters have continuously approved measures limiting the legislature's power to tax. They also

Table 1

Opinions about Washington State Legislature

What kind of job do you think the state legislature is currently doing, overall?

Very good	2.6%
good	34.3%
fair	48.4%
poor	10.2%
very poor	4.5%
Valid cases	382

Who do you think are better at making public policy, elected representatives, the voting public, or would you say that both are equally good?

Elected representatives	18.2%
Voting public	21.5%
Both are equal	57.3%
Neither	3.0%
Valid cases	380

Source: Author's survey of Washington voters Spring 1999 (n = 403) and Spring 2000 (n = 398). Conducted by Applied Research Northwest.

have approved initiatives authorizing spending programs that had not emerged from the legislative process, and have voted to limit legislative discretion in spending revenues. A proposal to limit state legislative terms was also approved in 1992, although it was later overturned by the courts.

In 2000 alone, voters approved separate initiatives that mandated further tax cuts (I-722), increased spending on teacher pay (I-732), and increased spending to reduce K-12 class sizes (I-728). In 2001, they voted again to limit property taxes (I-747), approved a tax on tobacco to help fund health programs (I-773), and established a new home care quality authority (I-775). Each of these measures were drafted outside the legislature, but had great effect on how the legislature could write the state budget. On occasion, voters also approve referendums that repeal laws the legislature had approved (e.g. R-48 of 1995 and R-53 of 2002).

All of these public votes might be seen as suggesting that the citizens of Washington are dissatisfied with state government in general, and their legislature in particular. Yet, as noted above, public opinion polls indicate that voters give their legislators relatively high marks. So, we have an apparent paradox—a well functioning, well regarded state legislature that is the frequent target of the public's wrath.

How might we reconcile public satisfaction with the legislature coinciding with movements to limit what the legislature may do? This paradox reflects the often awkward interaction between the legislature and Washington's tremendously popular citizens' initiative process. Supported by the state constitution, the idea remains widely popular in the state that citizens, rather than representatives, have the final say over policy. When asked in 1999, "Who do you think are better at making public policy, elected representatives, or the voting public?," a large majority of Washington voters replied that the public is just as good as the legislature; another one-fifth replied the public is better at making policy than legislators. Only 18 percent claimed that the legislature was better suited for the task (see Table 1). A similar poll found that a majority of Washington voters agreed that representatives should do what their district wants, even if the representative thinks it is a bad idea (only 38% disagreed).[3]

The Legislature Under the Shadow of Initiatives

These attitudes of the Washington public, although flowing from the long Populist and Progressive tradition of the Pacific Northwest, represent a trend toward greater participatory forms of governing now emerging in many states. Indeed, state politics scholar Alan Rosenthal warned in 1998, "Representative democracy as the states had experienced it for several centuries is now in decline" (1998:5). Others observe that since the initiative plays such a large role in setting the agenda in Washington, the legislature is less relevant than before.

Given this political environment in Washington, the state's legislature may be even more responsive to the voting public than legislatures in many other states. Major legislative policy initiatives are often vetted with an eye toward how potential initiative proponents might respond. Since voters approved Tim Eyman's I-695 in 1999, the fear of voter backlash—against acts passed by the legislature as much as against individual legislators—has become more pronounced. Despite a court ruling that overturned I-695 and its requirement that future taxes receive voter approval, legislators and the governor have operated under the assumption that major revenue proposals need to be referred to the public (e.g. R-51, a gas tax proposal legislators sent before voters in 2002). Indeed, some observers suggest that a new breed of Republican legislative leaders has emerged, who expect that tax proposals should go to the voters for approval (Ammons 2002).

Others, such as former Senate Democrat Leader Sid Snyder, report being "extremely frustrated" with voter initiatives that handcuff the legislature when it needs to deal with fiscal crises such as budget deficits (Hadley 2002). Another influential Democrat, a candidate for governor in 2004, suggested that if initiative proponents such as Eyman "want to write the state budget, he ought to run for Legislature or run for Governor" (Ammons 2002).

For their part, legislators and legislative candidates mirror the voting public in reporting high levels of support for the initiative and referendum process.[4] Legislators and voters, however, differ in their evaluations of how the initiative process should work. State legislators on the west coast are much more likely to support reforming the initiative process than are voters. Just 21 percent of Washington voters approved granting the legislature more discretion in amending voter initiatives, yet two-thirds of legislators and legislative candidates approved such a reform (Bowler et al. 2001).

A growing body of academic research demonstrates that initiatives have important effects on what a state legislature does. At one level, the initiative process opens the door for groups and individuals to promote "governance" or "reform" policies that constrain how legislators govern and seek office: campaign finance regulations, term limits, limitations on taxing, and limitations on state spending. One direct effect of initiatives is that states such as Washington are more likely to adopt such "governance" policies (Tolbert 1998; Pippen et al. 2002).

Professionalization

Provisions for direct democracy were adopted when reformers viewed the legislature as too easily corrupted by powerful economic interests. In the 1960s many felt that legislatures were still ill-equipped for representing the public (Rosenthal 1998:50-54). Most legislators had little staff, no research budgets, and little time in session. Legislators were often paid very little, which required that they keep their "regular" jobs and spend limited time at the capitol. Prior to the mid 1960s, many state legislatures met for sessions that lasted for just a few weeks. Few legislators served in office very long and, for many, their jobs were limited to processing personal concerns of constituents. To some observers, the combined effect of these factors left state legislatures ineffective, and placed disproportionate power in the hands of the governor. Worse, these "unprofessional" legislators could more easily be corrupted by interests seeking special treatment from the legislature.

The movement to professionalize state legislatures focused on building the institutional capacity of legislatures. By increasing salaries, reformers hoped to attract more talented people. Formal and "interim" legislative sessions were increased in Washington and many states. Alan Rosenthal (1998) argues that increased numbers of staff personnel was the reform that produced the single greatest boost to legislative capacity. Other reforms included building more space for committee hearings and members' offices at the capitol and in their district. Legislatures that adopted most of these reforms are known today as "professional," while those that adopted few or none are referred to as "citizen" legislatures. Compared to other states, Washington's legislature remains a hybrid between a pure professional and pure citizen legislature—but it ranks well above average in terms of several measures of professionalization (Hamm and Moncrief 1999).

As measured by levels of legislative staff, average salary, length of session, and other indicators of professionalism, Washington ranks well above a pure, part-time citizen legislature, and slightly below the most professional, full-time state legislatures. By 2003, the average members' salary was $33,556, with the formal legislative session lasting about 100 days.[5] In contrast, the average legislator in the most professionalized of all state legislatures (California) would be paid $75,000 for a 265-day session.

Although Washington has about nine staff people per state legislator, a highly professionalized legislature such as New York has 25 per member (Hamm and Moncrief 1999:145). This does not mean that each individual legislator has nine staff people at her disposal. A large proportion of these non-partisan staffers in Washington work for legislative policy committees (e.g., House Agriculture and Natural Resource Committee, Senate Transportation Committee), and for departments and agencies of the legislature (e.g., Legislative Ethics Board, the Code Revisers Office). These are people with training in law, economics, accounting, policy analysis and many other fields, as well as clerical staff, who organize committee hearings, conduct specialized policy research, and serve the needs of the elected legislators. The average Washington legislator may be assigned just one full time staffer to work in their capitol office during the session. The same staffer may also work in the district office during the rest of the year. Washington is one of only eight states that provide legislators year-round personal staff for their capitol and district offices, for both Senate and House members (Rosenthal et al. 2001:16). Interns from the state's universities also augment the personal staff available for legislators.

The legislative party caucuses in Olympia tend to have substantial discretion over how staff are allocated. Party leaders tend to be given more staff. Allocation of staff may also be used by party leaders to reward and punish individual members. If a representative of one party falls out of favor with her party's caucus, the party may leave the member without any staff.

Two studies (Squire 2000; Hamm and Moncrief 1999) placed Washington as the fourteenth most professionalized legislature in the United States. Professionalization has its consequences. For one thing, legislators in professionalized states tend to come to office with more political experience. In the early 1990s, one-third of Washington's "freshman" state legislators came to Olympia after previously holding another office (Hibbing 1994). They also tend to stay longer in professionalized legislatures, and are likely to be more insulated from the corrupting influences of interests who have business before them. Professionalization increases the legislator's independent access to information—which means legislators need not always rely on lobbyists. It also means that legislators have an income source that is not dependent on the interests that lobby them.

The relatively short legislative session in Washington (compared to the most professionalized state legislatures) does not mean that Washington's legislators work a part-time job. One study estimated that a Washington legislator's year-round duties were the equivalent of three-quarters of a full-time job. This includes work spent in regular session, special session held to extend the regular session, work on "interim" committees that meet outside of the regular and special legislative sessions, year-round constituency service, and campaign work (Rosenthal et al. 2001:7).

It is somewhat ironic that Washington's initiative system was born from the fears of an unprofessional legislature. The legislature has now been professionalized to the extent that last century's Populist/Progressive concerns about extensive corruption are no longer as relevant as they were in the early 1900s. Direct democracy lives on, nonetheless, and its effects on the legislature are substantial. As we see below, populism and legislative professionalism collided in the 1990s in the movement to limit legislative terms.

Turnover and Competitiveness of Legislative Elections

Since the movement to professionalize state legislatures produced greater institutional capacity, legislative careers became more attractive, and there was a 30-year national trend of state legislators remaining in office longer (Patterson 1996). One critique of professionalism is that it may insulate representatives from the pressure of elections. As Table 2 illustrates, however, the Washington State legislature retained a large measure of membership turnover after each session through much of the 1990s. At the start of each new session, there has been a healthy proportion of veterans returning, and also a substantial number of new members.

Table 2 illustrates that 67 percent of those serving in the House of Representatives after the 1972 election had been there in the previous legislative session—a 33 percent turnover rate since 1970. In 1982, 54 percent of House members who began the session that year were returning members—a 46 percent turnover rate since 1980. In 1992, the turnover rate was 39 percent for the House. After the 2002 election, 80 percent of those who had served in the House in 2000 returned for the next session—a 20 percent turnover. Turnover rates in Washington were above the national average in the 1990s (Rosenthal 1998, 74).

Democratic theory suggests that legislators are more responsive to the public when they face the prospect of electoral defeat. Competitive elections, it is

Table 2

Turnover in the Washington State House of Representatives: 1972–2002

Year	Turnover
2002	20%
2000	23%
1998	24%
1996	n/a
1994	42%
1992	39%
1990	24%
1988	20%
1986	19%
1984	28%
1982	46%
1980	26%
1978	24%
1976	36%
1974	10%
1972	33%

Sources: 1972–1994; *Book of the States,* various years. 1994–2002; author's calculations from secretary of state's data.

assumed, strengthen the bond between the public and their representatives, since representatives know they may be turned out of office if their actions deviate too much from what their constituents prefer. By extension, competition between candidates of rival parties should produce representatives who reflect the concerns of a wider segment of voters.[6] The potential for election-induced turnover is thus seen by some as a sign of a healthy polity. As former Speaker of the U.S. House Tom Foley (D - Spokane) commented on his own defeat in 1994:

> The threat of turnover is a useful discipline on a parliamentary party. Otherwise it's very hard to convince members that decisions have to be made, not only to accommodate differences, but that they involve real adjustments...The threat of the ax isn't necessarily sufficient, you have to actually feel the blade (Biggs and Foley 1999:244).

The majority of turnover reported in Table 2, however, is not the product of legislators "feeling the blade" of defeat, but of their retiring after a few sessions (or moving on to seek other offices). Only a handful are defeated at each general election. The decision to retire, however, may be a strategic consideration affected by perceptions of electoral vulnerability (e.g. Jacobson and Kernell 1983).

Representatives may also be more sensitive to the threat of the electoral ax if they fear their party might lose control of the legislature as the result of losing a few key seats.

Nevertheless, most legislators in Washington now come from districts that are apportioned to be quite safe for just one political party. By 2002 over one-third of all of Washington's state legislative races were so one-sided that they were contested by a candidate from just one of the main parties. "Safe" districts are largely unavoidable in much of the state; it is difficult to find areas of urban Seattle or eastern Washington where equal numbers of Democratic and Republican voters reside side by side.

Table 3 demonstrates rates at which the two major parties faced each other in legislative races. From 1968 to 1995, Washington's state legislative contests were among the most competitive in nation—whether measured by the proportion of seats contested by both major parties, or by the proportion of candidates elected by something less than a landslide (Hamm and Moncrief 1999). By 2002, however, the percentage of seats contested by both parties dropped from an average of 87 percent to 66 percent. By itself, this does not mean that legislators face less pressure from voters. Many districts are still quite competitive—evidence of this can be seen in the relatively constant proportion of seats where the loser receives at least 40 percent support.

High levels of safe incumbents reflect districting practices, but also reflect on incumbents who do a good job representing their constituents and/or deterring challengers. It is not rare for an apparently safe seat to become a tight two-party contest after a popular incumbent moves on. As safe as most incumbents are, more Washington legislators are defeated in general election contests than members of the U.S. House of Representatives. In 1998, 93.7 percent of in-

Table 3

Competitiveness of Washington Legislative Races

Year	Seats with two-party competition	Loser received 40% or more	
		Washington	*U.S. House*
1968–1995	87%	43%	
1996	83%	41%	36%
1998	70%	43%	27%
2000	80%	38%	23%
2002	66%	37%	17%

Note: Figures for Washington include House and Senate contests.

Sources: 1968–1995: Hamm and Moncrief 1999. Washington, 1996–2002: author's calculations from secretary of state's data. U.S. House data: Center for Voting and Democracy.

cumbents seeking office were reelected to the Washington House. That same year, 99 percent of incumbents were reelected to the U.S. House. Table 3 demonstrates, furthermore, that fewer Washington legislators are elected by landslides than members of the U.S. House. By these measures, Washington's legislative elections are at least more competitive than the U.S. House contests.

Despite this, the composition of the Washington legislature may be more polarized today than in previous eras, with a large block of fairly liberal Democrats elected from safe urban and west-of-the-mountain seats competing against a large block of fairly conservative Republicans elected from safe rural and eastern seats. Few seats are left to be contested by moderates. In a state once famous for independent, "maverick" politicians, few can be found in the current state legislature.

Escaping Term Limits

Critics of legislative professionalism (e.g., Will 1992) argue that it led to bigger government, and claim that long-serving incumbents stand as a barrier between citizens and their government. Advocates of "citizen legislatures" contend that frequent rotation of those in office establishes a stronger bond between the public and their government. Some early American revolutionaries advocated rapid rotation of those in office to guard against tyranny (Petracca 1992).

In the early 1990s, legislative term limits were seen by some as a means to undo the alleged problems of legislative professionalism. Advocates offered it as a way to make legislators more responsive, and make elections more competitive. Backed by popular opinion and a few wealthy conservative donors, term limit initiatives were quickly approved in 14 states by the mid 1990s (Donovan and Snipp 1994).

Washington residents voted on three separate term limits initiatives in the 1990s. In 1991 Washington voters rejected one of the most restrictive of these proposals, I-553. The measure would have limited members of the U.S. House of Representatives to six two-year terms, and state House members to three two-year terms (Olson 1992). The election set a record for turnout, and Washington still stands as the only state to have rejected one of the "first wave" term limit measures.

The very next year, however, Washington voters approved a similar but less restrictive measure (I-573) that limited terms of the state legislature and Congress. Provisions of that initiative were found to be unconstitutional by the Washington State Supreme Court and by a federal court. In 1996 Washington voters rejected a proposal (I-670) that would have required that ballots list whether legislative candidates were in favor of term limits.

Turnover figures displayed in Table 2 should not be seen as suggesting that term limits would have little effect in Washington. The difference between a term limited legislature and a non-limited legislature hinges on the 10–20 percent of members who remain in the legislature for a decade or more. These tend to be high "quality" members who survive the "filtering" of the electoral process (Mondak 1995), and the committee chairs and party leaders who comprise the institution's memory and expertise. Carey et al. (2001) suggest that when these leaders are removed, the equilibrium—or balance of power—that might exist between the legislature and the executive is upset. Novice legislators come to rely more upon lobbyists, legislative staff, and the executive branch for information, rather than their own experience.

Organization of the Legislature: Committees

The party with a majority of seats in a house of legislature controls how that house is organized, and modern legislatures are organized around committees. Thousands of bills are introduced in a legislative session, and at least one standing committee must review every bill proposed before it reaches the floor of its house of origin. Committees allow for specialization of tasks according to policy areas; bills are usually assigned to a committee having jurisdiction over the policy topics included in the bill. Table 4 lists the standing committee in each house as of 2003, and the number of legislators on each committee.

After an election, particularly when a new party takes control of a majority in a house, the list of committee jurisdictions might shift a bit, with old committees split or merged. For the most part, however, the committee structure is fairly static across time. Before each session, the party caucuses in each house attempt to respond to legislators' preferences when placing members on committees. Given frequent departure of representatives from the legislature (see Table 2), the rank-and-file membership of committees, as well as some chairs, change after each election. If a change in partisan control of a house occurs after an election, then the entire leadership of that house—committee chairs, speaker, majority leader, whips—shifts to the new majority party.

Committees have the ability to report a bill to the floor with a recommendation that it be passed or amended. They may also refer a bill back to its sponsor to be re-drafted, or they may allow a bill to die in committee. Bills eventually reported out of committee may look quite different from their original form (Wolsborn 1992). These committees are where much of the hard work of the legislature is done: research, hearings, investigations, and bargaining. Rules grant chairs of committees some discretion in affecting the fate of any bill, since chairs control meeting agendas and have influence over when (or if) a bill will have a hearing or be put to a vote.

Chairs must have these tools, given the number of bills processed by the legislature, and given the relatively short length of the session. Business in the legislature—in committees and on the floor of each house—is oriented around a session calendar that stipulates when committee reports must reach the floor.

Table 4

Committee Organization, Washington House and Senate, 2003

House	
Rules	(19)
Appropriations	(27)
Agriculture and Natural Resources	(13)
Capital Budget	(25)
Children and Family Services	(9)
Commerce and Labor	(9)
Criminal Justice and Corrections	(7)
Education	(11)
Finance	(9)
Financial Institutions and Insurance	(11)
Fisheries, Ecology and Parks	(9)
Health Care	(13)
Higher Education	(15)
Judiciary	(9)
Juvenile Justice and Family Law	(6)
Local Government	(9)
State Government	(17)
Technology, Telecommunications and Energy	(10)
Trade and Economic Development	(10)
Transportation	(29)
Senate	
Ways and Means	(17)
Rules	(19)
Agriculture	(5)
Children and Family Services & Corrections	(7)
Commerce and Trade	(5)
Economic Development	(9)
Education	(8)
Financial Services, Insurance and Housing	(7)
Government Operations & Elections	(7)
Health and Long Term Care	(7)
Higher Education	(7)
Highways and Transportation	(12)
Judiciary	(9)
Land Use and Planning	(5)
Natural Resources, Energy and Water	(9)
Parks, Fish and Wildlife	(8)
Technology and Communications	(7)

The calendar is essential, since bills must be heard in their house of origin, as well as the opposite house, in a timely manner if they are to reach the floor before the end of session. Despite the calendar, there is often a crush of business on the floor of each house toward the end of session, and the session adjourns before all bills that cleared the committee process can be brought to a vote. In the end, most bills fail to pass in their chamber of origin, and only those that pass in *both* houses go on to the governor.

Parties and the Legislature

Scholars note that party unity in a legislature becomes well developed in two-party competitive states, where parties control the legislative process through their party caucuses (Jewel and Olson 1988). Washington, being a fiercely two-party competitive state, has a legislature structured overwhelmingly by unified party caucuses. David Olson, a political scientist at the University of Washington, wrote that "it is the party that sets the agenda, establishes a hierarchy of leadership, and adopts the working rules and procedures" in the legislature.

Both party's rank-and-file members (or caucus) elect leaders for each house at the start of each session, and grant them substantial discretion in setting the party's goals and strategies. Legislative leaders in Washington have far greater ability to maintain party unity than leaders in many other western states. Leadership tools for maintaining unity include influence over staff assignments, committee assignments, and, now more than ever, control of campaign resources. It is no surprise then that observers of the Washington legislature note that party affiliation is the single greatest determinant of how a representative votes on a bill (Nice 1992; Seeberger 1989; Olson 2001).

Party leadership in the House centers on the speaker, who assigns members to committees and who chairs the powerful Rules Committee. Other leaders in the House include the majority leader, the majority party caucus chair, the majority floor leader, and majority whip. These party leaders, and the caucus vice-chair and assistant whips from the majority party consolidate their control over the institution by holding many—if not most—of the majority party's seats on the Rules Committee, as well as many seats on the Appropriations Committee, the major budget-writing committee. The minority party maintains a similar, parallel leadership structure. The leadership structure in the Senate is similar to that of the House, although there may be no single Senate leader with as much influence there as the speaker has in the House (Wolsborn 1992). Party leaders in the Senate consolidate power by holding seats on the Rules Committee, and the Senate's major budget committee, the Ways and Means Committee.

Leaders work to coordinate the pace and content of legislation as it moves through each house. If a party controls a majority in a house, then it chairs every committee, and holds a majority of seats on every committee in that house. In each house, the majority party has much greater control than the minority party over the bills that flow through it. If one party holds a majority in *both* the House and Senate, that party's leadership is relatively well-positioned to insure that its priority bills will emerge from the legislative process enact, and in a timely manner.

However, as Figure 1 illustrates, recent elections rarely have given either party unified control of both houses. The figure plots the proportion of seats in each house held by Democrats from 1974 to 2002. When *both* data points for seats in the House and Senate show above or below the 50 percent line in a given year, an election gave one party unified control of both houses. Prior to 1988, this was not uncommon. In seven elections from 1974 to 1986, six left one party controlling both the House and Senate: five times for Democrats and once for Republicans (in 1978 there was a tie in the House). Since 1988, however, divided control has been the norm. Four of eight elections prior to 2004 produced a Democratic majority in one house, serving with a Republican majority in the other; two other elections produced ties in the House. The close partisan balance in the legislature reflects the fact that, by the late 1990s, Washington was one of the nation's most "two-party competitive" states (Bibby and Holbrook 1999).[7]

Divided control means that Senate leaders and House leaders often have policy goals that are the ideological mirrors of each other—with the leaders of neither party in a position to coordinate the workings of the legislature in an efficient manner. The situation was further complicated in 1998 and 2000 when those elections produced consecutive ties in the House of Representatives. This required that each House committee have two chairs (or "co-chairs"), one from each party, and that the House have "co-leaders," with a Democratic and a Republican speaker sharing power. Another complication to smooth legislating results when the parties are split between control of the legislature and the governor's office. For example, when Republicans managed to win unified control of the legislature in 1996–1998, they had to anticipate a potential veto from the Democratic governor when advancing their agenda.

Put simply, from 1980 to 2003 it has been rare for the political stars to align such that a single party has had enough voter support to control both houses of the legislature, while also controlling the governor's office. This may be one explanation for the frequent use of referenda and initiatives in the 1990s and 2000s. Close partisan balance in either house potentially increases the power of any group or individual to delay, block, or modify what the legislature might otherwise accomplish—potentially forcing some policy choices onto the state's ballot via initiatives. But the tight partisan balance has also created strong incentives for each party to maintain discipline over its members in order to remain cohesive and unified in the face of a strong partisan adversary.

Parties and Legislative Campaigns

One way that a party caucus remains unified is by controlling campaigns. Washington's parties are probably the primary recruiters of legislative candidates (Seeberger 1989; Olson 2001), and are clearly a major source of campaign funds.

In the 1980s, Washington's legislative party organizations ranked among the strongest nationally in terms of candidate recruitment and service to candidates (Cotter et al. 1984). They have grown even stronger since then. Looking back over two decades in 2001, Olson wrote that "the single greatest change in the party in [the Washington legislature] has been the emergence of legislative campaign committees [LCCs] and leadership PACs [political action committees]."

Control over campaign finance is one of the major vehicles party leaders have for maintaining caucus discipline. Seeberger noted that the two party organizations ranked fifth and seventh among the top contributors to Washington legislative candidates in 1990. By the year 2000, as Table 5 illustrates, several different state party organizations ranked as the top six largest contributors to legislative candidates. For many candidates seeking office in a contested legislative seat, a party organization was by far the single largest donor to the campaign.

The new dominance of parties in legislative races is a byproduct of campaign finance laws established by an initiative that voters approved in 1992 (I-134). The initiative, co-sponsored by then state legislator Linda Smith (R-Vancouver), opened the floodgates for party "soft-money" spending in legislative races. Campaign finance laws resulting from I-134 limit direct individual and PAC contributions to candidates to $625 per election (primary and general). There are no such limits, however, on the amount any individual can give to the state party or to party LCCs, and limits on PAC contributions to parties and LCCs are much looser than limits on direct PAC donations to candidates.[8]

Party leaders have great flexibility in using these vehicles to channel funds to their candidates, since there are no limits on transfers across the various party organizations. This last part is crucial, because it allows legislative leaders and aspiring leaders—many who come from safe seats—to raise cash that they then spend on behalf of candidates via several party bank accounts. The party organizations and LCCs are allowed far more direct spending on behalf of a candidate than any single PAC or individual is allowed. The law permits two types of party organizations (LCCs and state party organizations) to each spend up to $.62 per voter in a district, while two other types of party organizations (county and legislative district) can spend up to $.32 per voter in the district. In practice, the law limits a PAC or an individual to $1,250 in direct contributions to a candidate per election, while allowing the candidate's party to spend well over

Table 5

Top Contributors to Washington State Legislative Races, 2000

Group	Number of candidates funded	Total $$	avg. $$ per candidate
Washington State Democratic Central Committee	99	891,501	9,005
House Democratic Caucus Campaign Committee	43	652,123	5,165
House Republican Organization Committee	21	566,000	26,925
Washington State Republican Party	40	512,137	12,803
Senate Democrat Campaign Committee	20	257,476	12,873
Senate Republican Campaign Committee	7	161,598	23,085
Washington Education Association PAC	102	106,241	1041
Public School Employees PAC	118	101,400	859
Washington Restaurant Association PAC	114	96,810	849
Washington Medical PAC	100	95,685	956
Washington Optometric PAC	132	95,500	723
Puget Sound Energy	127	90,375	711
Weyerhaeuser	97	85,280	879

$100,000 in a legislative race.[9] All of this means that donors seeking influence via large campaign contributions must contribute to party organizations. Parties have thus become more efficient at raising money than individual candidates, and large contributions flowing to candidates are controlled by party elites.

Table 6 places this in context by listing the average cost of recent legislative races. In contested seats with an incumbent, the winner's average spending to win exceeded $120,000 in 2000. On average, candidates spent about $56,000 each in 2000, with average spending levels increasing steadily since 1994. In open seats targeted by both parties, spending is much higher. Four House races cost over $300,000 in 2002, one Senate race broke the $735,000 mark in 2002, and two other Senate races cost over $400,000 each.

The major parties tend to direct funds to the same contests. In races in 2000, candidates received as much as 70 percent of all campaign funds from their party organizations.[10] The Washington Public Disclosure Commission (PDC) reported that parties, and "party-linked PACs," spent $5.456 million on legislative races in the 1999–2000 election cycle. This represents 33 percent of all spending in legislative races for 2000.

Table 6

Average Legislative Election Campaign Expenditures, 2000
(General election candidates only)

State Senate		
Winners	26	$111,363
Losers	18	72,930
Incumbents in contested seats	19	121,839
Challengers in contested seats	15	63,084

State House of Representatives		
Winners	98	79,263
Losers	71	52,682
Incumbents in contested seats	77	80,903
Challengers in contested seats	59	46,179

Source: Election Financing Fact Book 2000. Washington State Public Disclosure Commission.

Cost of Legislative Races 1992–2002
(All legislative candidates, primary and general elections)

Year	Total spending	Number of candidates	Per candidate spending in 2002 dollars
1992	13,465,718	343	50,460
1994	10,516,508	316	40,486
1996	13,064,270	313	47,974
1998	12,994,043	267	53,834
2000	16,257,511	303	56,183
2002	15,500,000	n/a	

Source: Election Financing Fact Book 2000, and data from PDC web site (2002). Washington State Public Disclosure Commission.

Lobbying

Organized groups are well positioned to express their concerns to individual legislators, and to the legislative committees that do the hard work of crafting the content of proposed laws. These groups have several methods of communicating with legislators—from face-to-face meetings, drafting sample bills, testifying at committee hearings, mobilizing grassroots supporters, and by contributing to campaigns. Different groups may make use of different mixes of lobbying methods.

Table 7

Most Active Interests—Lobbying Expenditures in 2002 (through August)

Health care industry (providers, practitioners, products)	$3,442,900
Utilities (electric, telephone, water, waste)	$1,562,900
Unions (teachers, public employees, trade)	$1,550,000
Local governments (and tribes)	$1,503,700
Transportation (air, land, and marine interests)	$1,403,300
Business (general)	$1,285,400
Manufacturing firms	$1,115,051
Construction industry	$973,200
Insurance industry	$972,500
Forest/wood products industry	$802,300
Financial industry	$788,600
Food, beverage and lodging industry	$775,500
Real estate & development interests	$622,400
Law and justice (lawyers, prosecutors, judges)	$595,200
Agriculture	$537,200

Source: Washington State Public Disclosure Commission on-line data base.

The better funded interest groups and business lobbies have a permanent presence in Olympia, with office space, full-time staff, and professional lobbyists who interact with the legislature. Firms and individuals who are paid to lobby in Olympia must register with the state's Public Disclosure Commission. Table 7 lists the most active interests lobbying in the state, in terms of spending by groups that are categorized into distinct types of economic interest. Groups and firms that are placed into these 15 categories spent nearly $18,000,000 on lobbying in the first 8 months of 2002—about 80 percent of all expenditures recorded by the PDC.

The top 15 most active lobbying interests are largely private firms and industries that are directly affected by state laws and regulations. Industries such as health care, utilities, insurance, construction, real estate, and finance are affected by state laws that shape the scope of their business practices and affect who may compete with them. Consumer-oriented interests that might seek to re-define health care regulations, insurance practices, or lending practices typically have much less of a funded, professional presence in Olympia than the industries affected by such regulations. The interest groups most active in Washington State are quite similar to those that have a presence in other state capitals. Researchers have found that business groups, teachers' unions, and utility companies had reputations as the most effective interest groups in most states, with trial lawyers, health care organizations, and insurance companies following these in the rankings.

Conclusions

It is important to remember that the state's constitution grants legislators in Washington less discretion over policy and budgets than their counterparts in many other states. The Washington legislature faces the task of balancing the need to govern with expectations that it will be highly responsive to the public's preferences for policy. Unfortunately, the public's preferences are not always well articulated. Rather, public sentiments are transmitted in fits and starts via initiatives that are not easily reconciled. The tension between the public and legislature that is enshrined in the state constitution—between populism and representative democracy—remains. Voters are offered opportunities to cut some taxes, raise others, and approve spending; and the legislature is left to sort through the pieces and craft budgets and long-term policies. Despite all this—with the political context of close partisan balances in the legislature, citizens committed to legislating via the ballot box, and frequently divided partisan control of the legislature—the Washington State legislature can be considered to be functioning reasonably well.

Endnotes

1. Details about this are available from the Washington Redistricting Commission Web Site, at http://www.redistricting.wa.gov/
2. These data are from the Center for American Women in Politics at Rutgers University. http://www.cawp.rutgers.edu
3. Opinion data cited here are from polls conducted for the author in 1999 and 2000 by Applied Research Northwest.
4. Eighty-one percent of Washington voters respond that "statewide ballot propositions are a good thing for the state." Seventy percent of candidates and legislative candidates offered this response.
5. Major budget legislation is done in odd number years, when sessions have a 105 calendar day limit. Even numbered years have a 60 calendar day limit. "Special" sessions are held when these limits need to be exceeded.
6. Key and Downs serve as examples.
7. Ironically, as the state remained competitive, individual legislative districts became less two-party competitive.
8. A single PAC may give $3,000 to "major and minor political party committees," $3,000 to a party county central committee, $3,000 to a party legislative district committee, and $600 to a legislative caucus committee. The law seems to allow a single PAC to contribute to multiple county and legislative district committees.
9. If we assume 78,000 voters per district—the law allows a party's organizations to combine and spend $1.88 per voter ($1.88 x 78,000 = $146,640).
10. Geraghty 6th District House Position 2. All campaign finance data from Washington State Public Disclosure Commission 2000 Fact Book.

References

Ammons, David. 2002. "Eyman's Initiative Would Make It Hard for Legislators to Raise Taxes." *Seattle Times* (October 24), B2.

Bibby, John F., and Thomas M. Holbrook. 1999. "Parties and Elections." In *Politics in the American States: A Comparative Analysis,* seventh edition, ed. V. Gray, R. Hanson, and H. Jacob. Washington, D.C.: CQ Press.

Biggs, Jeffrey R., and Thomas S. Foley. 1999. *Honor in the House: Speaker Tom Foley.* Pullman: Washington State University Press.

Bowler, Shaun, Todd Donovan, Max Neiman, and Johnny Peel. 2001. "Institutional Threat and Partisan Outcomes: Legislative Candidates' Attitudes toward Direct Democracy." *State Politics and Policy Quarterly* 1(4): 364–79.

Bowler, Shaun, and Todd Donovan. 2003. "Direct Democracy in the American States." In *Politics in the American States: A Comparative Analysis,* eighth edition, ed. V. Gray and R. Hanson. Washington, D.C.: CQ Press.

Carey, John M., Richard Niemi, and Lynda W. Powell. 2001. "The Effects of Term Limits in State Legislatures." *Spectrum: The Journal of State Government* 74: 16–19.

Cotter, Cornelius P., James L. Gibson, John F. Bibby, and Robert J. Huckshorn. 1984. *Party Organizations in American Politics.* New York: Praeger Publishers.

Donovan, Todd, and Joseph Snipp. 1994. "Support for Legislative Term Limitations in California: Group Representation, Partisanship and Campaign Information." *Journal of Politics* 56: 492–501.

Gerber, Elisabeth R. 1999. *The Populist Paradox: Interest Group Influence and the Promise of Direct Legislation.* Princeton, N.J.: Princeton University Press.

Gerber, Elisabeth R. 1996. "Legislative Response to the Threat of the Popular Initiative." *American Journal of Political Science* 40: 99–128.

Hadley, Jane. 2002. "Voters Rejecting Eyman's Latest Cuts on Car Tabs." *Seattle Post-Intelligencer* (October 24), A1 and A7.

Hamm, Keith, and Gary Moncrief. 1999. "Legislative Politics in the States." In *Politics in the American States: A Comparative Analysis,* seventh edition, ed. V. Gray, R. Hanson, and H. Jacob. Washington, D.C.: CQ Press.

Hibbing, John R., and Elizabeth Theiss-Morse. 1995. *Congress as Public Enemy: Public Attitudes toward American Political Institutions.* Cambridge, Mass.: Cambridge University Press.

Hibbing, John R. 1994. "Modern Legislative Careers." In *Encyclopedia of the American Legislative System,* ed. J. Silbey. New York: Scribner's.

Jacobson, Gary C., and Samuel Kernell. 1983. *Strategy and Choice in Congressional Elections.* New Haven, Conn.: Yale University Press.

Jewel, Malcolm E., and David M. Olson. 1988. *Political Parties and Elections in American States,* third edition. Chicago: Dorsey Press.

Mondak, Jeff. 1995. "Elections as Filters: Term Limits and the Composition of the US House." *Political Research Quarterly* 48: 701–27.

Nice, David C. 1992. "Political Parties in Washington." In *Government and Politics in the Evergreen State,* ed. David C. Nice, John C. Pierce, and Charles H. Sheldon. Pullman: Washington State University Press.

Olson, David J. 2001. Expert Witness Statement of David J. Olson. *Washington State Democratic Party et al. v. Sam S. Reed, Secretary of State of the State of Washington et al.* United States District Court. Western District of Washington at Tacoma.

Olson, David J. 1992. "Term Limits Fail in Washington." In *Limiting Legislative Terms,* ed. G. Benjamin and M. Malbin. Washington, D.C.: CQ Press.

Patterson, Samuel C. 1996. "Legislative Politics in the American States." In *Politics in the American States: A Comparative Analysis,* sixth edition, ed. V. Gray and H. Jacob. Washington, D.C.: CQ Press.

Petracca, Mark P. 1992. "Rotation in Office: The History of an Idea." In *Limiting Legislative Terms,* eds. G. Benjamin and M. Malbin. Washington, D.C.: CQ Press.

Pippen, John, Shaun Bowler, and Todd Donovan. 2002. "Election Reform and Direct Democracy: Campaign Finance Regulations in the American States." *American Politics Research* 30: 559–582.

Rosenthal, Alan. 1998. *The Decline of Representative Democracy.* Washington, D.C.: CQ Press.

Rosenthal, Alan, Karl T. Kurtz, John Hibbing, and Burdett Loomis. 2001. *The Case for Representative Democracy: What Americans Should Know about Their Legislature.* Denver: National Conference of State Legislatures.

Seeberger, Edward D. 1989. *Sine Die.* Seattle: University of Washington Press.

Squire, Peverill. 2000. "Uncontested Seats in State Legislative Elections." *Legislative Studies Quarterly* 25: 131–46.

Tolbert, Caroline. 1998. "Changing Rules for State Legislatures." In *Citizens as Legislators: Direct Democracy in the United States,* ed. S. Bowler, T. Donovan, and C. Tolbert. Columbus: Ohio State University Press.

Will, George F. 1992. *Restoration: Congress, Term Limits, and the Recovery of Deliberative Democracy.* New York: Free Press.

Wolsborn, Kay Gausman. 1992. "The Legislature." In *Citizens as Legislators: Direct Democracy in the United States,* ed. D. Nice, J. Pierce, and C. Sheldon. Pullman: Washington State University Press.

| Chapter Ten |

Budgeting and Public Finance in Washington

Lance T. LeLoup and Christina Herzog

Introduction: Budgetary Challenges of the 2000s

IN THE FIRST DECADE of the new millennium, the state of Washington found itself in a prolonged budget crisis where revenues were insufficient to meet program demands and mandates. Solving these recurring problems were made more difficult by a string of voter-approved initiatives that both limited state government's ability to raise revenues and mandated additional spending. This "ballot box budgeting" significantly reduced the discretion of the governor and legislature in making difficult fiscal choices. Despite the prosperity of the 1990s, that decade saw a gradual reduction of the state's tax base and a gradually shrinking public sector.

The most dramatic reversal of budgetary fortune came in the biennial budget covering 2003–2005. In just a few short years, the state of Washington went from a budget with a surplus of $1.3 billion to a deficit of $2.5 billion. Certainly, much of the reason for the most severe budget crisis in a generation was the recession intensified by the September 11, 2001, terrorist attacks. But the Washington governor and legislature were also accused of "binge and purge" budgeting: spending and cutting taxes rather than creating reserves during times of surplus, then making draconian cuts when deficits appeared (Postman 2002, A19). Responding to these budgetary challenges was also·made more difficult by the political environment in the state, specifically the close division between Republicans and Democrats. From the late 1990s through the turn of the century, the legislature was either closely divided or tied, often with split party control between one or both houses and the governor.

This chapter examines budgeting and public finance in the state of Washington. We begin by looking at demographic and economic trends in the state.

Next, we examine the budgetary history of the state, particularly the ways in which revenues have been raised and the tradition of restricting state government's taxing capacities. We then consider more closely the numerous voter initiatives of the 1990s and early 2000s that significantly changed overall budget trends in the state. How do Washington's taxing and spending patterns compare to other states? We look at comparative data to put the state's tax system and spending priorities in context. We review the overall political environment of the state in recent years and how it has affected budgeting and look at some of the budget options to close the structural deficit that is projected through the decade. In the conclusion, we consider the difficult challenges facing the state in the coming years caused by voters' contrary desires to have high levels of services while limiting or lowering taxes.

Demographic and Economic Trends in Washington State

Washington is among the faster growing states in terms of population, experiencing annual growth rates of 1.5 percent. Population has doubled since 1960. At current rates, population will exceed 6.5 million by 2010. Both younger and older age cohorts are increasing in the state. Children under 15 currently constitute 22.7 percent of the population while people over 65 compose 11.6 percent of the population. Population trends suggest that demand for public services, particularly education, will grow substantially in the 2000s. Colleges and universities will face increased demand as the number of high school graduates is expected to increase by 50 percent by 2010. As population grew during the 1970s and 1980s, so did state government and services. General fund expenditures increased from $7.9 billion in 1983–85 to $14.9 billion in 1991-93. In 1993, however, voters passed the first of several tax limitations, Initiative 601 (see below). After 1993, biennial increases in spending were smaller both in absolute and percentage terms.

The state of Washington had one of the nation's most robust economies in the 1990s. It was a leader in the dot-com boom and developed a more diversified economy than that of a generation earlier when traditional manufacturing led by Boeing dominated the state's economy. Aerospace employment remains a vital part of the state economy and the decline of jobs in that sector contributed to the economic woes of recent years. In 1998, 110,000 people worked in the aerospace industry in Washington. This was projected to decline to 69,000 by 2005 (Schumacher 2002).

By the 1990s, manufacturing constituted only 13.5 percent of gross state product. Employment also declined in traditional areas such as fishing, agriculture, mining, and forestry, while expanding in services, instruments, and wholesale and retail trade. Washington was home to the corporate headquarters of companies such as Microsoft and Weyerhaeuser. By 2000, Washington had an unemployment rate under 4 percent, one of the lowest in the nation.

This growing economic diversity seemed to provide some hope that the state would not be as vulnerable to a recession and cyclical swings in traditional industries such as airplane manufacturing, agriculture, and forestry as it had in the early 1980s and early 1990s. The events of 2001 proved that to be a false sense of security and the state economy would show it was still vulnerable to boom and bust cycles. Beginning with the decision by Boeing to move its corporate headquarters to Chicago, the year 2001 also saw the continuation of the dot-com collapse. Dozens of high-tech enterprises in the Seattle area went bankrupt. Microsoft shares declined in value significantly, reducing net wealth. By the beginning of 2002, Washington unemployment had jumped to 7.5 percent, second only to neighbor Oregon as the highest in the nation. Figure 1 compares growth in personal income in Washington to that in the rest of the nation. It shows that before 2000 Washington was growing faster, but then dropped more suddenly. These projections show that the state economy will recover more slowly than the rest of the country through 2005.

Figure 1

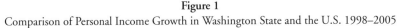

Comparison of Personal Income Growth in Washington State and the U.S. 1998–2005

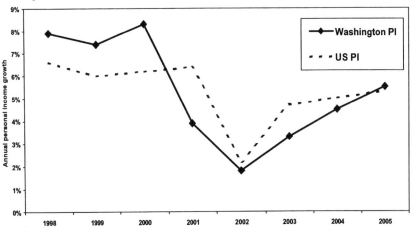

Despite the greater diversification of the state economy, state revenues proved highly responsive to the economic downturn. By fall of 2001, only months after the legislature approved the $22.8 billion budget, the governor's budget office projected a $1.3 billion deficit. By the time the legislature convened to struggle with a supplemental budget in 2002, the gap had grown to $1.6 billion. By the 2003–2005 biennium, the gap had grown to some $2.5 billion. Washington State was not alone in its difficulties. Across the country, the combined state budget deficits were expected to reach $85 billion, as much as 10 to 20 percent of total budgets in some states, the worst financial crisis for states in forty years (Wilgoren 2003).

Budgetary History of Washington

Since its earliest years, Washington State has relied heavily upon property and sales taxes, while avoiding a state income tax. The state originally relied solely upon property taxes until the Great Depression in the early 1930s. The tax burden on property owners increased at a rapid rate at the same time owners faced increasing inability to pay. This resulted in declining state revenues while growing unemployment increased demand for governmental services (Burrows and Taylor 1985). This led to the first formal limitation on taxation in state history, one placed by the legislature itself. Legislators voted to reduce the rate of property taxes and place a ceiling on permissible rates. This eventually became part of the state constitution when it was adopted as Amendment 17 in 1944 (Sanders 1992, 187).

Although this further decreased state revenues from property taxes, at the same time the legislature broadened the tax base by enacting a business activity tax (on the gross receipts of all investments), which functioned as a variable-rate excise tax. The state also turned to borrowing through the issuing of bonds (Sanders 1992, 188). In total, the 1935 legislature enacted 14 new taxes and reinstated two others in the Revenue Act of 1935, six of which remain today: retail sales, public utilities, tobacco, alcohol, business and occupation, and use taxes. Today the state, as well as many cities and counties, relies on sales taxes as its primary source of revenue. Washington's state and local tax collections as a percentage of personal income has remained consistently higher than the national average over the past decade, but appears to be on the decline (Washington State Department of Revenue 2002).

Today, Washington is one of seven states that have no personal income tax. Nonetheless, it remains among the one-third of the highest per capita tax states. Taxation per capita in Washington was $3,148, above the national average of $2,992, and just below California (Washington State Department of Revenue 2002). Without an income tax, Washington has to rely heavily on sales taxes and property taxes. Sales tax alone provides 46 percent of state revenues as compared to a national average of 27 percent (Washington State Department of Revenue 2002). As a result, the state has a relatively regressive tax structure which was coming under increased attack in the early 2000s.

Ballot Box Budgeting: Voter-approved Initiatives

One of the most important elements in budgeting and finance in the state is the importance of voter-approved initiatives on state taxing and spending patterns and the reduced discretion it has given decision-makers. The Washington voters in the last decade have acted as if they were being overtaxed. They have enacted a number of tax limitations and roll-backs, while at the same time mandating additional spending in a number of areas. In at least one instance, the results of one initiative undermined the results of an earlier initiative. Some of the most significant measures are reviewed below.

- *I-601:* Perhaps the most important budget constraint imposed on elected officials by the voters was I-601, enacted in November of 1993. It was a direct reaction to a tax increase of over $1 billion the prior year to cover the budget deficit caused by the 1991–92 recession. The philosophy of the measure was expressed by one of the I-601 steering committee members, Ann Donnelly, in 1993: "During a downturn, savings are inadequate and fast-expanding programs must be reined resulting in a 'purge crisis.'" (Postman 2002, A19) What they proposed was a plan where biennial spending increases would be limited by a formula based on population growth and inflation. Revenues collected above that amount would be placed in a reserve fund. If the reserves grew to 5 percent of the biennial budget, the surplus would go into a special account for school construction. The voters enacted the initiative by a narrow margin. Since 1993, it has had a pronounced effect on the state budget. Before 1993, spending increase percentages were routinely double-digit and jumped as much as 32 percent. After 1993, average increases were about half as large. Figure 2 looks at the percent change in general fund expenditures since 1965–67. With the robust economy of the 1990s, the reserve fund burgeoned. The legislature responded with a number of tax cuts, including repealing many of the business taxes that had led to the initiative in the first place. The legislature in 1994–95 enacted a number of tax breaks to encourage high-tech industries and traditional manufacturing firms.

- *Referendum 47:* In a referendum approved in 1997, voters placed a set of restrictions on the growth of property taxes in the state. The main impact was on counties and local governments.

- *Referendum 49:* A statewide ballot measure was enacted in November 1998 to reduce car tabs (auto license plate renewals) and to divert car tab monies to a number of transportation projects around the state. Washington has an increasing transportation and infrastructure problem. Annual taxes on automobiles had been assessed at 2.2 percent of each car's value, meaning that many taxpayers with newer, more expensive vehicles paid as much as $600–$1,000 yearly. The revenues from car tabs were a major source of support for local governments around the states. Sweetened by the car tab reduction, voters supported increased spending for transportation: $2.4 billion in bonds without new taxes.

- *I-695:* A measure approved by voters in November 1999, I-695 required a rollback of car tab fees in the state to a uniform rate of $30. It also required a vote on any tax or fee increase of any kind by voters in the

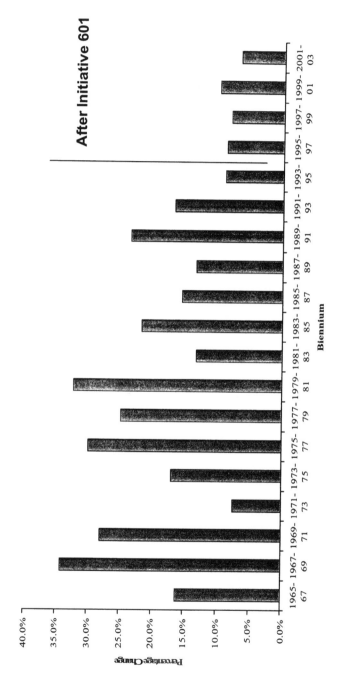

Figure 2
The Decline in Spending Growth after Initiative 601

future. The initiative was led by Tim Eyman, a watch salesman from Mukilteo, Washington, and a charismatic populist. Eyman would go on to author a series of successful ballot initiatives cutting state revenues. I-695 was ultimately ruled unconstitutional by the state Supreme Court because it included two different measures in the same proposition. But hearing the clear message of the voters on car tabs, the legislature, with the support of Governor Gary Locke, approved legislation to implement the $30 fee. I-695 had a dramatic effect on public finances, particularly local government, costing over a billion dollars each year from state and local treasuries when fully implemented. I-695 also had the effect of undoing the vote for Referendum 49 by making it impossible to fund the newly approved transportation projects.

- *I-728 and I-732*: These initiatives, written and proposed primarily by public school teachers and their supporters, mandated that the state dedicate money to reduce class sizes in all schools in the state and that teachers receive guaranteed pay raises every year. Recognizing the growing trend of ballot box budgeting, teachers and school districts decided to capitalize on public support for education and earmark additional resources for themselves. Facing a severe budget crisis in 2003, Governor Gary Locke proposed that these initiatives be suspended, which the legislature can do by majority vote two years after an initiative has taken effect.

- *I-747*: Enacted in November, 2001, this initiative sponsored by Tim Eyman put a new limitation on local property taxes, making sure that they could increase no more than 1 percent per year. The continued popularity of these constraining initiatives with voters was surely demonstrated by I-747. It received 56 percent of the vote despite the fact that it took place six weeks after September 11, 2001, and would potentially hurt police and firefighters! In 2002, Eyman admitted that he had diverted money from his nonprofit organization, Permanent Offense, for personal uses. He was ultimately fined by the state's Attorney General's Office in an out-of-court settlement. This scandal did not seem to reduce the appeal of his initiatives, however, as another passed in the November 2002 election.

- *I-776*: Returning to license tabs, I -776 reiterated that all license tab fees be set at thirty dollars. This would have the effect of repealing voter-approved excise taxes in four counties for high-capacity transportation. Critics questioned the fairness of using a statewide vote to undo what voters had approved for their own counties. Approved with 52 percent of the vote, I-776 eliminated $700 million in public transportation funds in King, Pierce, Snohomish, and Douglas counties. In February 2003, a King County Superior Court judge ruled I-776 unconstitutional because it impermissibly linked two subjects on the same ballot title (Mitchell 2003).

The sum total of these voter-approved referenda and initiatives has had huge consequences for the Washington State budget. Figure 3 shows the amount of revenue lost by these various measures. In 2002, it cost $1.5 billion—approximately the size of the budget deficit. By 2007, the cost will grow to $2.5 billion. When deficits appear, the provisions of I-601 and other initiatives make it difficult for the state to raise revenue in other ways.

Figure 3
Budgetary Consequences of Referenda, Initiatives, and Tax Cuts

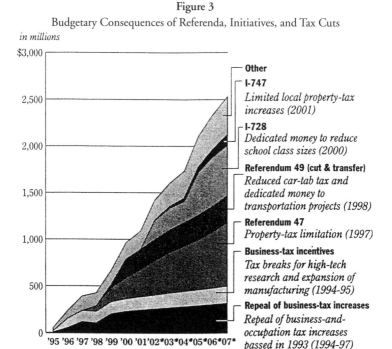

in millions

Other

I-747
Limited local property-tax increases (2001)

I-728
Dedicated money to reduce school class sizes (2000)

Referendum 49 (cut & transfer)
Reduced car-tab tax and dedicated money to transportation projects (1998)

Referendum 47
Property-tax limitation (1997)

Business-tax incentives
Tax breaks for high-tech research and expansion of manufacturing (1994-95)

Repeal of business-tax increases
Repeal of business-and-occupation tax increases passed in 1993 (1994-97)

*Projected figures

An analysis of I-601 by Michael New of the Cato Institute concluded that the Washington tax and spending limitations had succeeded in limiting the growth of state expenditures (New 2001, 12–13). However, despite the significant effect that these restrictions have had on state budgeting, legislators and governors have been able to undermine the effectiveness of I-601 in a number of ways. Democrats in particular believe that the I-601 limits are too low to adequately fund state services (Postman 2002, A19). One tactic was to transfer monies from the general fund to outside accounts not limited by I-601. Monies were shifted to sports facilities and economic development aid without counting against the I-601 limit. In 2001, these transfers allowed the state to spend an additional $300 million (Postman 2002, A19). In 2000, the state legislature—where both parties shared power—enacted legislation to revise the law, allowing the 5 percent reserve requirement to apply to one year of the biennial budget rather than both (Senate Ways and Means Committee 2002a: 17). This allowed $240 billion that was above the reserve requirement to go towards school construction. Finally, in 2002, the legislature passed a bill suspending the part of I-601 that requires a supermajority (two-thirds) to raise taxes or break the spending limit, and required only a simple majority vote instead (Associated Press 2002, B3). This temporary measure extends until June 30, 2003, the end of that biennial budget cycle.

What explains voters' penchant for adopting these various tax cutting and earmarking initiatives? The state's Progressive-era, anti-party traditions and the particular political culture of the state has much to do with it. However, many in Washington were getting increasingly fed up with ballot budgeting. In an effort to mock the initiative process and its main adherent, an initiative was filed with the Secretary of State's Office to officially declare, "Tim Eyman is a horse's ass." Surprised by the initial positive response, the sponsor decided to collect the requisite number of signatures for the November 2003 election, but it was not allowed on the ballot. In the legislature, a joint resolution was introduced to require a supermajority to pass future initiatives that had major budgetary consequences. Any initiative or referendum with a financial impact greater that 25/1000ths of one percent of the state budget (about $5.5 million) would require 60 percent voter approval (Queary 2003). As of press time, the future of this resolution is uncertain, but the passage of this resolution reflects the growing frustration with the initiative process.

State Political Environment for Budgeting

Competitive Political Parties: The state of Washington has one of the most competitive party systems in the country, although in recent years the Democrats have done marginally better in statewide elections. Democrat Gary Locke, the nation's first ethnic Chinese governor, was elected easily to his second term in office in 2000, but declined to try for a third term in 2004. Bill Clinton carried Washington in 1992 and 1996 and Al Gore won the state in 2000, but in each case both national parties considered the state to be "in play." In the 1994 mid-term elections, where Republicans swept to an historic victory in Congress for the first time in forty years, Washington State had more turnover in its congressional delegation than any other state. It went from a delegation overwhelmingly Democratic to one dominated by Republicans. U.S. House Speaker Tom Foley was defeated for reelection, the first time a sitting speaker had been defeated in a century and a half.

Parties are competitive in Washington for a number of reasons. First, political parties are relatively weak. With its Progressive-era tradition, Washington's blanket primary system does not allow the parties to control their own nomination processes. Second, philosophically, the state is somewhat torn between between a sense of social responsibility and a western fiscal conservatism and individualism. Geographically, the state is divided between the more Republican, conservative agricultural areas east of the Cascades and the more liberal, Democratic I-5 corridor west of the mountains. Finally, the state's reformist tradition is revealed in the redistricting process that is used every ten years after the census. A bipartisan commission, with the oversight of the state Supreme Court, draws up what are generally fair and neutral district lines for congressional and state legislative districts. The kind of partisan gerrymandering that occurs in Texas, Michigan, California, or Indiana does not pass muster in Washington State.

Close Divisions in the State Legislature. This competitiveness between the two parties produced a series of remarkable election results in 1998 and 2000. Both years, the state House ended up in a 49–49 tie between Republicans and Democrats. The state Senate, which cannot be tied because it has 49 members, was controlled by the Democrats by a slim 25–24 margin. On an issue like budgeting, where the two parties tend to define themselves to voters, partisanship and conflict run high. Although there are ample examples of bipartisanship and cross-partisan votes, it appears that the nearly equal divisions have increased the tendency for party voting in the legislature.

Since 1988, divided party control has been the norm (see chapter 9—"The Legislature"). This has particularly encumbered the budget process. With the House of Representatives twice tied during Governor Locke's tenure, committees labored under co-chairs, and procedural matters had to be agreed upon by co-speakers. Performance seemed particularly poor in 2001, the third consecutive session with a 49–49 split. The legislature was unable to pass a budget in a timely fashion, could not come up with a compromise on a desperately needed statewide transportation plan, and failed to reform the blanket primary system despite a U.S. Supreme Court decision invalidating a similar plan in California. Governor Locke had to call the legislature back for four extra sessions, running months beyond the prescribed constitutional limit. Finally, a compromise budget was passed, but nothing was done about transportation.

The chance to break the tie came for the Democrats in November 2001 when a vacancy in a Republican-held seat led to a special election. Both parties brought out the big guns to win the election, including money from out of state. On election day, the Democrats prevailed, and along with their slim margin in the Senate, took control of the House 50–48, beginning with the short session that started in January 2002. Unified government did not last long. In November 2002, the Democrats increased their margin in the House but the Republicans recaptured the Senate by 25–24. This meant that the difficult decisions necessary to reconcile the $2.5 billion shortfall for the 2003–2005 biennium would have to be bipartisan.

The State Budget Process

Washington has a biennial budget process, as do a number of American states, with a fiscal year that runs from July 1 until June 30. The state has a fairly standard budget process compared to other states, in terms of the relationship between agencies and departments, the governor and budget office, and the legislature. Like most states, Washington is required to have a balanced budget. However, the state is allowed to borrow for capital projects and in other special instances.

The process begins in the late summer and early fall each even-numbered year, when agencies and department submit their budget requests to the Office of Financial Management (OFM). This office works with the governor to make the decisions on the specific numbers to be included in the governor's budget requests to the legislature. By law, the governor must submit a budget by December. In odd-numbered years, the governor reviews revenue receipts and other budget trends and recommends a supplemental budget to the legislature. The budget consists of a number of funds, but the main components are operating, transportation, and capital budgets. The most important source of revenue is the general fund. Those specific budgets will be looked at in more detail below.

The legislature receives the governor's budget and begins to formulate its own budget when it convenes in January. The legislature considers the biennial budget in odd-numbered years and is required to finish before the start of the fiscal year on July 1. In even-numbered years, the legislature considers a supplemental budget. In a year such as 2002, when the state suffered from a serious economic and budget crisis, the supplemental budget becomes particularly important.

The legislative budget process centers on the House Appropriations Committee and the Senate Ways and Means Committee, although other committees review the transportation portions of the budget. During odd-numbered years, when the legislature meets in a longer session, the objective is to pass the budget by the end of April. In even-numbered years, the legislature meets in short session and has only until the middle of March to pass a supplemental budget to avoid a special session. After both the House and Senate pass their version of the budget, it goes to a conference committee of six members representing both parties. The final budget must be passed in identical form by both legislative houses before it is sent to the governor.

The governor of Washington possesses a line-item veto for budget legislation and uses it often. In vetoing legislation, the governor cannot eliminate any provisions smaller than a section of the law. He can veto all or any part of a money bill but cannot add funding for programs that the legislature has not provided. The legislature can override a line-item veto, as any other veto, with a two-thirds vote of both houses. The governor can reduce the budget without prior legislative approval as long as reductions are made across the board (Book of the States, 1990–91). Figure 4 shows the overall timeline of the budget process in Washington.

Figure 4
Washington State Budget Process

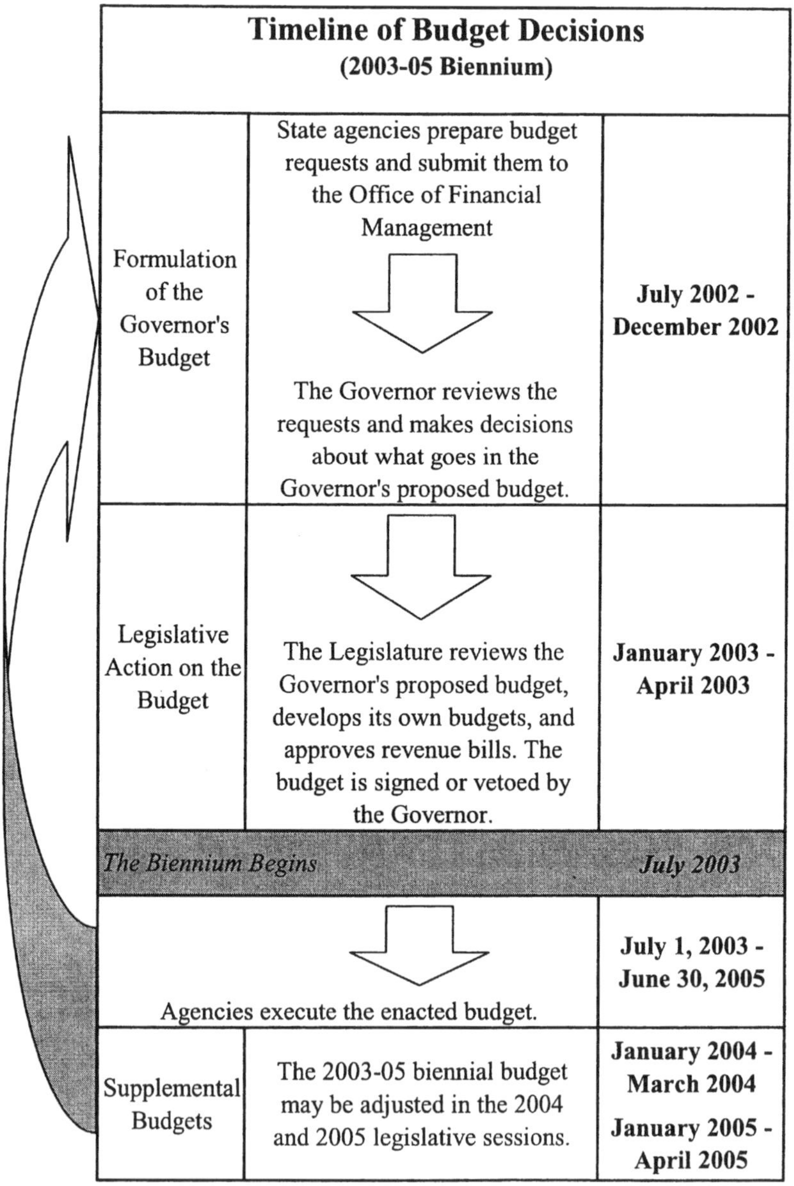

Timeline of Budget Decisions **(2003-05 Biennium)**		
Formulation of the Governor's Budget	State agencies prepare budget requests and submit them to the Office of Financial Management ⬇ The Governor reviews the requests and makes decisions about what goes in the Governor's proposed budget.	**July 2002 - December 2002**
Legislative Action on the Budget	⬇ The Legislature reviews the Governor's proposed budget, develops its own budgets, and approves revenue bills. The budget is signed or vetoed by the Governor.	**January 2003 - April 2003**
The Biennium Begins		*July 2003*
	⬇ Agencies execute the enacted budget.	**July 1, 2003 - June 30, 2005**
Supplemental Budgets	The 2003-05 biennial budget may be adjusted in the 2004 and 2005 legislative sessions.	**January 2004 - March 2004** **January 2005 - April 2005**

Budget Overview and Comparisons

Revenues: In the budget for 2001–2003, the state of Washington spent a total of $49.7 billion. That included an operating budget of $43.4 billion, a transportation budget of $3.8 billion, and a capital budget of $2.5 billion (Senate Ways and Means Committee 2002b). The revenues to support this came 50.3 percent from taxes ($25.1 billion), 25.6 percent from federal grants ($12.8 billion), 15.9 percent from licenses and user fees ($7.9 billion), with the rest from borrowing (4.3 percent) and transfers.

As we have noted, since the early 1990s Washington voters have behaved as if they were overtaxed. How does the tax burden in the Evergreen State compare to other states? Though there is no state income tax, Washington's tax burden was relatively high compared to other states in the mid 1990s. In 1995, Washington ranked eleventh in terms of state and local tax collections per $1,000 of personal income. As the effects of I-601 and subsequent measures kicked in, however, this ranking began to drop sharply. In the latest comparison, 1999, Washington was twentieth among the states in tax burden (Washington Department of Revenue 2002).

Spending: Overall, measured as a percent of the state economy (gross state product), total expenditures in the state have been on a gradual but steady decline since 1993. That year, state spending was 8.0 percent of the economy. In 2001, this had fallen to 7.1 percent of the economy. The largest category of outlays in the state budget (38 percent) is human services, which include a variety of social programs including Medicaid and welfare programs. As shown by Figure 5, this is followed by elementary and secondary education, higher education, government operations, transportation, natural resources and various other costs.

Figure 5
State Spending Priorities

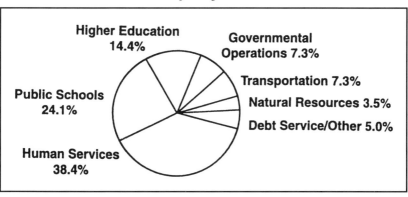

Higher Education 14.4%

Governmental Operations 7.3%

Transportation 7.3%

Natural Resources 3.5%

Debt Service/Other 5.0%

Public Schools 24.1%

Human Services 38.4%

Although state expenditures have increased across the nation steadily, the pattern of spending for major categories in Washington State has remained relatively stable. Expenditures in the area of natural and human resources, as a percentage of the budget, have increased slightly, while percentages for education, transportation, and the cost of general government have declined slightly (Sanders 1992, 181–2). Inflation, aging, population growth, urbanization, increasing prison populations, and the movement from agrarian to a high-tech, industrial economy has caused shifts in demands for governmental services.

Washington's long-held and constitutionally protected priority of providing for public education is clearly reflected in the state's largest budget allocation. However, there has been significant growth in the area of human resources (social services, public assistance, public health services, corrections, and public safety), which has resulted from increased urbanization and crime, as well as an aging population with dramatically rising health care costs (Sanders 1992, 184).

Health care costs compose the fastest growing area of the state budget. Health care costs per person have grown at 2.5 times the average rate of inflation, and caseloads in the state have grown nearly three times more than the growth in state population. Spiraling health care costs are one of the main factors creating the state's structural deficits. The state's health services account is afflicted with declining revenues from taxes, transfers, and the tobacco settlement while, at the same time, with costs that are projected to increase 11.4 percent per year through 2007 (Senate Ways and Means Committee 2002c, 15). The projected deficit in the health services account for 2003–2005 was projected to be over half a billion dollars.

Education for K–12 constitutes nearly a quarter of state spending, or $12 billion dollars. Budgetary growth in this area was in part mandated by voter-passed initiatives 728 and 732, requiring smaller class size and guaranteed teacher raises. Higher education follows, at 14.4 percent of spending, a budget share that has gradually declined throughout the past decade. The state is facing increased demand for higher education enrollments during the next decade: the 18-22 age group is growing at more than twice as fast a rate as the overall state population (Senate Ways and Means Committee 2002c, 11). State universities may not be able to meet this demand at current levels of funding. The presidents of the state's two research universities—the University of Washington and Washington State University—announced that neither institution would accept additional students without increased funding. However, committing more funds to higher education would be extremely difficult because of the expanding gap between spending commitments and revenues.

A Projected Structural Deficit: Budget problems in Washington since 2000 are similar to those in the other 49 states around the country. Medicaid and health care costs are driving up expenditures, and revenues took a dive due to the sluggish economy in the first half of the decade. By 2003, the collective gap between revenues and spending commitments in the states was $80 billion, the worst state fiscal crisis in 40 years. In addition, ending balances of the states fell by almost half between 2001 and 2002. In Washington, state economists forecast a recurring imbalance between spending commitments and revenues—a structural deficit that would grow from $726 million in 2002 to nearly a billion dollars by 2007 (Senate Ways and Means Committee 2002c).

Budget Options for the State of Washington in the Decade of the 2000s

The supplemental budget of 2002, the first to reflect the new budget realities of the decade, provides some clues about the budget options and political constraints on state leaders. One of the most controversial options was the "securitization" of the tobacco settlement, which sells an interest in the state's future payments in the tobacco settlement for cash today.

Tobacco Securitization: One of the most controversial means to bridge the budget gap is to "securitize" a portion of the state's stream of payments from the tobacco settlement. Securitization is a financial transaction where a stream of revenue is sold or assigned to a third party in exchange for a cash payment (Senate Ways and Means Committee 2002b, 9). The 1998 settlement was reached by the nation's largest tobacco companies and the attorneys general of 46 states. Washington's Attorney General, Christine Gregoire, was one of the prime architects of the master settlement (Derthick 2001). The General Accounting Office (GAO) found that a dozen states have already dipped into their tobacco settlement funds to help resolve general fund shortfalls (GAO 2001). Alabama tapped its funds for $30 million for Medicaid. Missouri used $139.2 million to offset its shortfall. Tennessee depleted its tobacco settlement reserve in FY 2001, so all payments have been counted as recurring revenue since FY 2000. Pennsylvania transferred $198.5 million from the Tobacco Fund to supplant general fund dollars used for medical assistance long-term care, and New Jersey securitized its tobacco settlement money to generate more than $1 billion.

In a single year, Washington sacrificed $890 million in future tobacco settlement funds in exchange for $450 million immediately in an attempt to balance the state's budget. Securitization has been lambasted from many quarters around the state. Attorney General Christine Gregoire criticized her fellow Democrats in the legislature and governor's mansion. Critics likened the decision to taking out a mortgage to buy food. The state could realize as little as 25 cents on the dollar to sell their interest in the settlement in the future. The settlement would only last for a few years at the rate utilized in 2002. There were other possible consequences as well. The state treasurer, Democrat Michael Murphy, announced that as a result of the tobacco securitization, Standard & Poor's had placed

Washington on a "credit watch." (Ammons 2002c, A5). The viability of to-bacco securitization as a budget option suffered a blow in 2003 when, in re-sponse to a court ruling against Philip Morris, Washington state's tobacco bonds plunged 13 percent (Fuerbringer 2003, 6). That meant that the state would have to pay higher interest and get less immediate cash.

Spending Reductions. Given the unpopularity of tax increases, significant spending reductions will have to be made to meet the balanced budget require-ment. After large cuts in 2002–2003, future cuts will not just be fat and waste, but rather will have to involve serious program and service elimination. This was the case with the 2003–2005 biennial budget. Governor Locke attempted to eliminate the gap using massive spending cuts without any tax increases. Possible reductions may include aid to cities and counties, not covering in-creases in health care costs for state employees and teachers, limiting or elimi-nating pay increases for state workers and college professors, and suspending I-728 and 732 and possibly other initiatives after two years in order to save money. Higher education may have to cover an increasing share of its costs through tuition, grants, and contributions. Massachusetts' governor, in response to his state's fiscal crisis in 2003, proposed a virtual privatization of the Univer-sity of Massachusetts (Butterfield 2003). In 2002–2003, Washington State Uni-versity and the University of Washington raised tuition by 16 percent, and planned to increase it by 9 percent the following year, significantly shifting the burden for the cost of higher education to students and their parents. More and more cuts may be made among the 50,000 state government employees. Agen-cies may be reorganized and merged. For example, in 2002 the state library was merged with the secretary of state's office and the state archives (Ammons 2002d, A3).

Tapping State Reserves: Half of available state reserves were used to solve the short-fall in the 2001–2003 budget. That left around $420 million in reserve for future years, which makes the utilization of state reserves less and less a viable option for the state.

Revenues: In adopting the supplemental budget to plug the gap in the 2001–2003 budget, revenues were only increased $80 million out of a total package of $1.5 billion. That was in part because, despite the dire fiscal situation, the leg-islature felt compelled politically to reduce estate taxes. The legislature voted to allow the state to join the "Big Game," a multi-state lottery that promised to raise $24 million per year. Unfortunately, as a result, revenues from the state's other lotteries fell, resulting in far less revenue gain overall. Other changes in gambling may still be considered. More aggressive tax collections were assumed to bring in an estimated $50 million, and closing tax loopholes was projected to increase collections by $30 million. The state tax code had exemptions for ev-erything from body parts to bull semen, and all have been fiercely defended by special interests. One likely option to increase future revenues will be to increase user fees. This could entail new and higher fees for the use of state parks, toll bridges, toll lanes on highways, and other charges.

Despite the serious gap between revenues and spending commitments, neither party has really wanted to look seriously at tax increases. For example, in 2002 legislators considered minor revenue enhancements such as a tax on candy and a tax on bar drinks (both rejected). In the end, only $80 million of the $1.6 billion would come from new revenues. The defeat of the 9-cents-per-gallon tax increase for transportation by *62 percent* of the voters in November 2002 showed the difficulty of proposing new taxes to solve budget problems. A few weeks later, despite the huge deficit facing the state in 2003–2005, the Democratic governor, Gary Locke, did not propose any new tax increases (Ammons 2002e, A6). Unless the political climate of the state were to change suddenly, the mix of items in the "budget fixes" is likely to be highly skewed toward spending cuts and gimmicks rather than tax increases. The only body willing to suggest a tax increase was the Washington State Tax Structure Study Committee, headed by Bill Gates Sr., father of Microsoft Chairman Bill Gates (Queary 2002, A1). The Commission suggested variants of a flat rate income tax to reduce the "unduly burdensome" taxes on the poor (Queary 2002).

Conclusion: Hard Budget Choices, Growing Constraints

The budget choices facing the state during the coming decade are among the most critical policy decisions that elected officials will face. Those decisions will shape the economic environment of the state, i.e., whether Washington retains an infrastructure that supports economic and population growth. They will determine what kind of education system emerges and what kind of opportunities for higher education that the state's high school graduates will find. Budget decisions, such as continuing to rely heavily on sales taxes rather than income taxes, will determine whether the tax system changes or not. These choices will take place in a political context of close partisan division in government and a healthy dose of citizen mistrust of elected officials.

Washington is a national leader in "ballot box budgeting," but this may increasingly become a dubious distinction if voter initiatives further limit the discretion of elected officials around the state. It is highly likely that other interest groups, seeing the success of public school teachers, home healthcare workers, firefighters, and police in getting their pay raises and pensions improved through successful initiatives, will try to get their own "piece of the pie" through the initiative process. This is a troublesome prospect in terms of fairness and the capacity of officials to balance various needs and interests around the state. Despite Tim Eyman's financial improprieties and personal punishment, voters in Washington have shown no signs of losing their taste for tax-limiting initiatives. Courts have so far ruled that there are no constitutional ways to stop groups and individuals from "buying" their way onto the ballot using paid signature gatherers. The problem is, of course, that choices become increasingly difficult and limited for elected officials as more funds are earmarked for special interests and more constraints on revenue options are stipulated. This may be part of a larger trend reflecting, in the words of political scientist Alan Rosenthal, "the decline of representative democracy" in the American states (Rosenthal 1998).

Running the state's finances on a daily basis may be the dominion of accountants, but budgeting itself is ultimately a reflection of democratic politics. Looked at over longer cycles, state taxing and spending patterns often take a long time to change. During certain epochs in Washington State's history, voters have supported raising taxes and higher levels of services. This scenario could conceivably return if the infrastructure of the state crumbles and young people and jobs begin to leave the state. For the last decade, however, and for the foreseeable future, the state finds itself in a very different situation—confronting serious fiscal imbalances for many years, but with fewer and fewer options for responsibly bridging the gaps. Unless the national and state economies return to boom times, the budget prospects in the state of Washington will be difficult.

References

Ammons, David. 2002a. "Governor Locke Closes Washington's Final Budget Gap—At Least for Now." *Moscow-Pullman Daily News* (April 6): 3A.

Ammons, David. 2002b. "Lawmakers Hope for On-Time Adjournment." *Spokesman-Review* (March 12): B2.

Ammons, David. 2002c. "Olympia's Chronic Headache: Endless Budget Woes." *Moscow-Pullman Daily News* (March 30): A5.

Ammons, David. 2002d. "Washington Legislature Sends Budget to Locke." *Moscow-Pullman Daily News* (March 14): A3.

Ammons, David. 2002e. "New Democrat Locke Unsheathes Budget Knife." *Moscow-Pullman Daily News* (December 21): A6.

Associated Press. 2002. "Legislature Passes Bill Suspending Initiative 601." *Spokesman-Review* (March 13): B3.

Book of the States (1990-91 edition): volume 28. Lexington, Ky.: Council of State Governments.

Burrows and Taylor. 1985. "Public Finance in Washington." In *Political Life in Washington: Governing the Evergreen State*, ed. T. Swanson, W. Mullen, J. Pierce, and C. Sheldon. Pullman: Washington State University Press.

Butterfield, Fox. 2003. "Romney's Campus Plan Would Cut Deficit, and a Political Foe." *New York Times* (February 27): A24.

Derthick, Martha. 2001. *Up in Smoke*. Washington D.C.: CQ Press.

Fuerbringer, Jonathan. 2003. "For Some, Tobacco Debt May Now Be Worth the Risk." *New York Times* (April 13): section 3, p. 6.

Galloway, Angela, and McGann, Chris. 2002. "Budget Deal a Short-term Fix." *Seattle Post-Intelligencer* (March 15): A1, A10.

General Accounting Office. 2001. Report GAO-01-851. June 29.

Mitchell, Melanthia. 2003. "King County Judge Rules I-776 Unconstitutional," *Moscow-Pullman Daily News* (February 11): 4A.

National Conference of State Legislatures. 2002. "State Budget and Tax Actions Report" (August 28), 6, 8.

National Conference of State Legislatures. 2002. "State Budget Gap Deepens to $58 billion." www.ncls.org (September 25).

New, Michael J. 2001. "Limiting Government Through Direct Democracy." *Policy Analysis* 420. CATO Institute (December 13): 1–17.

Postman, David. 2002. "State Failed to Put Away for Rainy Day Despite I-601." *Seattle Times* (March 3), A1, A19.

Queary, Paul. 2003. "Initiative Limit Proposal Sparks Senate Floor Fight." *Moscow-Pullman Daily News* (February 27): A4.

Queary, Paul. 2002. "Commission Foats Income Tax Idea." *Moscow-Pullman Daily News* (December 12): A1.

Roesler, Richard. 2002. "State Cashes in on Future Tobacco Settlement; Smaller Payment Now Helps Resolve Current Budget Woes." *Spokesman Review* (October 25).

Rosenthal, Alan. 1998. *The Decline of Representative Democracy.* Washington, D.C.: CQ Press.

Sanders, Debra. 1992. "Public Finances of Washington State." In *Government and Politics in the Evergreen State,* ed. D. Nice, J. Pierce, and C. Sheldon. Pullman: Washington State University Press. Pp. 181–198.

Schumacher, David. Sept. 19, 2002. "September Revenue Update." Olympia, Wash.: Senate Ways and Means Committee.

Senate Ways and Means Committee. 2002a. *A Citizen's Guide to the Washington State Budget.* (January): 1–18.

Senate Ways and Means Committee. 2002b. *Senate 2002 Supplemental Budget Summary.* (March): 1–46.

Senate Ways and Means Committee. 2002c. *Washington State 2003-05 Budget Preview.* (September): 1–21.

Washington State Department of Revenue. 2002. www.access.wa.gov.

Wilgoren, Jodi. 2003. "New Governors Discover the Ink Is Turning Redder." *New York Times* (January 14): A20.

Chapter Eleven

Environmental and Natural Resource Policy in Washington State

Edward P. Weber and Tetyana Lysak

I N THE FALL OF 1999 and the Summer of 2000, rural parts of the Pacific Northwest were abuzz with the controversial efforts of agencies to enforce the Federal Endangered Species Act (ESA) for the sake of salmon, steelhead, and suckerfish. The National Marine Fisheries Service (NMFS) in the Methow Valley of Washington State and NMFS, together with the U.S. Bureau of Reclamation in Klamath Falls, Oregon, opted for a confrontational, coercive approach. The agencies shut down irrigation ditches, thereby depriving farmers of water for their crops, and did little to encourage coordination and cooperation. While both efforts may have succeeded in saving at least some fish, they also alienated large numbers of citizens, injected new vigor into efforts calling for the revocation of the ESA, and stirred fear among other rural areas with similar at-risk fish populations (Weber, Lovrich, and Gaffney 2002).

Yet today, such top-down, government-goes-it-alone, coercive approaches to environmental policy are not the dominant storyline in Washington State and elsewhere. In what some have called the "next generation" of environmental policy (Chertow and Esty 1997), the emphasis now is on developing institutional capacity grounded in devolution, collaboration, citizen participation, and area-based (e.g., watersheds) comprehensive, integrated approaches to public problems. The message from policymakers is also changing. Instead of "save the environment at all costs," it is a positive-sum environment and economy message that seeks to save fish *and* traditional economic livelihoods, and build sustainable communities for the future.

This chapter explores the new environmental policy dynamic in Washington State by first developing the general changes in the ways environmental problems are perceived and examining the changing character of problem-solving approaches. The next section addresses the state-federal relationship and establishes Washington's reputation as a national leader in environmental affairs. We then turn to a series of illustrative, and innovative, new policy and enforcement initiatives—the Watershed Planning Act of 1998, the Growth Management Act of 1990, and a cooperative approach to ESA compliance by NMFS and the Washington Department of Fish and Wildlife (WDFW). The examples show how Washington State policymakers are maintaining their leadership in environmental policy.

Reframing and Expanding the Problem Set

During the 1960s and 1970s, environmental policy targeted a fairly simplified and bounded problem set, such as belching smokestacks, large industrial sites (e.g., large factories, power plants, oil refineries), and logging clearcuts that mowed down vast expanses of forest. Characterizing pollution and ecological harm (or benefit) in these ways simplified the task for policymakers because the problems were clearly identifiable (visible), emanated from a more manageable subset of "major" pollution sources, and could be (and were) easily categorized as posing direct harm to human health and nature. At the same time, problems were generally confined to a relative handful of actual pollutants and to those emissions "capturable," hence measurable, in standard industrial pathways, or "point" sources such as pipes and smokestacks (Rabe 1986; Weber 1998).

The decisions of elected officials and regulators further bounded the environmental problem set. Problems were divided into more manageable parts and specific authority over particular problems was given to different bureaucratic units. In pollution control, for example, legislation and agency structure reflected the separation of problems according to media—air, water, or land.[1] The fragmentation, or specialization, extended to the relationship of environmental policy to other policy domains (Davies 1990; Torgerson 1998). Environmental policy tended not to incorporate considerations of economic development, social or community health, or other non-environmental policy domains.

Starting in the late 1980s and 1990s, however, public pressure, advances in science, the relatively comprehensive control of major pollution sources, and the limited effectiveness of earlier policy combined to expand the definition of just what qualified as an environmental problem. The list of pollutants under regulatory control has grown exponentially from a handful to thousands, and the focus on direct harm and visible pollution has expanded to include indirect harm and invisible pollution such a radon gas and chlorofluorocarbons, the compound primarily responsible for the hole in the atmosphere's ozone layer. Indirect harm stems from human activities slowly, but inexorably, and cumulatively exerts negative impacts on human health and on the ecological support systems connected to natural resource health. Yet indirect threats are not as visible as direct harm, are hard to measure except over long periods of time, and often involve individuals (e.g., farmers) whose net impact on the larger problem is negligible. Moreover, indirect harm is "different from violations involving direct threats because [it does not] necessarily involve bad people doing bad things. In fact, …it's often the result of good people doing good things, like building roads and communities or growing food to feed the masses" (Bireley 2001, 3).

As definitions have changed, so too has the propensity to target only point sources and major sources of environmental degradation. Instead, fugitive emissions—those that escape from a pipe—and non-point sources such as farms, ranches, and construction sites occupy attention. Moreover, problems are increasingly characterized and treated as connected to a geographic area—watershed, habitat, ecosystem, coastal zone, community (McGinniss 1995; Kettl 2002).

Adopting a Robust Array of Problem-Solving Mechanisms

The dominant form of environmental policy problem-solving since the 1960s has involved centralized, stringent, and rigid government control that emphasizes an adversarial, coercive approach and incorporates limited public input during implementation (Mazmanian and Kraft 1999b; Beierle and Cayford 2002). The command-and-control approach is one where government uses its authority and expertise to "command" compliance with mandated policy goals and to fill in the details of regulatory programs. Government then "controls" behavior by limiting the discretion of the regulated community regarding the available means for solving problems, and by enforcement actions based largely on punitive sanctions. Success in this model tends to emphasize compliance with the regulatory rules as the proxy equivalent of policy success—a cleaner, healthier, or protected environment—rather than actual environmental results (Weber 2000).

Alternative approaches to environmental problems have begun, however, to supplement and replace command-and-control as policymakers strive to provide a better match between the design of government programs and the changing nature and understanding of public problems (Mazmanian and Kraft 1999b). The alternatives emphasize decentralization, collaboration, flexibility, robust citizen participation, and ongoing (iterative) deliberation. In essence, society is brought back in to work in partnership with bureaucratic experts to determine what the public interest actually is and/or what policy mechanisms work best. The expected benefits include increased trust in government, increased citizen capacity for problem solving and self-governance, new information for making improved policy decisions, more customized and effective "fits" between problems and solutions, and, for some, the prioritization of environmental protection and sustainability at or near the top of the public policy agenda (Beierle and Cayford 2002; Dryzek 1987; Kemmis 1990, 2001; Paehlke 1995; Weber 2000).

Contemporary policymakers are also focusing their efforts on preventing environmental degradation rather than simply reacting to it after the fact. In some cases this means that chemical compounds or mechanical processes are changed in order to eliminate particular forms of pollution. Key examples include the removal of lead from gasoline, changes in paint formulas to remove toxic volatile organic compounds (VOCs), and the adoption of new technologies like zero-emission vehicles (ZEVs).[2] Others are promoting a comprehensive industrial ecology, or life cycle approach to the use and management of raw materials and products.[3]

Expanding the List of Responsible Parties

The changing problem set and the adoption of a robust array of new approaches to problem solving have combined to redefine the list of parties responsible for environmental degradation. The new approaches operate from the premise that "us is them," that all have a role to play in cleaning up. The change in perspective recognizes that individual citizens—as consumers of plastic, cars, wood, computers, ever-larger homes, and a growing array of mechanical gadgets—contribute to pollution and the devastation of natural resources and thus share responsibility. The change also recognizes that policy success requires persuading an ever-expanding universe of actors, many engaged in behaviors that have been codified and legitimated through custom and law, to voluntarily accept the environmental protection mission as their own and to change their behavior accordingly. Correspondingly, emphasis increasingly is placed on partnerships, or what some have termed "coalitions of the unalike" (Snow 1996).

The State-Federal Relationship

Prior to the 1960s, and much like other policy areas, environmental policy was largely a state matter. Yet beginning in the 1960s there was a push for national, centralized control of environmental policy because most state governments lacked the political will to enact laws of their own and were ill-equipped administratively to manage the growing number of problems. Support for the shift in authority was almost universal in the U.S. Congress. Votes in both chambers of Congress on federal laws related to clean water, clean air, endangered species, toxic and solid wastes, and pesticides garnered supermajorities of support with few votes in opposition.

Within only a few years, however, and prompted initially by the election of President Ronald Reagan, a counter-trend, environmental federalism, took hold. Over the last two decades, the success of environmental federalism, although embraced by presidents across the ideological divide and state regulators seeking greater flexibility and discretion in program management, has been a mixed bag. On the one hand, states have been handed greater responsibility, both administratively and financially, and have greatly strengthened their administrative decision-making machinery. In addition, a number of federal agencies are now embracing community-oriented strategies of problem solving. The EPA has established the Community-based Environmental Protection Office, the U.S. Bureau of Land Management (BLM) has created a community-based collaborative planning program, and the National Marine Fisheries Service, for example, is developing a cooperative approach to compliance that engages community resources in voluntary support of ESA goals. On the other hand, there has *not* been a commensurate devolution in decision-making control over either the substance (the "what") or means (the "how") of achieving environmental policy goals.

The response of Washington State to contemporary environmental problems, while fitting the overall pattern in state-federal relations over the past forty years, nonetheless has exhibited an aggressiveness and progressiveness matched by few states. From its initial willingness to create extensive new institutional capacity and to adopt a broad array of programmatic initiatives, to its ongoing political and financial support for environmental policy, the state has earned a reputation as a national leader in environmental affairs. As a result, the state has been much better prepared than most for environmental federalism and the added demands it places on the importance of state capacity (Lester 1994). The evidence supporting the conclusion that Washington state is committed to environmental policy *vis-à-vis* other states shows up in a variety of different areas.

First, there is the Green Index. The Green Index is comprised of 179 indicators that measure "green" conditions state-by-state, and another 77 indicators focused on state-level "green" policies. States are ranked by individual indicators and according to several composite-scoring mechanisms (Hall and Kerr 1994). Table 1 presents the total scores and rankings for twelve Western states according to the three main composite indices—the total Green Index, green conditions, and green policies. Oregon leads all fifty states in the Green Index, while California ranks fourth and Washington places ninth nationally. Key issue areas contributing to Washington's top-ten ranking include a first place for the amount of municipal waste recycled (29% of all waste), a first place for the amount of renewable energy sources as a percentage of all energy consumed (53.5%),[4] and a second place score for the amount of mass transit used in urban areas (Hall and Kerr 1994, 55, 56, 77). Washingtonians also have a decided preference for efficient automobiles compared with other states. The 17.2 miles per gallon average ranks fifth (54). In addition, herbicide usage is comparatively low at 0.4 pounds per acre of cropland (eighth place) as are carbon emissions (209 tons per year per $GSP; eleventh place) (52). Areas of weakness for Washington include the per capita amount of toxics released to surface water (2.9 pounds per person; forty-sixth place out of fifty), the percentage of water systems violating the Safe Drinking Water Act (66.6%; forty-eighth place), and a general lack of investment for sewers throughout the state (forty-seventh place) (35, 36, 38).

Second, few are aware that state governments do the vast majority of environmental protection work. More than 70 percent of federal programs that *can* be delegated have been. States conduct 97 percent of all environmental inspections, 90 percent of enforcement actions, and gather 94 percent of all environmental data. State governments are also responsible for roughly two-thirds of the environmental program funding expended at the state level (Roberts 2001, vi; Brown 2002, 26).

Washington again ranks in the top tier of states in resources expended on environmental programs. As of 1991, on a per capita basis, Washington ranked fifth nationally in state spending to manage hazardous waste and seventh in overall program spending (Hall and Kerr 1994, 76, 148). From 1991 to 1996, however, Washington State lost ground in both the national and regional rankings (see Table 2). While per capita spending on programs increased from $53 to $57 per person, the state dropped from seventh to fifteenth in the national rankings for per capita expenditures, and from eighth all the way to twenty-second in terms of the percentage of total state budget spent on environmental programs.

Table 1

Green Index Scores, 12 Western States

State	FINAL Green Index (256 Indicators) Total score	FINAL Green Index (256 Indicators) NATIONAL RANK	Green Conditions (179 Indicators) Total Score	Green Conditions (179 Indicators) NATIONAL RANK	Green Policies (77 Indicators) Total Score	Green Policies (77 Indicators) NATIONAL RANK
Oregon	4,583	1	3,487	3	1,096	2
California	4,931	4	4,167	19	764	1
Washington	**5,473**	**9**	**3,867**	**13**	**1,606**	**14**
Colorado	4,931	16	3,780	10	2,330	26
Idaho	6,513	19	3,805	11	2,708	36
Montana	6,546	21	4,013	15	2,533	31
Nevada	6,670	22	3,753	9	2,917	43
New Mexico	6,998	28	4,200	20	2,798	38
Utah	7,122	33	4,234	22	2,888	41
Alaska	7,173	34	4,130	18	3,043	47
Arizona	7,342	35	4,540	26	2,802	39
Wyoming	7,445	38	4,521	25	2,924	44

Table 2

Environmental Program Expenditures, 12 Western States

State	1991 $ per Capita	Rank	1991 % of Total State Budget	Rank	1996 $ per Capita	Rank	1996 % of Total State Budget	Rank
Wyoming	272	1	7.73	1	213	2	5.66	1
Montana	87	3	4.29	2	108	3	3.47	5
Alaska	257	2	4.00	4	400	1	4.74	2
Idaho	62	6	4.22	3	91	6	3.51	4
Oregon	68	4	3.03	6	66	13	2.18	15
Washington	**53**	**7**	**2.63**	**8**	**57**	**15**	**1.80**	**22**
California	53	8	2.60	9	83	9	2.69	9
Nevada	34	17	2.57	10	74	10	2.95	6
Utah	30	24	1.80	24	71	12	2.52	12
Colorado	23	34	1.65	24	58	14	2.49	13
New Mexico	30	27	1.48	29	39	33	1.06	42
Arizona	13	45	0.96	43	18	50	0.72	50
National Averages	**30**		**1.90**		**48**		**1.67**	

Source: Hall and Kerr 1994; Council of State Governments 1999.

Third, and perhaps a better method of measuring a state's commitment to environmental quality, is the idea of an environmental need-policy response measure (Davis and Lester 1989). The "need" ranks states by the potential for pollution, or problem severity, on a 10-point scale, with 1 being "highest" need or problem severity, and 10 equaling "lowest" need. The "policy response" measures overall institutional capacity, and is defined as the combination of political, financial, and administrative support. Political support refers to the enactment and strength of over a dozen policies from the adoption of environmental impact analyses, hazardous waste programs, endangered species protection, and surface mining reclamation to comprehensive land-use planning and agricultural preservation. Financial support refers to the amount of money contributed to various environmental programs and administrative support refers to the type of institutional structure and personnel available to administer federal environmental programs (71-72). Using the need-response framework, Davis and Lester (1989) developed a comparative index of all fifty states. Washington state has a "low" pollution potential score of 9 relative to other states, and ranks sixth out of fifty in strength of policy response. When environmental need is combined with policy response, Washington State ranks third nationally (tied with Massachusetts and Maryland), behind only Minnesota (No. 1) and Oregon (No. 2) (78-79). Regionally, Washington comes in second behind Oregon, with Montana and California following in close order, and the other

Table 3

States' Commitment to Environmental Quality, 12 Western States

State	Pollution Potential (Scale of 1-10)	Institutional Capacity Indicators Rank (National)	Need-Response Index Score (Column 1- Column 2)	Need-Response Index (*National* Rank)	Need-Response Index (*Regional* Rank)
Oregon	9	5	4	2	1
Washington	9	6	3	3	2
Montana	9	7	2	6	3
California	2	2	0	9	4
Colorado	9	27	-18	26	5
Alaska	10	33	-23	32	6
Arizona	9	32	-23	32	6
Utah	9	33	-24	35	8
Wyoming	9	33	-24	35	8
Nevada	9	39	-30	41	10
Idaho	10	47	-37	46	11
New Mexico	9	46	-37	46	11

eight western states scoring in the bottom half of the national rankings (see Table 3).

Maintaining Leadership in Environmental Policy

Washington State has maintained its progressive environmental policy reputation in recent years by embracing the changing definition of problems and the alternative approaches that go with them. In this way, the state has continued to expand its institutional capacity, albeit with an important twist. State resources are now increasingly devoted to policies promoting collaboration among stakeholders, additional citizen input and control, and the prevention of future degradation. The new policies also try to manage a multiplicity of environmental problems from an area-based perspective using a comprehensive, integrated approach to information gathering, assessment, planning, and implementation.

The goal is the creation of communities and landscapes capable of maintaining or improving environmental health, while simultaneously sustaining the livelihoods of the state's citizens. Although there are a number of policy examples to choose from, including the Fish and Forests initiative and the Salmon Recovery Act among them, three key policy and enforcement initiatives representative of the larger pattern are covered here.

Organizing for Action According to Biophysical Boundaries: The Watershed Planning Act

In 1998, amid growing concerns about deteriorating anadromous fish runs and conflicts over water quality and use, the legislature passed the Watershed Planning Act (WPA) (RCW 90.82) to more thoroughly integrate policy efforts for streamflow and water use (water resource issues), water quality, and fish habitat issues (primarily salmon and steelhead). The Watershed Planning Act organizes Washington according to 62 water resource inventory areas (WRIA), emphasizes cooperation among citizens, government agencies (federal, state and local), and Indian tribes,[5] and aims "to provide local citizens with the maximum possible input concerning their goals and objectives for water resource management and development" (RCW 90.82.005). Stakeholders and citizens in each WRIA form watershed management planning units that assess environmental problems related to water and habitat, identify and rank policy concerns, develop goals and a comprehensive plan that specifies resource management strategies, identify the various stakeholders' roles and responsibilities, and establish a time frame for implementation. As part of this, the management units are required to prepare a detailed assessment of the watershed's current and future water supply and uses, and recommend long-term strategies for providing minimum, sustainable surface flows for fish and out of stream uses. The management units are also responsible for plan implementation as well as monitoring and evaluating the plan's effectiveness.

State agencies are key players in watershed planning. The law requires that said agencies provide the locally based watershed units with technical assistance, and encourages agencies to coordinate their efforts on watershed planning through use of a Memorandum of Understanding (MOU) so that government can speak with a single voice when it participates in the planning unit meetings. Twelve agencies and commissions, including the Governor's Salmon Recovery Office; the Department of Community, Trade, and Economic Development; the Department of Natural Resources; the Department of Ecology; and the Department of Fish and Wildlife[6] signed the cooperative MOU and have also taken the next step of identifying a lead staffer to represent their agency in these proceedings. The dominant player, however, is the Department of Ecology (DOE). Fully two-thirds, or $7.9 million, of all state technical assistance money has been allocated to DOE. Others taking a prominent role in technical assistance efforts are the Department of Transportation ($940,000), Department of Fish and Wildlife ($840,000), Department of Agriculture ($480,000), and the Department of Natural Resources ($500,000) (Washington Office of Financial Management 2001, hereinafter cited as WOFM 2001; Washington Department of Ecology 1998, hereinafter cited as WDOE 1998).

Funding for technical assistance also has increased over the years, from a low of $1.12 million in the 1998–99 biennium, to $4.64 million in 2000–2001, to almost $5.6 million for 2002–2003. A second area of state funding for WPA involves grants to local planning units. Every WRIA is eligible for these funds according to three different activity areas: (1) initial planning group organization costs (up to $75,000); (2) watershed assessments (up to $200,000); and (3) development of a watershed management plan (up to $250,000). To date, $24.0 million has been allocated, with $11.1 million of that coming in the 2002–2003 biennium (WOFM 2001).

The three phases of funded activities—planning group organization, watershed assessments, and plan development—when combined with a measure of planning scope provide a rough calculus for assessing individual WRIA progress toward WPA goals. Planning scope references the degree to which a planning effort goes beyond the required water quantity component of the law to address the three optional objectives—water quality, instream flows, habitat. In Table 4, all 62 WRIAs are categorized according to where they are in the process and with respect to "beyond compliance" planning. "Star" status is accorded to those watersheds that are clearly committed and making rapid implementation progress. They have advanced to Phase 3 and are mounting comprehensive planning efforts covering all three optional goals. Progressives are engaged in both Phase 2 and Phase 3 activities, and are covering all three goals. A "Good Faith Effort" ranking is awarded to watersheds that are either at Phase 2 and addressing all three goals, or working in both Phase 2 and 3, but only planning for two of the three goals. "Strugglers" are those where the commitment beyond the primary water quantity goal is limited. They have made definite progress in planning, either having completed Phase 1 for all three goals; Phase 2, but for only two goals; or having advanced beyond Phase 2, yet only for a single goal. "Laggards" are those areas that, even after four years, have barely begun to organize, much less assess watershed problems or plan for other than the required water quantity component of the law.

The variance in the responses to the Watershed Planning Act is more than just a measure of commitment to its process and goals; it is also a product of a series of problems encountered in implementing the law. A basic concern is that more money is needed, especially for assessment. Some WRIAs have expressed concern that unless more money is forthcoming, the water quantity and quality assessments will be of a general nature, hence of limited value, and only focused on certain parts of the larger WRIA, rather than a systematic, comprehensive

Table 4

WRIA Progress toward WPA Goals, 2001

Status	WRIA
STARS (total of 3)	37 Lower Yakima; 38 Naches; 39 Upper Yakima
PROGRESSIVES (total of 10)	01 Nooksack; 13 Deschutes; 17 Quilcene-Snow; 18 Elwha-Dungeness; 25 Grays-Elokoman; 26 Cowlitz; 27 Lewis; 28 Salmon-Washougal; 59 Colville; 62 Pend Oreille
GOOD FAITH PLANNERS (total of 18)	02 San Juan; 11 Nisqually; 12 Chambers-Clover; 15 Kitsap; 19 Lyre-Hoko; 20 Soleduck-Hoh; 22 Lower Chehalis; 23 Upper Chehalis; 29 Wind-White Salmon; 32 Walla-Walla; 44 Moses Coulee; 50 Foster Creek; 45 Wenatchee; 46 Entiat; 48 Methow; 55 Little Spokane; 56 Hangman; 57 Middle Spokane
STRUGGLERS (total of 4)	03 Lower Skagit-Samish; 04 Upper Skagit; 06 Island; 30 Klickitat
LAGGARDS (total of 27)	5 Stillaguamish; 07 Snohomish; 8 Cedar/Sammamish; 9 Duwamish/Green; 10 Puyallup/White; 14 Kennedy Goldsborough; 16 Skokomish-Dosewallip; 31 Rock Glade; 33 Lower Snake; 34 Palouse; 35 Middle Snake; 36 Esquatzel/Coulee; 40 Alkaki/Squilchuck; 41 Lower Crab; 42 Grand Coulee; 43 Upper Crab/Wilson; 47 Chelan; 49 Okanogan; 50 Foster; 51 Nespelem; 52 Sanpoi; 53 Lower Lake Roosevelt; 54 Lower Spokane; 58 Middle Lake Roosevelt; 60 Kettle; 61 Upper Lake Roosevelt

Source: Washington Office of Financial Management. Watershed Planning Report, 2001.

review. In some areas, tribes have been reluctant to participate for fear that doing so will infringe on their sovereignty to manage their own lands and resources as they see fit. Others have reported there is little state guidance and much confusion associated with efforts to integrate watershed planning with the requirements of other state laws, including growth management planning, salmon recovery, and water system planning, among others (WOFM 2001; WDOE 1999).

Further, limitations in the Watershed Planning Act circumscribe its potential to foster the institutional change likely to be necessary for the achievement of long-term policy success. For example, the plan cannot affect or interfere with ongoing negotiations over water rights, the planning groups cannot change existing local ordinances or existing state rules or permits, and the plan is subsidiary to forest practices rules related to water quality under the Forest Practices Act (RCW 76.09) and cannot create obligations or restrictions on forest practices (RCW 90.82.120).

Despite these problems and weaknesses in the law, and as the progress report in Table 4 duly notes, many WRIAs are overcoming these obstacles and making significant *planning* progress just as the law intended. Whether the progress continues into the plan *implementation* phase is another question and one that cannot be answered here since the first completed plans are due in Fall 2003. In addition, the process of assessment and planning is generating valuable new information that, by itself, is helping to identify gaps in existing regulatory programs, increase the public's awareness of their watersheds, and facilitate and support habitat protection and restoration efforts more generally. The success has been such that Governor Gary Locke went out of his way to recognize the Whatcom Watershed program in the "progressive" Nooksack WRIA with the state's Service and Quality Improvement Award for the year 2000. Locke described the watershed program as "a model of excellence. It shows what can be accomplished in our communities when citizens, businesses and government work together to solve problems" (WDOE 2000).

Smart Growth, Targeted Growth: The 1990 Growth Management Act

The uncoordinated and unplanned growth of economic development and human settlement patterns became a high priority policy issue for Washington State after three decades of 20 percent population increases (per decade). According to the legislature, such growth, which is expected to double over the next fifty years, posed a threat to environmental quality, sustainable economic development, and the quality of life. In response, the state passed the controversial—some argued unconstitutional—Growth Management Act (GMA) in 1990. At the time, Oregon, Florida, Maryland, and New Jersey were the only other states with similar laws (Washington Office of Financial Management 2002, hereinafter cited as WOFM 2002).

The GMA is designed to encourage wise land use and planning, to retain and enhance open space and recreational opportunities, and to address a myriad of associated public problems such as environmental problems, traffic congestion, the loss of farmland and forests, and urban sprawl. The law also recognizes that growth management efforts will likely increase housing costs and so includes language "[e]ncourag[ing] the availability of affordable housing." In addition, the GMA explicitly recognizes the inviolability of private property rights by stating that such property "shall not be taken for public use without just compensation" (RCW 36.70. A.020; see Table 5).

Table 5

Planning Goals of the 1990 Growth Management Act

(1) *Urban growth.* Encourage development in urban areas where adequate public facilities and services exist or can be provided in an efficient manner.

(2) *Reduce sprawl.* Reduce the inappropriate conversion of undeveloped land into sprawling, low-density development.

(3) *Transportation.* Encourage efficient multimodal transportation systems that are based on regional priorities and coordinated with county and city comprehensive plans.

(4) *Housing.* Encourage the availability of affordable housing to all economic segments of the population of this state, promote a variety of residential densities and housing types, and encourage preservation of existing housing stock.

(5) *Economic development.* Encourage economic development throughout the state that is consistent with adopted comprehensive plans, promote economic opportunity for all citizens of this state, especially for unemployed and for disadvantaged persons, promote the retention and expansion of existing businesses and recruitment of new businesses, recognize regional differences impacting economic development opportunities, and encourage growth in areas experiencing insufficient economic growth, all within the capacities of the state's natural resources, public services, and public facilities.

(6) *Property rights.* Private property shall not be taken for public use without just compensation having been made. The property rights of landowners shall be protected from arbitrary and discriminatory actions.

(7) *Permits.* Applications for both state and local government permits should be processed in a timely and fair manner to ensure predictability.

(8) *Natural resource industries.* Maintain and enhance natural resource-based industries, including productive timber, agricultural, and fisheries industries. Encourage the conservation of productive forestlands and productive agricultural lands, and discourage incompatible uses.

(9) *Open space and recreation.* Retain open space, enhance recreational opportunities, conserve fish and wildlife habitat, increase access to natural resource lands and water, and develop parks and recreation facilities.

(10) *Environment.* Protect the environment and enhance the state's high quality of life, including air and water quality, and the availability of water.

(11) *Citizen participation and coordination.* Encourage the involvement of citizens in the planning process and ensure coordination between communities and jurisdictions to reconcile conflicts.

(12) *Public facilities and services.* Ensure that those public facilities and services necessary to support development shall be adequate to serve the development at the time the development is available for occupancy and use without decreasing current service levels below locally established minimum standards.

(13) *Historic preservation.* Identify and encourage the preservation of lands, sites, and structures that have historical or archaeological significance.

Source: RCW 36.70A.020

The Growth Management Act requires 29 counties and 215 cities to develop and adopt comprehensive plans that accord with *all* 13 statutory goals. The remaining ten counties and 62 cities are subject to partial GMA planning requirements (Washington Office of Community Development 2002, 5-7, hereinafter cited as WOCD 2002). Planning groups must identify and protect critical areas and resource lands,[7] identify urban growth areas where high density growth will occur, inventory public facilities and services (e.g., transportation), work within 20-year growth and land use/development projections provided by the state Office of Financial Management (OFM),[8] and develop regulations that carry out local GMA plans. Planning efforts must provide for public participation so that citizens can help to establish priorities and provide policy recommendations that reflect their values and aspirations for their particular area. In addition, the GMA requires coordination with neighboring jurisdictions, and local governments must reassess their plans every ten years, with the exception being six high-growth counties—Clark, King, Kitsap, Pierce, Snohomish, and Thurston. Amendments to the GMA in 1997 require the high-growth counties to prepare a "buildable lands analysis *every five years* that determines whether [they] are achieving their planned densities, if sufficient buildable lands are available to meet [new] population projections, and whether [new] measures need to be taken to accommodate the project growth" (1000 Friends of Washington 2002, 4). If all goes according to plan, "citizens and elected officials will work together, along with neighboring local governments and state agencies, to prepare a shared vision for the future, plan together for that future, and then work together to make that plan a reality" (1000 Friends of Washington 2002, 1).

As with the Watershed Planning Act, state agencies primarily play an assistance role—offering technical and financial help to local governments. And although local GMA planning units must submit plans and regulations to the Washington Department of Community, Trade, and Economic Development, the agency does not have the authority to accept or reject such plans. Plans are presumed valid upon adoption, or unless and until one of the three regional growth management hearings boards—Central Puget Sound,[9] Eastern Washington,[10] and Western Washington[11]—decides that they are not in compliance with the GMA. Each regional hearings board meets regularly and has three members that are appointed by the governor. Board members must be residents of the region over which their board has jurisdiction (Washington Department of Community, Trade, and Economic Development 1997, hereinafter cited as WDCTED 1997).

Table 6 details the implementation progress to date for "fully planning" counties and cities under the 1990 Growth Management Act. Large supermajorities of both cities and counties have developed comprehensive growth

Table 6

GMA Planning Progress Report, "Fully Planning"
Counties and Cities only, 2001

	Counties	Cities
Comprehensive Growth Management Plan (GMP) in Place	25 of 29	210 of 215
Development Regulations in Place that are Consistent with Comprehensive GMP	21 of 29	191 of 215
In Full Compliance with GMA	10 of 29	186 of 215

management plans and a corresponding set of regulations, yet only about 35 percent of the counties are in full compliance (full compliance is defined as having adopted a comprehensive plan with matching regulations, and having no outstanding Hearing Board noncompliance orders). In addition, all 39 of the state's counties and 258 of its 277 cities have met the GMA requirement to designate and protect critical areas (e.g., wetlands, wildlife habitat, etc.), while 35 of 39 counties have designated resource lands—agricultural and forest—as required (WOCD 2002, 6). Finally, the three regional hearings boards have been petitioned to resolve hundreds of disputes in the local GMA planning processes and decisions. As of 1996, the hearing boards had received 396 petitions challenging 181 plans and/or regulations. Fully 70 percent of board decisions upheld local government actions, with roughly half dismissed outright and the other half finding local governments in compliance with state law. Of the remaining decisions, 80 percent found noncompliance and remanded the case back to the local government with an order to correct the plan, while only 20 percent of the noncompliance decisions, or 6 percent of the total, went so far as to find local decisions invalid (WDCTED 1997, 35-36).

Despite the signs of progress, a number of concerns have been raised over the years suggesting that the promise of the law is not being met. Judith Runstad, appointed by Governor Locke as one of the co-chairs of the Washington Competitiveness Council, was one of the more forceful critics. She argued "[t]hat the core of the urban Growth Management Act assumed…that there would be rewards to the cities that planned and met their goals under the Growth Management Act. And…it assumed that there would be permit streamlining, which would allow development to occur in those denser urban cores." Runstad concludes: "The fact of the matter is that not one of [the] premises upon which growth management is based has been met, and this is a serious and ongoing issue" (Washington Research Council 2001, hereinafter cited as WRC 2001).

Others point to the internal inconsistency of a law that enshrines the politics of compromise within the 13 goals by "embracing property rights and economic development while mandating efforts to curb sprawl and protect the environment, ...provid[ing] no...guidance on priorities and tradeoffs, and... enshrin[ing] the aspirations of opposing interest groups without taking sides" (WRC 2001, 1). At the same time, comprehensive growth management has met with stiff citizen and taxpayer resistance in a number of areas. The push for higher urban densities comes into conflict with the preference of many citizens to live in places that limit compact development and multi-unit housing—just the opposite of GMA goals. Nor have Washington voters supported the necessary investments in transportation infrastructure that most agree is needed to support GMA success. Voters repealed the Motor Vehicle Excise Tax in 1999 and rejected by a wide margin the multi-billion dollar transportation-based gas tax initiative in 2002. Moreover, in the same year that the legislature passed the GMA, voters, by a margin of nearly three to one, rejected an initiative *upon which much of the GMA was based* (WRC 2001).

Finally, even champions of the GMA recognize its shortcomings, especially the seeming unwillingness of the state to follow through by funding and taking the kinds of actions required to make such a comprehensive, integrated effort successful. In a 1999 review of the law, 1000 Friends of Washington (1999, 3) wrote:

> It is difficult to conduct an accurate assessment of the State's achievements under growth management because the State has not established and monitored key benchmarks. The state does not collect pertinent data related to urban growth boundaries, farm and forest land loss, wetland loss, and other key indicators.

Saving Fish in the Walla Walla Watershed Using Cooperative Compliance

By the 1980s, the Pacific Northwest and virtually all of the Columbia River drainage had a full-fledged anadromous (ocean-going) fisheries crisis on its hands (Johnson et al. 1997; Nehlsen et al. 1991). The combination of dozens of dams which have obliterated 55 percent of spawning habitat and created a myriad of other problems affecting fish survivability, commercial fishing operations, gillnetting by Native Americans, predator-prey issues involving arctic sea terns and sea lions, additional silt loads from logging operations, and chemical pollution from industrial and farming operations have led to dramatic declines in salmon and steelhead stocks. A major federal initiative, the Pacific Northwest

Power Act of 1980, although designed to help stem the decline by, among other things, elevating the protection of fish as a policy value to a par with hydroelectricity production and irrigation, had limited effect (McGinnis 1995). By the late 1990s, the problem had worsened to the point where fifteen different runs of salmon and steelhead throughout the Columbia River Basin were listed as either threatened or endangered under the federal ESA. In response, Washington State has crafted a series of initiatives, including the 1998 Salmon Recovery Act and a new Salmon Recovery Board, chaired by ex-U.S. EPA Administrator William Ruckleshaus, that is charged with reviewing and funding proposals designed to promote fish survivability.

A lead agency in the battle to save salmon and steelhead, the Washington Department of Fish and Wildlife (WDFW), has partnered with the lead federal agency responsible for protecting endangered anadromous fish runs, the National Marine Fisheries Service (NMFS). These two agencies are experimenting with an innovative new enforcement approach in the Walla Walla watershed located in southeast Washington State. The new approach starts from the premise that success in saving fish requires prevention of harm and massive coordination and cooperation across traditional political and agency jurisdictions, and among a broad spectrum of stakeholders. Those involved in the Walla Walla effort include administrators and elected officials from all three levels of government, local and state environmentalists, agricultural interests (e.g., Farm Bureau; local irrigation districts), small businesses, the local community college, and the individual farmers and water users most directly affected by the program.[12]

The two agencies forged a plan—cooperative compliance—that encouraged voluntary action first, followed by a series of steps to notify and eventually prosecute holdouts. They selected Captain Mike Bireley of the WDFW's Environmental Protection Division to lead implementation efforts. The cooperative compliance plan focused on a state requirement for fish screens, a law on the books for seventy years that had never been enforced, especially for small surface-water diverters using electric pumps (as opposed to gravity-flow diversions). A properly sized and designed fish screen allows withdrawal of the legally certified amount of water, while preventing juvenile fish from getting sucked into irrigation pipes or otherwise harmed. The end result of seventy years of neglect was a "screening" compliance rate of zero for pump diversions (90% of all diversions) in the Walla Walla watershed (this is typical for rural areas of Washington). Yet the lack of a properly designed screen constituted a violation, or "take" under the ESA.

In the Walla Walla case, Captain Bireley had a plan—cooperative compliance—but no program of implementation. How was he to accomplish cooperation among so many people given that his agency's traditional modus operandi, and his own training, was adversarial—writing tickets, handing out fines, and taking people to court once they had been caught breaking the law? And how was he to approach the delicate task of convincing farmers to change century-old water diversion practices all for the sake of saving fish? After all, Mark Twain's wry observation still held true in the American West, that "whiskey is for drinking, and water is for fighting."

In 2000, Bireley started his cooperative efforts by holding open public forums to educate and cajole farmers into joining the fish screen program. The WDFW agreed to pay 85 percent of the cost in exchange for an assessment and adjudication of the diverter's water right (needed in order to size the screen). Amnesty also was offered to those willing to stick their necks out and admit they were breaking the law, and cooperative farmers were given signs identifying their property as a Fish Friendly Farm. Despite the incentives and the promise of amnesty, Bireley encountered stiff resistance fueled by widespread anger, apprehension, and fear—and only a handful of takers (interviews 2001; 2002). "People weren't sure if they could trust me, much less the WDFW to follow through on our word. Was the screening program just a Trojan Horse to identify violators, arrest people, and take control of water and property for environmental purposes?... Was WDFW going to hurt or help the community with this information" (interviews 2001; 2002)?

Captain Bireley took the challenge in stride. Within eighteen months he built bridges among former adversaries and across political and administrative divides, while helping to energize the broader community of stakeholders as active partners in saving fish. Bireley developed relationships with and engendered support from key leaders, and persuaded the main local paper, the *Walla Walla Union-Bulletin*, to provide a series of positive front-page stories and editorial support for the Cooperative Compliance program. He forged a critical partnership with Walla Walla Community College. Professors and students, instead of regulators, took responsibility for gaining access to farmer's properties for the purpose of assessing compliance and proper sizing of fish screens. When it became clear that the private sector had not developed screens of the type needed, and that WDFW's own screen shop was experiencing a severe backlog and budget cuts, Bireley jumpstarted the screen development process by engaging the private sector in a screen design competition. Further, Captain Bireley convinced a leading state-level environmental advocate, Rob Caldwell, the Executive Director of the Center on Law and Environmental Policy, that cooperation was the best way to go. Caldwell then used his influence to persuade state and national environmental groups to forego litigation and let the collaborative dynamic play out. In addition, Bireley engendered respect from the local community by tenaciously identifying and successfully pursuing, along with others, millions of dollars in program funds from the legislature and sources outside WDFW. Finally, he tirelessly promoted what became known as the "Walla Walla way" in public venues around the Northwest during 2001 and

2002. In these efforts, Bireley repeatedly transcended traditional organizational and jurisdictional boundaries, and persuaded organizations and people to commit energy and resources to the prevention-oriented resource protection mission (Khademian and Weber 2002; Weber, Lovrich, and Gaffney 2003).

To date, the WDFW cooperative screening program has signed up 300 landowners responsible for 450 diversions—60 percent of Walla Walla diversions. Moreover, 90 percent of these diversions are located on stretches of stream classified as the most ecologically important for saving fish (Priority 1 and 2 designations), so the "benefit is immediate" (interview 2002). The result of the cooperative approach, according to a senior NMFS official, is that

> unlike other ESA programs, we are on the ground, and we're saving fish now [2001], not five or ten years from now after the legal battles have been fought or after a more perfect, more comprehensive plan has been designed (interview 2001).

Conclusion

Over the past fifteen years Washington State has adopted a number of innovative new programs for solving environmental problems. The new policy approaches recognize the changing character of environmental problems, the need to approach such problems from an area-based, holistic perspective, and the value of involving more citizens in problem-solving efforts. Yet no one believes these approaches are panaceas applicable in all situations or as wholesale replacements for top-down approaches. Nor are these new approaches likely to be problem-free in their application. In fact, many consider the wide variance in implementation progress (i.e., too many laggards) for the Watershed Planning Act and the Growth Management Act as evidence of laws that are not working and that need either more incentives or more of the traditional regulatory hammer to speed up implementation. But is the variance failure? Or is it a reflection that in a state with widely varied ecological conditions some areas need a particular law more than others? At this juncture, we lack the information required to determine which interpretation is correct.

The experiences with the new approaches also raise questions that suggest much more time and effort is needed before we can determine just where these new approaches will prove most effective. For example, will all communities respond to collaboration in the same positive manner as Walla Walla residents, or is there something socially, economically, or politically special about the area? Do state and federal agencies have enough field-level employees capable of successfully managing the social relationships required in cases where society is brought back in to help manage public problems? Given the voluntary character of these cooperative arrangements, policy success ultimately involves a willingness on the part of those with established power and rights (e.g., property) to share power with others in the community. How many communities are there where the existing power elites are so ready to share power in such a fashion?

Further, the success of direct democracy in Washington via voter-sponsored ballot initiatives is posing serious challenges to the state's ability to implement effectively the legislatively sponsored collaborative, participative, and area-based problem-solving approaches. In the most obvious example, the passage of numerous initiatives that reduce the revenue-raising capacity of state government directly harm the ability of regulators to implement the new programs. As was clear with the Walla Walla example of cooperation for the sake of endangered fish, these new programs may prove to be more effective at protecting the environment, but they are likely to be just as costly as the old programs, at least in the short term. Moreover, voter initiatives typically approach policy dilemmas as if they are discrete problems unconnected to the whole, or a broader panoply of policy issues. Yet this is just the opposite of what is demanded by the more comprehensive and interconnected approach to policy that most agree is necessary if policy problems are to be addressed effectively over the long term.

Seen from another perspective, however, the legislature's success in crafting these new approaches to environmental policy may serve as a vehicle for defusing the ongoing tension between direct and representative democracy. The additional opportunities to participate in the policy process and shape outcomes may convince growing numbers of voters to view their elected representatives as more responsive to their needs and therefore less in need of the correctives provided by the initiative process.

In any case, the new approaches to environmental problem-solving, while having made significant headway in recent years, still play second fiddle most of the time to top-down approaches. This is due to the accretion of such policies over an almost 40-year period and to the support afforded the top-down strategy from many senior agency officials who earned their reputations as zealous enforcers of the approach in the environmental policy wars of the 1960s–1980s and who are less familiar than their younger colleagues with the new alternatives. It is also due to the fact that top-down tactics are still preferred by the vast majority of organized environmental groups. Even under the best of circumstances, therefore, the institutionalization of top-down policies ensures that the "next generation" of environmental policy is unlikely to tilt the policy balance in its favor for another decade or more.

Endnotes

1. At the federal level, the 1970 Clean Air Act, the 1973 Clean Water Act, and the 1976 Toxic Substances Control Act were managed by separate parts of the U.S. EPA—the Air Office, the Water Office, and the Solid Waste Office, respectively.

2. It is important to keep in mind that while the ZEVs are technically emission free, the batteries used to power such vehicles draw their power from polluting sources (i.e., coal burning power plants) and end up as toxic waste later on.
3. Chertow and Esty (1997). The life-cycle approach identifies the network of suppliers, materials, and mechanical processes (e.g., factory-based assembly line, transportation/ shipping system) required to produce and market a particular item. This integrated database is then used to manage, minimize, and, whenever possible, eliminate the flow of pollutants during the life cycle of the product.
4. A summary score for renewable energy use shows that Washington ranks 7th nationally. A caveat is in order here; many will object to the high score, given that in Washington State most renewable energy is provided by hydroelectric dams—the same dams that decimate ocean-going fish runs.
5. Whenever there are tribal lands within a WRA, tribes must be invited to participate.
6. Others include the Department of Agriculture, the Conservation Commission, the Department of Health, the Department of Natural Resources, the Department of Transportation, the Interagency Committee for Outdoor Recreation, the Puget Sound Water Quality Action Team, and the State Parks and Recreation Commission.
7. Examples include wetlands, habitat critical to fish and wildlife, frequently flooded areas, geologically hazardous areas, and areas with a critical recharging effect on aquifers used for potable water.
8. The Office of Financial Management produces a high, intermediate, and low population projection for each county. Counties must then adopt a projection for planning purposes that lies between the high and low projections.
9. King, Snohomish, Pierce, and Kitsap counties.
10. Includes all counties and cities east of the crest of the Cascade Mountins.
11. Includes all counties and cities west of the crest of the Cascade Mountains other than those included under the jurisdiction of the Central Puget Sound hearing board.
12. Weber, Lovrich, and Gaffney (2003). The watershed also encompassed parts of Oregon, but the cooperative compliance effort only focused on the Washington side of the border.

References

Beierle, Thomas C., and Jerry Cayford. 2002. *Democracy in Practice: Public Participation in Environmental Decisions*. Washington, D.C.: Resources for the Future Press.
Bireley, Michael. 2001. "Environmental Enforcement: Is That Our Role?" Speech to Washington Association of Game Wardens (October 15).
Brown, R. Steven. 2002. "States Put Their Money Where Their Environment Is: State Environmental Spending." Washington, D.C.: Environmental Council of States.
Chertow, Marian R., and Daniel C. Esty. 1997. *Thinking Ecologically: The Next Generation of Environmental Policy.* New Haven, Conn.: Yale University Press.
Council of State Governments. 1999. *Resource Guide to State Environmental Management*, 5th ed. Lexington, Ky.: Council of State Governments.
Davies, J. Clarence 1990. The United States: Experiment and Fragmentation. In *Integrated Pollution Control in Europe and North America,* ed. Nigel Haigh and Frances Irwin. Washington, D.C.: Conservation Foundation, 51-66.

Davis, Charles E., and James P. Lester. 1989. "Federalism and Environmental Policy." In *Environmental Politics and Policy: Theories and Evidence,* ed. J. P. Lester. Durham, N.C.: Duke University Press, 57–85.

Dryzek, John S. 1987. *Rational Ecology: Environment and Political Economy.* New York: Basil Blackwell.

Growth Management Act. RCW 36.70. (1990). Washington State legislature.

Hall, Bob, and Mary Lee Kerr. 1994. *1991–1992 Green Index: A State-By-State Guide to the Nation's Environmental Health.* Washington, D.C.: Island Press.

Johnson, Thom H., Richard Lincoln, Gary R. Graves, and Robert G. Gibbons. 1997. "Status of Wild Salmon and Steelhead Stocks in Washington State." In *Pacific Salmon and Their Ecosystems: Status and Future Options,* ed. S. Deanna, P. Bisson, and R. Naiman. New York: Chapman and Hall, 127–144.

Kemmis, Daniel. 1990. *Community and the Politics of Place.* Norman: University of Oklahoma Press.

Kemmis, Daniel. 2001. *This Sovereign Land: A New Vision for Governing the West.* Washington, D.C.: Island Press.

Kettl, Donald F. 2002. *The Transformation of Governance: Public Administration for Twenty-first Century America.* Baltimore: Johns Hopkins University Press.

Khademian, Anne M., and Edward P. Weber. 2002. "Throwing Out the Book: Building Collaborative Capacity to Tackle Paralyzing Public Problems." Paper presented to the Association for Public Policy Analysis and Management, Dallas, Texas (November 7–9).

Lester, James P. 1994. "A New Federalism? Environmental Policy in the States." In *Environmental Policy in the 1990s,* 2nd edition, ed. N. J. Vig and M. E. Kraft. Washington, D.C.: CQ Press, 51–68.

1000 Friends of Washington. 1999. "Get Smart Washington: Managing Growth in the New Millennium." Online at www.1000friends.org; Retrieved on October 15, 2002. Seattle, Wash.

1000 Friends of Washington. 2002. "Washington's Growth Management Act." Online at www.1000friends.org/smart_growth/gma.cfm; Retrieved on October 22, 2002. Seattle, Wash.

Mazmanian, Daniel A., and Michael E. Kraft, eds. 1999a. *Toward Sustainable Communities: Transition and Transformations in Environmental Policy.* Cambridge, Mass.: MIT Press.

Mazmanian, Daniel A., and Michael E. Kraft. 1999b. "The Three Epochs of the Environmental Movement." In *Toward Sustainable Communities: Transition and Transformations in Environmental Policy,* ed. D. A. Mazmanian and M. E. Kraft. Cambridge, Mass.: MIT Press, 3-42.

McGinniss, Michael V. 1995. "On the Verge of Collapse: The Columbia River System, Wild Salmon, and the Northwest Power Planning Council." *Natural Resources Journal* 35 (Winter): 63–91.

Nehlsen, Willa, Jack E. Williams, and James A. Lichatowich. 1991. "Pacific Salmon at the Crossroads: Stocks at Risk from California, Oregon, Idaho, and Washington." *Fisheries* 16(2): 4–21.

Paehlke, Robert. 1995. "Environmental Values for a Sustainable Society: The Democratic Challenge." In *Greening Environmental Policy: The Politics of a Sustainable Future,* ed. Frank Fischer and Michael Black. New York: St. Martin's Press, 129–44.

Rabe, Barry G. 1986. *Fragmentation and Integration in State Environmental Management.* Washington, D.C.: Conservation Foundation.

Roberts, Robert E. 2001. "A Letter from the ECOS Executive Director." Washington, D.C.: Environmental Council of the States (June).

Snow, Donald. 1996. "Coming Home." *Chronicle of Community*, 1 (1)(Autumn): 40–43.

Torgerson, Douglas. 1998. "Limits of the Administrative Mind: The Problem of Defining Environmental Problems." In *Debating the Earth: The Environmental Politics Reader,* ed. J. S. Dryzek and D. Schlosberg. New York: Oxford University Press, 110–127.

Trohimovich, Tim. 2002. *The Growth Management Act after More than 10 years: Another Look and a Response to Criticisms.* Seattle: 1000 Friends of Washington (April).

Washington Department of Community, Trade, and Economic Development. 1997. *Growth Management: It's Beginning to Take Shape* (January).

Washington Department of Ecology. 1998. Memorandum of Understanding for the Coordinated Implementation of Chapter 247, Laws of 1998: Watershed Management. Watershed Planning Act (RCW 90.82).

Washington Department of Ecology. 1999. Implementing the Watershed Planning Act: Report for 1998 and 1999.

Washington Department of Ecology. 2000. "Communities Use State Grants to Protect Local Water Supplies." *Confluence Newsletter* (Winter).

Washington Office of Community Development. 2002. Growth Management Services, Annual Report. Olympia: Washington Department of Community, Trade, and Economic Development (June).

Washington Office of Financial Management. 2001. *Watershed Planning Report.*

Washington Office of Financial Management. 2002. Official Population Estimates (April 1).

Washington Research Council. 2001. "Washington's Growth Management Act: Goals and Promises." Online at www.researchcouncil.org/Briefs/2001/PB01-29/WAGMAGoalsPromises.htm; retrieved on October 10, 2002.

Watershed Planning Act. RCW 90.82. 1998. Washington State legislature.

Weber, Edward P. 1998. *Pluralism by the Rules: Conflict and Cooperation in Environmental Regulation.* Washington, D.C.: Georgetown University Press.

Weber, Edward P. 2000. "A New Vanguard for the Environment: Grass-Roots Ecosystem Management as a New Environmental Movement." *Society and Natural Resources* 13: 237–59.

Weber, Edward P. 2003. *Bringing Society Back In: Grassroots Ecosystem Management, Accountability, and Sustainable Communities.* Cambridge, Mass.: MIT Press.

Weber, Edward P., Nicholas P. Lovrich, and Michael J. Gaffney. 2002. "Lessons from the First Application of ESA-Enforcement Involving Anadromous Fish and Communities in the Pacific Northwest." Report to the National Marine Fisheries Service and the Washington Division of Fish and Wildlife. Pullman, Wash. (September).

Weber, Edward P., Nicholas P. Lovrich, and Michael J. Gaffney. 2003. "Two Different Approaches, Two Different Outcomes: A Tale of Endangered Species Act Enforcement in Two Communities." Paper presented at the Annual Meeting of the Midwest Political Science Association, Chicago (April 3–6).

Contributors

Ammons, David
Associated Press reporter stationed in Olympia; has reported on Washington State politics and public affairs for the past decade.

Appleton, Andrew
Associate Professor of Political Science and Director of Graduate Studies in the Department of Political Science at Washington State University, Pullman.

Clayton, Cornell W.
Associate Professor of Political Science in the Department of Political Science at Washington State University, Pullman.

Donovan, Todd
Associate Professor of Political Science in the Department of Political Science at Western Washington University, Bellingham.

Ellwanger, Steven J.
Doctoral candidate in Political Science at Washington State University, Pullman.

Elway, Stuart
Principal representative of Elway Research, Inc. of Seattle. This firm is broadly considered to be a premier agency for public opinion research in Washington, and Stuart Elway is widely regarded as among the foremost experts on civic affairs-related public opinion in the state of Washington.

Gombosky, Jeff
Former state legislator (House of Representatives) [D, Spokane area], currently serves as the legislative liaison to the Washington State legislature for Eastern Washington University, Cheney.

Grosse, Ashley
Researcher at the Social and Economic Sciences Research Center and Adjunct Instructor in the Department of Political Science at Washington State University, Pullman.

Herold, Robert
Scholar-in-Residence, Political Science and Organizational Leadership, at Gonzaga University. Long-time activist in civic affairs in Spokane.

Herzog, Christina
Doctoral candidate in Political Science at Washington State University, Pullman.

LeLoup, Lance T.
Claudius O. and Mary W. Johnson Distinguished Professor of Political Science at Washington State University, Pullman.

Long, Carolyn N.
Assistant Professor of Political Science and the Coordinator of the Public Affairs Program at Washington State University, Vancouver.

Lovrich, Nicholas P.
Claudius O. and Mary W. Johnson Distinguished Professor of Political Science, and Director, Division of Governmental Studies and Services, at Washington State University, Pullman.

Lysak, Tetyana
Doctoral candidate in Political Science and Internship Program Coordinator for The Thomas S. Foley Institute for Public Policy and Public Service at Washington State University, Pullman.

May, David
Assistant Professor and Chair, Department of Government at Eastern Washington University, Cheney.

Meyer, Stephen
Doctoral candidate in Political Science at Washington State University, Pullman.

Nice, David
Professor of Political Science in the Department of Political Science at Washington State University, Pullman.

Otte, Erin
Doctoral candidate in Political Science at Washington State University, Pullman.

Pierce, John
Former Chair of the Department of Political Science and Dean of the College of Liberal Arts at Washington State University, Pullman; now serves as the Executive Director of the Oregon Historical Society in Portland, Oregon.

Stehr, Steven D.
Associate Professor and Chair, Department of Political Science at Washington State University, Pullman.

Weber, Edward P.
Associate Professor of Political Science and Director of The Thomas S. Foley Institute for Public Policy and Public Service at Washington State University, Pullman.